Howiewood

Howie Krakow

*For Suzanne & Philip
new friends.
what could be better)*

Howiewood
Copyright c 2023
By Howard Krakow

Cover Design: Peter Coutroulis
               Niko Coutroulis

All rights reserved. No part of this book may be reproduced or transmitted in any form or by any means, electronic or mechanical, including photocopying, recording or by any information storage and retrieval system without written permission from the author, except for inclusion of brief quotations in a review.

For more information contact Howard Krakow at krax@me.com

Printed in the United States of America

"Let go. Or be dragged."

For Jonah and Jesse

Who have always been mystified about what their father did all day.

Part 1

Peripheral Cinema Luminary

My dinner with Warren

I didn't even think about saying "no."

This was the question: Would you be willing to work with Paul Newman and Warren Beatty on some radio commercials for Jimmy Carter's presidential campaign?

Well, I'd already folded my underwear and read most of the sports section so I was confident I could fit these two guys into my schedule.

As it turned out, Paul (because we were obviously intended to be business associates, it seems only reasonable that we refer to each other by first names) was unavailable. He offered some rather flimsy excuse – something about being committed to film production in the South of France. I didn't buy it then and I don't buy it now. But I have no doubt that for the rest of his life he regretted missing out on the opportunity of working with me. Unquestionably, it's a loss that he took to his grave although from all accounts, it's pretty certain that "Damn, I blew my opportunity to work with Howie" is not etched on his headstone.

Warren however jumped at the opportunity. He was excited, eager and beyond accommodating. He only had a few minor requests: He didn't want to go to a recording studio, he didn't want to read anything that somebody wrote for him, he didn't want to waste more than an hour on the project, and he'd only be willing to do it if we came to his place.

At the time, a home was being built for him in Beverly Hills or Bel Air or some other Los Angeles area where the rich and famous maintain their distance from the rest of us. So, in the meantime, he was living at the Beverly Wilshire Hotel.

It came as no shock that he was not sequestered in a standard room, but it was at least somewhat surprising that his accommodations were not more lavish. He was staying in a one-bedroom cabana near the hotel's rooftop swimming pool. It was certainly a significant step up from Motel 6 but hardly a space befitting an internationally famous writer, director, and movie star.

Because he was expecting guests, Warren had gone out of his way to ready the living room. He had, if memory serves me correctly, taken the trouble to move his T-shirt from the sofa and place it where it obviously belonged – draped over the TV.

The room was small but fortunately, so was our production crew. I was half of it. The other half was a sound guy.

Our time was limited so we dispensed with much of the traditional small talk. My guess is that Warren wasn't really that interested in hearing about our ordeal of thwarting Rolls Royce and Mercedes limos in bumper-to-bumper Rodeo Drive traffic. And surely he was well aware of the parking nightmare regularly faced by guests attempting to gain entrance to the hotel parking lot. So the "hello", "how are you?" and "Nice to meet you" comments were kept to a minimum. OK, they were nonexistent.

He did introduce himself – which I thought was a nice, although somewhat unnecessary, gesture. After all, even if I hadn't recognized him immediately, because he was the only person in the room other than the soundman and me, by process of either deduction or elimination, I'm pretty sure I would have figured out who he was.

A common reaction when meeting film stars is that, in person, they seem surprisingly short. That's because we are so accustomed to seeing them on the big screen where they are always larger than life. If diminutive height is a factor – and it often is - adjustments are made by having the actors stand on apple boxes and only filmed from the waist up. Some brilliant cinematography and editing was definitely required to make us believe that, at 5' 7", Sylvester Stallone could reasonably portray a contender for the heavyweight championship of the world.

But Warren Beatty is definitely not short. He is over 6 feet. Well over. His height didn't make him imposing, just unexpected - about as unexpected as the modesty of his current, temporary, living arrangements.

His preparations for the production had been nothing short of meticulous. In addition to re-positioning his T-shirt, he had gone to the enormous trouble of preparing his own script by writing a few words on a sheet of scrap paper. Clearly, he viewed this radio commercial as an opportunity to propel his career to even greater heights and had therefore committed not only an hour to the actual production but quite possibly several minutes thinking about what he would say.

Because time limitations had been established as a significant consideration, the sound guy set up quickly, checked levels and, in short order, announced that we were ready to go.

I told Warren (by now we knew each other so well that I called him by his first name, and he reciprocated in kind by referring to me as "you") that we might as well start laying down tracks and just keep the tape rolling while we recorded everything. That way, we'd be able to use even bits and pieces that felt right and, of course, edit out anything that didn't.

For some reason he felt that was a brilliant way to proceed. Score one for Howie.

He had a few false starts, said "let me do that again" once or twice, and found himself drifting into phrases that he didn't like. Very soon it became apparent that, although he was a brilliant screen writer and perhaps an even better actor, this attempt at a making a radio commercial was simply not working. Even though he was absolutely certain about the information he wanted to communicate, he had no idea how to start the commercial. And the points he wanted to make took too long to develop. Within a few minutes it became painfully obvious that it would have been impossible to edit his ramblings into anything close to a comprehendible 60 second radio commercial.

I offered a few suggestions. He nodded, but it was more of an "I hear you" nod and less than of a "let's try it your way."

He made a few more attempts, but nothing worked. As someone who is used to succeeding, because that wasn't happening, his frustration continued to mount. We'd only been at it for a few minutes and already negativity threatened to take the recording session completely down the tubes.

So, I offered another suggestion. I'd use his thoughts, his ideas, his expressions and organize them into something that at least resembled the format of a radio commercial. This time his nod indicated that he'd be willing to give it a try.

Score a second point for Howie.

I asked if he had a typewriter. He gestured to the bedroom where there was an older portable that didn't appear to have been used for some time. The dusty plastic cover was my clue.

He handed me a few sheets of plain white paper and returned to the other room to let me write in privacy.

When I took the cover off, I noticed there was a piece of paper still in the roller. On it were some names. There were others, but these are two that I definitely remember:

Julie Christie
Dianne Keaton

Time for a reality check. For me, these are the names of beautiful, talented actresses I only know because I've seen them in Academy Award winning films. But that's not the case for the man whose typewriter I was about to use. They might be women he'd like to work with in the future, women he's worked with in the past or women with whom he had a romantic relationship. All of those possibilities existed - not in some fanciful dream but in the actuality of his normal, everyday life. For me, they were women on an inaccessible pedestal. For him, that pedestal is where he has his morning cereal.

With great care, I removed Julie Christie and Dianne Keaton from the typewriter. I felt as if I was dismissing them unfairly – and had no right to do so.

Then I got to work.

I might have been in Warren Beatty's hotel suite, and I might have been in full cognizance of the rarified air in which he operates, but as I sat in front of the typewriter and began constructing a radio commercial, I was totally in my element. I knew exactly what to do.

When I brought the script to him, he looked it over slowly and carefully. I think he probably expected something else – something more like a typical hard sell radio spot. But that's not what I gave him. What he held was a script with his words and his thoughts – just condensed and re-structured.

He nodded appreciatively. And then nodded again. Howie scores point number three.

After that, the recording went smoothly. He did several takes – all of them good. He was pleased because he knew he did well. And even happier because he knew that he was done.

Not quite.

I had a thought. Because I'd scored a few positive points already, he was willing to listen. I chose my words very carefully because I was about to offer performance direction to one of the most famous actors in the world.

This is essentially what I explained to Warren Beatty:

"What you've done is good. That's obvious. You know it and I know it. We can certainly stop right here and feel more than satisfied about what's been accomplished. But I think the commercial can actually be even better."

"It feels as if the information you're providing comes from a seasoned expert – someone well versed in the political landscape and who has come to a very reasonable conclusion about what the next obvious steps ought to be. But there may be a way to make an even more powerful, more effective commercial. Instead of providing information as if you were a dispassionate observer, I think the words would have much greater impact if they seemed to be coming from your heart. In other words, I believe that a more personal performance – a genuine request from Warren Beatty – could take this commercial to another level."

He was quiet for a while. Then he nodded and said, "I understand what you're saying, and I agree. That kind of reading probably would be more effective."

In my head I was already marking point number 4 in my column of hits. But my chicken counting turned out to be premature.

He paused a bit before he finished. "But I'm not going to do it."

Another reality check. And, unquestionably, no additional point for Howie. As a director, I'd never been in that position before. Whenever I asked an actor to do something, it was done. That's because there is an established production hierarchy, and the director sits at the very top of the pecking order.

But not here. Not this time. Although I was an active participant, this was most assuredly not my show. Warren Beatty did say "no" very nicely. But he definitely said "no."

With that one word, there was nothing for us to do but wrap up and leave. We had what we came here to get. End of story.

Again. Not quite.

He invited me to dinner. Maybe he was just hungry and didn't want to eat alone. Maybe I had impressed him at least enough to think I might have something interesting to say. No matter the reason for the invitation, there was no chance I wouldn't accept.

We took the elevator downstairs to the hotel's restaurant. He obviously had chosen the restaurant more for convenience than for cuisine. He was unquestionably comfortable there – pretty much unnoticed and left alone. At upscale places like the Beverly Wilshire Hotel, the staff had been well trained about how to treat celebrities ... act as if they're just ordinary people and hope for a big tip.

Before we were shown to our table, he chatted a bit with the hostess. She clearly knew who he was (as did just about everyone at the restaurant even though they pretended not to). As instructed, she knew that she shouldn't be making a big deal about talking with him.

When we sat down, before we ordered and even before we looked at the menu, he gestured towards the hostess with his head and told me that he'd been semi flirting with her for a while and wondered if I thought she'd be willing to go out with him.

Another reality check. And like so many of them, this one was totally unexpected. It turns out that even one of the best known, best looking, most successful men in the entire world is, at least in some ways, just like the rest of us – insecure about how he might be perceived by an attractive woman.

I told him that he didn't have a chance. "She doesn't look like the type who'd be interested in tall, handsome movie stars. I think I'd have a much better shot. She's definitely someone who'd go for a short, bald Jew."

I got an appreciative laugh. And Carter got elected.

Touch the Future

The year was 1990.

The Berlin Wall, the last horrific existing symbol of the Nazi regime was joyously dismantled and, for the first time in decades, East and West Germany reunited. It was a monumental re-coupling, and the entire world took notice.

After the cheers subsided and the rubble cleared, it became obvious that there was actual work to be done. For starters, the unified country needed a new government and a new president. Because being the very first leader was assurance of a permeant place in German history and a name that every school kid would be required to memorize, there were no shortage of candidates. One of them was Helmut Kohl, a politician whose limited qualifications included having been the youngest elected member of Parliament, a party leader for decades, chair of the G7 Conference, and the current Chancellor. Vegas had him as a prohibitive favorite, but Helmut didn't want to take any chances, so he chose the members of his campaign team with scrupulous care. Obviously, I was at the top of his list.

The fact that he didn't know who I was, knew nothing about me, had never met me and, in fact, never would, was only a minor inconvenience. The key – not only to victory but the future of the newly cohesive Germany as well - clearly rested in my hands.

With my total lack of knowledge about German history, my inability to either speak or comprehend a single word of the German language and, frankly, my complete unfamiliarity with Helmut Kohl, I might not seem to have been the obvious choice to be the lynchpin of his presidential campaign.

But it was politics. And stranger things have happened.

There are apparently only two strategies to be considered when instituting a plan to run for political office. First time candidates proudly point to their outsider status, unencumbered by a system that has obviously failed so miserably without them. Those running for re-election tout their proven ability to negotiate hidden pathways within the existing political morass. In addition, they know the secret handshake.

Although a well-considered platform of ideas designed to improve the lives of every man, woman and child is of some importance, it is outweighed by other less obvious factors. High on that list is the ability to make outlandish promises without smirking and a willingness to feign interest when listening to the inane thoughts and ideas offered in coffee shops when mingling with the public.

For every election campaign, there are specific needs as well: a clear, simple rationale for announcing the candidacy ("I am a good, God fearing person; my opponent is a known devil worshipper"), a memorable slogan that fits comfortably on a button or baseball cap ("Nixon sucks"), and a rousing campaign song that inspires confidence, hope, and an unshakable desire to be part of a winning movement.

Understanding all that, someone deep within the bowels of the Kohl campaign took assessment of the situation and determined that recent German history left more than a bit to be desired. He had a point: the atrocities of World War II and the country's humiliating defeat made it difficult to look backwards with any sense of pride. Clearly, because things could hardly have been worse for so long, the focus needed to be on the hoped-for good times that lay ahead. Looking forward made sense but, given the country's impatience to get moving in the right direction, it was important not to look very far ahead. The future needed to be now – in fact, so close that every German citizen could almost reach out and touch it.

Ergo Koh's campaign slogan: Touch the Future.

I don't know how that phrase is spoken in German. But, as it turned, out, such translation proved to be unnecessary. My mono-linguistic ability was more than sufficient.

Kohl, his campaign strategist, or perhaps someone hankering for a free trip to America, determined that the future of Germany would be inexorably tied to the United States and that the importance of the English language could not – and should not under any circumstances – be undervalued. The decision was made, therefore, that the campaign song – the one intended to rouse the German electorate and begin the surge towards Kohl-mania, should be sung - not in German - but in English. By fortunate happenstance, English was the one language in which I was at least reasonably fluent.

Once the decision was made to create a campaign song in English, Kohl's crackerjack team began assembling the dominoes that needed to fall in reasonable sequence. I have no idea how many music companies or individuals in the U.S. were contacted, but I know, without question, that at least one of them was Killer Music, a talented and successful Los Angeles group responsible for creating and producing a slew of well-known advertising jingles – including a few that I had written.

Killer Music, and probably other music houses as well, was invited to participate in a competition for the Kohl anthem. They were asked to write the lyrics, compose the score, and ultimately produce the campaign song that would propel Kohn to victory.

With no writers on staff, combined with a crushing need for lyrics, Killer Music turned to writers they had worked with in the past. Obviously, I was their first call. Or perhaps the second. Maybe the third. They never told me, and I never asked.

What they did tell me was the title of the song and the day the lyrics needed to be delivered. I think the request was essentially this: take your time. We don't need it until tomorrow.

So that night, after making dinner, watching a ballgame on TV, putting my sons to bed, doing the dishes, and pretty much frittering away the rest of the evening, I eventually remembered that there was something else I was supposed to do. In the half hour between that realization and the time I dozed off for the rest of the night, I wrote the words destined to change the course of German history or at least get me to the next round of the competition.

The following morning, I showed the lyrics to my 14-year-old son. Although it would be correct to say that his critique was unduly harsh, it would also be difficult to say that he wasn't correct. Nevertheless, while not exactly brimming with confidence due to a teenager's lackluster review, but knowing that at least the assignment had been completed before the deadline, I stopped by the Killer Music offices, handed over my submission, and awaited a formal rejection.

Not only did the rejection fail to appear, but the unexpected response was surprisingly positive. Mine was one of 3 sets of lyrics that, after being reviewed by someone or perhaps more than one someone, was being moved on to Door #2. A composer from Killer Music was now assigned to write the melody. Following that, a singer and piano track would be recorded, and the resulting demo would be passed on to the Kohl team for further judgement.

A few days later, as promised, the demo was delivered to my home. Once again, my son was less than impressed. If memory serves correctly – and in this case, unfortunately it does - his assessment was that my uninspiring words were hardly enhanced by the hum drum quality of the music. For him the demo did not so much represent an improvement as much as a reinforcement of his original critique. He felt that the addition of a mediocre melody to mediocre lyrics was hardly a step in the right direction. Instead, the combination only doubled down on the bad.

Given my son's analysis and my own concerns, the next call I received from Killer Music was more than a little unexpected. For unaccountable reasons, my lyrics – and their music – had won the day. Together, ours was the winning entry. A full-blown recording session was scheduled for the following week.

Because, at the time, I was the creative director of one of the largest ad agencies in Los Angeles, it was impossible for me to take a full day off to attend the recording. But I did manage an elongated lunch break and was more than rewarded for my time away from the office.

The recording session was a big deal. A very big deal indeed. Killer Music put the word out that production of the theme song for a united Germany was taking place. So this wouldn't just be a musical event – it was international news. Their PR effort got the attention of the three major TV networks – ABC, NBC, and CBS. All of them sent reporters and cameras to cover the event. And because the owners of Killer Music wanted to make the most of the massive coverage, they prepared quite a show.

Usually when laying down the music tracks for a jingle, the process is straight forward. There is an orderly sequence. First to record is the rhythm section – piano, bass, and drums. Next come wind instruments, followed by strings. To create a fuller sound, most of the instruments and all the strings are recorded at least twice – and often more than that. So, even though there may be only 2 or 3 violin players, when doubled (or tripled), the string section sounds as if it is comprised of many more. After the instrumental tracks are completed, the singers are recorded (and often doubled as well). Once the instrumental and vocal tracks have been laid down, the mixing session begins. Sound levels are adjusted for optimum effect, and the whole piece comes together.

By the time I arrived at the studio many of the early musicians had already left and recording the strings was in full progress. I was surprised to see that instead of just a few players, a much larger group had been assembled. They not only sounded like the full string section of a symphony orchestra, because of their numbers, they actually looked like one as well.

Next came the singers. And, again, the ante had been upped. Instead of a soloist, a chorus of 4 backed up the two leads. Even their first take was impressive, but I knew that when the mixing session was complete, this group would sound like the Mormon Tabernacle Choir.

I was totally unprepared for my own emotional response. It's one thing to write a few words that vaguely resemble some sort of poetry, but quite another to hear them belted out by professional singers supported by a full orchestra. Even though my son was correct that the lyrics were considerably less than brilliant, as I heard the whole piece come together, the total effect was impressive – certainly to me.

Because I had a job to return to, I wasn't able to stay for the mix session. That would have been nice, but it was hardly important because I'd already heard more than enough. I floated back to the office.

About a week later I received a call from one of the producers at Killer Music. He told me that because he had come up with the title of the song, he felt entitled to half of the writing credit and half of the payment for the lyrics . Frankly, even though I knew that wasn't true because the title had been part of the original assignment, I was OK with that. Because I had never considered either getting credit or payment, learning that I'd get half of both was actually a plus.

Epilogue.

Kohl won.

Sadly, Germany has yet to repay the debt it owes me, and the failure to acknowledge my immense contribution is surely a constant subject of consternation for the current leadership. In retribution for that oversight, I have cut down drastically on my consumption of schnitzel, continue to boycott Oktoberfest, and refuse to participate in any singing that involves raised or waved beer steins.

Even after hearing the beautifully recorded version, my son never changed his mind about the lyrics or the song.

He was right about my words. As an example of just how forgettable they are, I do not remember any of them and have been unable to locate either a hard or digital copy. Even my good friend Mr. Google has been unable to verify proof of their existence.

That absence is hardly tragic. This may be one of the few instances when the phrase "being lost for words" is in everyone's best interest.

Here's Johnny!!!
(And why, exactly, is Howie here?)

For decades, film has been the preferred method of determining status in Hollywood. And yet, even though he never made a film in his entire life, there was a time when Johnny Carson was the most powerful man in town.

That point was made unequivocally when he renegotiated his deal with NBC.

At the time, his show – The Tonight Show – was NBC's top money-maker. It didn't draw the highest ratings, but its bottom line was staggering. That's because, other than Johnny's salary, the cost of producing the show was minimal. There were a few staff writers, a sidekick (Ed McMahon), a small live band, and a small set that often went for years without an upgrade. All the guests – and many were among the biggest stars in the entertainment industry – were paid almost nothing. According to the legal phrase "favored nations" they all received the same amount – the SAG (Screen Actors Guild) minimum payment of a few hundred dollars for their appearance.

Compared to half hour situation comedies, full hour dramas, and 90-minute, made-for-TV movies, producing the Tonight Show was practically free. But, because Johnny was so well loved, and because his guests had such a huge following, the ratings were consistently high – especially for a show that didn't air until close to midnight. But, after the nightly news was over, the Tonight Show ruled the airways. Late at night there was Johnny and a whole bunch of also-rans. NBC's return on their investment in the Tonight Show was beyond impressive. It was, by far, their most profitable venture.

Even better, the program was a total win/win for everyone. For NBC, the Tonight Show served as an ideal platform to generate interest in their own upcoming shows or to stimulate viewership for programs that were faltering. All of Johnny's guests were happy to come on the show to promote their latest project – often a film, a book, or an upcoming Las Vegas performance. Their appearance required little preparation and no lines to memorize. Even better, they knew they'd enjoy the experience because Johnny always – ALWAYS – made it a point for them to have a good time. Booking guests was almost effortless. The producers of the show could virtually pick and choose from a Who's Who of the biggest names in show business. There was hardly an A-lister on the planet who didn't look forward to being on the Tonight Show.

Long before his contract was scheduled to run out, Johnny and his representatives (his agent, manager, attorney, financial advisor and possibly his wife, perhaps a few of his friends and, if he wanted, his tennis coach and therapist) made a casual appraisal of the situation, assessed the opportunity, and drew up a ridiculous wish list in preparation for what would surely be a lucrative negotiation. Then they added to it. Their reasoning was pretty sound. Given his enormous contribution to NBC's bottom line, anything he asked for – no matter how outrageous - was certainly within the realm of possibility.

Request number one was for a raise. Knowing his leverage, the amount he came up with was certainly outrageous. Then he doubled it. For some reason he didn't feel the need to share the actual figure with me but it's safe to say that it was, by leaps and bounds, more than anyone else on TV was earning. Much more.

But having the Brinks truck stop at his front door to drop off his weekly salary was just a warm-up. He also wanted some serious perks.

He no longer was interested in maintaining a grueling 5-day weekly schedule. He thought he should work less. OK, a lot less. Takings Fridays off seemed reasonable. And he also wanted some vacation time. A full month off during the summer felt just about right. Really who could blame him for wanting a break? Chatting with celebrities for an hour and a half is no easy task. And if Johnny deemed the effort to be exhausting, who was to argue?

The network was prepared for all of that. They anticipated a significant salary request and probably could have guessed about a lessened work schedule. But Johnny was just warming up.

He also wanted to start his own company and had gone to the trouble of naming it: Johnny Carson Productions. Because of his long relationship with NBC, he felt it was only fair that the network should participate. His idea about participation was clear: NBC foots the bill for everything. By everything he meant 3 on-the-air shows, all guaranteed for a minimum of 13 episodes. By actual count, those 13 guaranteed episodes were 12 more than almost any other production company was ever offered. Most considered themselves lucky if they just got a go-ahead for a single pilot. If the pilot tested poorly, that was the end of that. So, a guarantee of 3 shows with 13 episodes each was quite an ask – actually, it was totally unprecedented.

It would have been nice to be a fly on the wall when the negotiations took place. But even without being there, it's easy to imagine the sound of the NBC executive's jaws dropping and smashing on the conference table. They obviously knew beforehand that they would have to give him a lot – but they could not possibly have been prepared for what requested. And they also knew, despite their justifiable protestations, they had brought water pistols to a gun fight.

The result was a foregone conclusion. NBC said "yes" to everything. Undoubtedly there was a lot of hemming and hawing, whining, and complaining. But everyone knew that Johnny held all the cards. NBC certainly wasn't going to risk airing "The Tonight Show Without Johnny Carson". And, even with the healthy chunk of dough they'd be sending to his personal account on a regular basis, when all was said and done, the network was still going to make a very handsome profit on the program.

The moment the new contract was signed, Johnny Carson was – unquestionably - the most powerful person in Hollywood.

Once the deal was done, and he was able to stop giggling about his victory, Johnny turned his thoughts to the programs he wanted to produce and, just as importantly, who was going to star in them. There was no shortage of possibilities. His Rolodex was crammed with film stars, TV stars, and every established and up-and-coming comedian in the country. Simply stated, he had the pick of the litter.

It didn't take him long to reach two decisions. He wanted to build a half hour situation comedy around Angie Dickinson, and he wanted Allan Katz, executive producer of the MASH TV show, to create it.

Asking Allan to be the show runner was a no-brainer. His TV credentials were impeccable. For years, he'd created, written, and produced a slew of successful comedy series and had worked with some of television's biggest stars. But television was only part of his comedy repertoire. Anyone who knew him would instantly agree that Allan was – hands down - the funniest person they'd ever met. He was certainly capable of being serious. But, given an opening – anywhere, anyplace, or any time – he'd come up with something hysterical. The more uncomfortable the situation, the more embarrassing the opportunity, the quicker he was to find the funny. It was beyond impossible for him to be on an elevator with a friend and any other person without immediately saying or doing something totally inappropriate and laugh-out-loud funny. His EMMY acceptance speech in front of a national audience remains a 10 second classic.

The decision to bring Allan on board was easy. But, to say the least, Angie Dickinson was a curious choice. Not because she was unknown. She had recently been the lead actor in Police Woman, a highly rated TV series that had been on the air for years. In that role she was tough, sexy, and the first woman to star in a cop or detective show. She had also recently earned rave reviews as the female lead in Brian de Palma's film, <u>Dressed to Kill</u>. She was in almost every scene and, even though she had very few lines, always looked gorgeous and sometimes petrified – precisely what the part called for.

Angie had been Johnny's frequent guest on the Tonight Show. The two of them had an easy, comfortable rapport. Her laughter was spontaneous and infectious. It was obvious that they had a good time together. Though definitely not a comedian, whenever she was on the show, there was always plenty of laughter.

Still, there was ample reason to question her ability to do the heavy lifting necessary as the star of a sit-com.

More on that later.

After Allan Katz signed on to create the show, I was his first hire. To say the least, I was almost as peculiar a choice as Angie Dickinson. Among other inadequacies, I lacked even a single reasonable credential. I had never written a TV show, never written a film, and never come close to earning my spurs as a member of the Comedy Fraternity. But Allan and I had worked together for years doing radio and TV commercials and he knew with absolute certainty that, whatever my shortcomings might be, I'd always have his back.

I also knew a lot of jokes. Here's proof:

A man was going on vacation for a few weeks and asked a friend to care for his cat while he was away. When he returned, quite naturally he asked his friend about the cat. He was unprepared for the abrupt answer, "Your cat is dead."

The man was crushed. He'd rescued the cat from a shelter when it was just a kitten and had lovingly shared his home with it for more than a decade. He was too distraught to even speak for a while but eventually composed himself and attempted to give his friend some indication about the significance of his loss. "That was devastating news. What's worse is that you delivered it in such an unemotional manner. The way you told me of my terrible loss was beyond cruel."

His friend was incredulous. "Your cat died. What was I supposed to say?"

"Well, you could have at least tried to lessen the blow. You could have told me that you had a good time playing with the cat. Then, one day you mistakenly left the door open, and it got outside and somehow climbed up on the roof. It seemed quite happy up there for a while until there was a sudden, terrible rainstorm. The wind swept the cat towards the edge of the roof where it struggled for a while but eventually lost its grip and tragically slid to its death. Do you see how a little warning could have made the bad news easier to take?"

His friend nodded. He clearly understood the message. Then the man asked, "Did anything else happen while I was gone?"

"Well, your grandmother was on the roof...."

There are some jokes that every comedian knows. That's definitely one of them.

I was given the title "Creative Consultant" because it sounded both official and sufficiently nebulous to grant me admission to all the meetings that Allan attended. Nobody really knew what I did or was supposed to do – including me. But it made Allan feel good to have me around, so I was his constant shadow at network conferences, casting sessions, and all the production meetings with the director, cast and crew.

Although everything about television was entirely new to me, I was beyond comfortable in the meetings with the executives at the network and the production company. Even though I was meeting them for the first time, after many years in the advertising business, I knew them all by type. They were all mightily impressed by their titles, well versed in entertainment jargon, and readers of the daily trade magazines from cover to cover. They dressed and postured very well but provided little substance to any discussion. Many, despite their lofty positions and inflated salaries, knew very little about production - including the guy who was supposed to be in charge.

Here's a for-instance:

I assured the head of production that we were very conscious of the budget and were doing everything possible to keep costs under control.

For starters, that was beyond an outrageous lie. I had absolutely no idea what the budget was, how it was created, or what the consequences might be if we exceeded it. But I knew that the word "budget" is something that all executives tend to understand. So, he'd certainly appreciate hearing that it was a priority for us.

I carefully explained one of the ways we were keeping costs under control. Apparently when the budget was initially created, the show was going to be shot on videotape. At the time, 3-camera taped shows were relatively standard, so it was reasonable to allocate videotape costs as part of the initial budget. But Allan felt that shooting on film would improve the quality of the over-all product. Even though a film shoot would increase production costs significantly, NBC had agreed to the new plan. I assured the executive that we had come up with a very clever way to save money. I told him that even though we'd be shooting on film we'd keep the video cameras and run the film through them – an absolutely absurd, impossible, totally ridiculous concept.

Despite the fact that his title was Head of Production, he had no idea what I was talking about. He nodded appreciatovely and told me, "Good idea." It was hardly the response I had anticipated. But it removed any concern that I was the only one who was in over his head.

Because I had written, produced and directed many TV commercials and worked with celebrities on a lot of them, I was hardly awe struck by the thought of working with well-known actors on a sit-com. Frankly, I've always felt that acting seemed like an awfully easy way to earn a living. When a 6 year-old girl can win an Academy Award, it's hard to dignify what actors do by calling it a profession.

Nevertheless, meeting Angie Dickinson most assuredly felt like a big deal. Along with a lot of other men, I find beautiful women intimidating. And famous beautiful women raise the stakes even higher. Before we met, I had no idea what to expect. I didn't know if she'd have an attitude, an entourage, or a slew of peculiar demands (like, for example, no licorice jellybeans). I wasn't concerned, but I was surely apprehensive.

Angie instantly swept aside any possible trepidation. She was welcoming, friendly, self-assured, totally at ease with everyone, and an absolute pleasure to be with.

Whether we met at her house, the studio, or a conference room, she was always agreeable and positive. She was helpful, energetic, and anxious to do anything she could to make the show work. Even better, she wanted to help make everyone enjoy the process.

In person, just as on screen, she definitely had a presence. There are undoubtedly women who are as attractive as she is, but very few who exude her confidence and sex appeal.

Judged only by her looks, Angie could easily be mistaken for a dumb blonde. But that would be an enormous mistake. Although she was solidly entrenched in the entertainment industry and palled around with the heaviest of heavyweights (think Frank Sinatra, the rest of The Rat Pack and others for whom the phrase "move star" is woefully insufficient) she almost never spoke about her experiences with them. Instead, when she dropped a name (which she did not so much to impress but usually to add weight to the point she was making) it was likely to be someone of substance - President John F. Kennedy or world-famous economist, diplomat and liberal, John Kenneth Galbraith

The information she passed along was not gleaned because she'd read their books or studied their writings. She knew their thoughts because she'd had dinner with them and was not only fascinated by what she'd heard but also because she had been an active participant in the conversation.

I was surprised, but enormously pleased, to realize that discussions with her would hardly be limited to topics related to the show, the script or wardrobe. We may not have solved hunger or world peace, but her information was always appreciated and often enlightening.

That isn't to say there weren't issues.

Just as I had no background in writing or producing television, Angie had no background in performing comedy. I should have known that there was trouble ahead when I told my barber that I was working on a sit-com pilot starring Angie Dickinson and he said, "She's got timing?"

His concern turned out to be rooted in reality. The unfortunate answer to his question became all too obvious at the first table reading and was continually reinforced as the show went into rehearsal. As attractive as Angie was, that's how funny she wasn't.

Nevertheless, we pressed on.

Practice did not make perfect. It didn't even make mediocre. Although the handwriting of doom was clearly on the wall, we went through the motions and ultimately filmed the show in front of a live audience. As is customary, we shot the entire performance twice and did pick-ups for scenes that we felt could be improved. But even an audience stacked with friends and well-wishers had difficulty forcing helpful laughter. Well written jokes landed flat, sight gags went unappreciated, and even the most optimistic participants had to reach deep down to find something positive to say about the performance.

Still, there was hope. There are many things that can be accomplished with adept editing. Flubbed lines can be replaced, responses can be slowed down or sped up, carefully placed sound effects and music can alter the mood considerably, and a talented operator of sophisticated "laugh box" technology can make it seem as if the audience's merriment is uncontrollable.

All of that helped. None helped enough. The show was lifeless and decidedly not funny. It didn't take a show business veteran to realize that the Angie Dickinson show was completely dead in its tracks.

The network's formal decision to abruptly halt everything was hardly a shock. Despite a guarantee of 13 on-the-air episodes, there was no question that the ride was over. Even the pilot would probably never see the light of day. 12 additional episodes were totally out of the question. All of us knew it. Well, everyone except Johnny.

That information needed to be passed on to him. Delaying the bad news would only prolong the agony. So, a meeting was quickly scheduled. Although there were many available offices and conference rooms at the network, there was never a question about location. Obviously, the most convenient place to meet with Johnny was at his house.

Four of us from the production side (the president of Johnny Carson Productions, the director, Allan and me) drove there together. Johnny's agent and lawyers were to meet us there. Mercifully, Angie would not be in attendance.

None of us had any illusions about the meeting. There was no question that it was going to be a disaster.

The scope of the problem was enormous. While not exactly akin to a mass shooting or a tornado wiping out a coastal city, in Hollywood, there is no tragedy like the cancellation of a show. From a financial standpoint this one certainly was a doozy. In addition to the money that was wasted on the pilot (an amount well in excess of $1 million and probably twice that) there were other significant issues. Angie's contract was for 13 shows – easily several million dollars. She'd receive every penny whether or not there were any further episodes. And there were plenty of other additional costs. Contracts had been negotiated and signed by a full cast, a staff of writers and members of the production crew. Every one of those contracts was for a full slate of 13 episodes.

NBC would take a significant hit. Millions of dollars were down the drain. With the cancellation of his first show, Johnny Carson – the man who could do no wrong - had failed spectacularly. Everyone associated with the show shared in the failure. Nobody was exiting this experience with ego or reputation intact.

In the car on the way to Johnny's house, doom and gloom permeated every conversation. Although the others were distraught, my take on the situation was somewhat different.

While everyone contemplated the prospect of a monumentally uncomfortable meeting in which the most powerful man in Hollywood was going to learn about a terrible blow to his reputation, my mind went to an entirely different place.

I couldn't help thinking, "I'm going to Johnny Carson's house."

I was actually pretty excited. For me, the fact that I would soon be unemployed was already old news. But I knew my friends would be impressed when I told them that I met with Johnny Carson in his living room. I could go out to lunch on that experience for a long time.

We passed through the gates of Bel Air and drove past estates that were mostly hidden from view by impressive walls and towering greenery. Eventually we wound up at our destination. As anticipated, the house was impressive – and guarded by an intimidating gate. Although, at the time, most of the group would have been pleased if entry had been denied, after announcing ourselves, the gates opened, and we drove into the Carson compound.

Johnny had been alerted about our visit but was hardly in a rush to see us. That was understandable given the important responsibilities he was involved with at the time. When we arrived, he was still in the midst of a tennis match (on his own private tennis court, of course) and for obvious reasons could not leave until the crucial set had been completed. But immediately after the final point was decided, he raced to meet us, pausing only to have some iced tea with his tennis partner, check with his assistant to make sure that dinner reservations had been made, and consider how to avoid apologizing for keeping us waiting.

We gathered in his living room, a visually assorted lot. The director, Allan and I were in jeans. The others – Johnny's lawyers, agents, and advisors - wore suits and ties. Johnny was impeccably dressed for the occasion. He remained in his tennis shorts, continually wiping away perspiration with a towel.

I don't think he knew the full extent of the bad news, but he obviously realized that a celebration was not forthcoming. Given the unusual gathering at his house in the middle of a weekday afternoon, it would have been remarkable if he didn't realize that it was something important, serious, and almost certainly not good. Not good at all.

No one else wanted to start the conversation, so he cut to the chase:

"What's up?"

The suits looked down and remained uncomfortably quiet. Someone was going to have to break the news, but it was painfully clear that there were no volunteers. The awkward silence continued and became even more awkward. No one wanted to look at Johnny. Every eye in the room seemed transfixed on the intricate weave of his carpet.

Even though the responsibility for delivering the news should have come from one of the executives, none of them were up to the assignment.

I had no idea what was going to happen, but I did know Allan very well. And I knew that when the situation is truly uncomfortable, he's always at his best, and certainly at his funniest. He simply can't help himself.   He has to go for the funny.

So, in the living room of the most successful man in the history of television - a room filled with some of the highest paid entertainment executives and attorneys - it fell to Allan to break the news. This was the moment when he had to tell Johnny that what he might have suspected would be bad news, was almost certainly even worse than he could possibly have anticipated.

Allan broke the painful silence by telling Johnny, "Well…. Angie was on the roof…"

Carson cracked up.

The suits couldn't fathom why he was laughing but they knew that the awful spell of darkness had been broken.

What followed were the predictable discussions about who was going to follow through with NBC, who was going to tell the cast, and who was going to speak with Angie.

There were undoubtedly all sorts of important lessons to be learned that day. I may have learned a few, but the one that impressed me most was one I already knew: rules are meant to be broken.

There is a long-standing, proud tradition that is steadfastly adhered to by everyone in the entertainment business: "The show must go on."

But sometimes it doesn't.

Scarlet Ribbons.
Finally, a Christmas film
with a realistic ending.

The idea for my first film script came from the song "Scarlet Ribbons". If not a huge hit or anything close to a popular standard, at least it was moderately well known. The most familiar version was sung by Harry Belafonte.

"Scarlet Ribbons" is a lovely song that tells a very sweet story about a man who overhears his young daughter saying her bedtime prayers. In addition to the standard "God bless the usual subjects" she has a special request: she'd like some scarlet ribbons. Why? We don't know. But her desire for the ribbons is clear. Moved by her request he immediately sets out to buy them. But because it's late at night, all the stores are closed. He returns home empty handed, checks on his sleeping daughter, and is overjoyed to see that the ribbons she wanted so badly are lying at the foot of her bed. He has no idea how they appeared. He is amazed and, of course, pleased that his daughter's prayers were answered.

That's it. That's all there is to it.

Because the melody is lovely and the story is sweet, I've always liked the song. And, perhaps like others, I wondered how the happy ending came about. Clearly, something happened. In real life, ribbons don't appear out of nowhere.

Whether I conceived the right solution to the mystery is a matter of opinion. But I came up with an explanation that made sense to me. As a bonus, I felt it made the story even sweeter.

So, I started my script with an ending. In fact, at that point, it's all I had. With the last sentence of the last scene essentially written, the only thing I needed to do was fill in everything else.

I started to solve the mysterious appearance of ribbons by assuming that there was no sorcery, witchcraft, or otherworldly intervention. So, how did the ribbons get there? Who bought them? Who brought them? How? Why?

Even though Christmas was never mentioned, I somehow thought of it as a Christmas song. That didn't seem like much of a stretch because the daughter was asking for something – and what she requested could easily be considered a Christmas present.

Because ribbons don't seem like much of a gift – especially for a young girl - why did she want them so badly? Answering that question became the key to the story I decided to tell.

In my mind, the entire event was conceived by the daughter. She knew that any Christmas present from her father would have to be inexpensive because he couldn't afford very much.

She thought long and hard about what he could get for her. It had to be both economical and something he knew she'd really want. Eventually she landed on ribbons she could wear in her hair. Surely, even on a tight budget, he could afford ribbons. So, as Christmas approached, she continued to drop subtle hints. Unfortunately, none of them were picked up.

As the final days before Christmas approached, she began to realize the possibility that no ribbons would be forthcoming. So, she decided to buy them herself. At the time, I had no idea how she was going to pay for them but, because they weren't an extravagant purchase, I figured she'd find a way.

When they opened presents on Christmas Eve, as expected, there were no ribbons. But the daughter knew what to do. When, as usual, her father listened in as she said her nightly prayers, she made sure he overheard her desire for red ribbons.

Once he closed the door to her room, she took the ribbons from the closet where she had hidden them, placed them on the foot of her bed and, satisfied that she had accomplished her mission, drifted peacefully off to sleep.

She had no idea whether her father was going to try to buy the ribbons that night. But it didn't matter. All she needed was for him to see – either when he checked in on her later in the evening or when he woke her up in the morning – that the ribbons had appeared and that her fondest wish for a Christmas gift had come true.

That's all I had. It seemed like a decent place to start. But, since most films have a beginning a middle and an end, there were holes that needed filling. Essentially, I had a punch line but was still missing the entire setup for the joke.

I began asking myself some questions.

For starters, who were this father and daughter? Where did they live? Was there a mother and, if not, where was she? If they didn't have much money, why not? Did the father work and, if he did, why was he so unsuccessful? How could I make him likeable even though he wasn't much of a breadwinner? More importantly, assuming that two people by themselves aren't sufficient to tell a compelling story, who were the others? Was there a woman in their lives? Neighbors? Friends? Conflict? Tension? Romance?

Gradually, the blanks began to fill in.

I decided that the father was a singer/songwriter - not an easy way to earn a living and not an easy business to break into. That explained the financial difficulties. It also meant there would be music in the film, so he needed to be talented. Bad songs and bad singing get old very quickly. Because talent - even extraordinary talent - is no assurance of success, it would be understandable that earning a living as a performer could be difficult. So, to pay the rent and put food on the table, I made him a cabbie. If the film took place now, he'd probably be an Uber driver.

For several reasons, I decided that there would be no mother. At the very least having the two of them living alone would create an unusual family situation and allow for a compelling father/daughter relationship. I briefly considered a divorce, but thought it was best to keep a wife out of the equation entirely. So, mama died giving birth. (Boom. There went the lead actress role). For the father, that loss was heavy, and for a long time, he was both uninterested and incapable of another relationship.

But, because even a Christmas story could use some romance, eventually he meets a woman. She is a passenger in his cab.

Father and daughter live on the second floor of a small apartment building. The cast expands. A widowed, older woman has an apartment downstairs. She and the daughter form a relationship and spend time together when the father is driving the cab or playing a gig. If needed for interest, humor or diversion, there are other apartments and other renters who can wander in and out of the story.

That seemed like a decent start. All I needed was the only thing that really matters - a story line. I know that there are writers who claim they are merely the scribe, and the story tells itself. I was poised and ready to let the characters show me the way, but that never happened. The plot didn't unfold easily. Action and complications refused to spontaneously occur. But, eventually, after considerable coaxing, events began to surface and, after many false starts and frustrating dead ends, something at least resembling a story started to form.

It took about 6 months to get there, but eventually I was able to put a check mark in box number one. I had a screenplay. Now all I needed to do was fill in the other 99 empty squares. At the rate of 6 months per box, my great, great, great grandchildren might get to see the film.

Even someone who knows next to nothing about the movie business realizes there is value to having a bankable star attached to the project. Surprisingly, not a lot of bankable stars called me and asked to participate. Finding one became my next assignment.

I quickly learned an unsurprising truth: getting a script to someone of consequence is not easy. The bigger the star, the more difficult the access. Agents, lawyers, and a plethora of assistants serve as gate keepers because there is an infinite number of people who would like to have someone of consequence attached to their project. To keep from being inundated by truckloads of inappropriate scripts, all the major stars have an orderly process in place. Their barrier is even more solid than Trump's Mexican wall. Any screenplay that manages to get all the way through has been heavily vetted.

Because this was my first script, I was only vaguely aware of the uphill climb I faced. Believing that anything was possible, I tried to think of the right person to play the lead.

I knew that, for various reasons, there are performers who don't particularly enjoy the idea of being type cast. After pulling down millions for their comic antics, it's not uncommon for a comedian to want to take on a completely different role. Just as often, actors known for their dramatic portrayals on Broadway often want the challenge of doing comedy. Everyone wants to play someone with a serious illness. Apparently, a speech impediment is the direct route to an Academy Award.

But even though I realized that actors often like to demonstrate their chops by accepting atypical roles, I had no idea if a Shakespearean actor or an action hero would even be remotely interested in the part I had written.

Because singing was a critical element of the story, I knew it was important that whoever played the lead had to be an accomplished singer. I assumed that there were actors who could sing, but I had no idea who they might be and didn't even bother to find out. But I thought that perhaps a singer – even a singer of some note - might find an acting role in a film to be at least somewhat appealing.

Two singer/song writers who immediately came to mind were personal favorites: Randy Newman and Paul Simon. As far as I knew, neither of them had ever acted, but perhaps the idea of playing the lead in a film might spark some interest.

Randy Newman was my first choice. I had been a fan for a long time and knew his songs very well. Even better, the lyrics to some of them seemed to fit nicely into the story. So, as I wrote the film, I inserted them. As the script evolved, Randy's music became the soundtrack for the entire film.

Next step: meet with Randy Newman. The goal was clear. As expected, accomplishing it proved to be a bit more difficult.

It seems that along with the contact information for the top Victoria's Secret models, I managed to misplace Randy's personal phone number. And since he seemed inclined to continue his long-standing tradition of never calling me, getting in touch with him was problematic.

But here's a left turn that you might find to be as surprising as I did: I met him. In person. In his house.

I can't recall exactly how it happened, but in talking about the script (something I did frequently with friends, acquaintances, and anyone with a working knowledge of conversational English), I eventually met someone who said that he knew Randy or knew someone who knew Randy or had some vague connection with him. Even better, that someone claimed to be capable of arranging a meeting.

The theory about 7 degrees of separation is perhaps at its apex in Hollywood. Names are dropped with abandon and purported linkage is happily bandied about. But, when push comes to shove and proof is required, what usually rises to the fore are excuses. Those are followed immediately by explanations and more excuses.

Once in a great while – a very great while – promises made in Hollywood are actually kept. Don't spread this around too freely, but in turns out that if you look under the correct rock, it is possible to find some people in the film business who can be trusted. Although I didn't truly appreciate my good fortune at the time, an honest to goodness meeting with Randy Newman was arranged. At least in theory, I was going to meet him. The fact that I never questioned the reliability of that theory is an accurate indication of my naivete about Hollywood protocol.

I was given an address, directions, and a time to arrive. Because I foolishly trusted that information, I drove towards what I confidently believed was Randy Neman's house. I had my script in hand and was ready to explain in as much detail as he was willing to hear about the brilliant film in which he would certainly want to star.

As I think about that day, I probably should have been more surprised than I was when I rang the doorbell and Randy Newman appeared. At that moment, whether or not my script ever became a film was a minor issue. Just meeting Randy Newman was more than sufficient justification for the months I'd spent writing. In my mind, as the two of us sat and talked in his living room, I felt I'd already achieved success.

Randy was ... let me put it this way – understated. He was quiet, introspective, attentive, and extremely reserved. That made sense. I think that's his normal personal style. But, in this case, he had plenty of reason to be less than enthusiastic. He knew nothing about me – all he knew was that someone suggested we meet. As we talked, he realized something else - I was a big fan. It didn't take very long to convince him that I knew his music – and especially his lyrics – almost as well as he did.

Maybe that's why he asked me a curious question. He was scheduled to be the music guest on Saturday Night Live a few days later and wanted my thoughts about what he should sing. He was considering "Rider in the Rain" – not one of my absolute favorites and not one of his very best, but certainly a good song. I encouraged him to do it mainly because he was already leaning in that direction. A few days later, when I watched the show, that was the song he performed. Obviously, I was a big influence on him. It's almost impossible to fathom how his career would have deteriorated into oblivion if he had not heeded my advice.

About a week or so later, I went back to his house to pick up the script and hear what he had to say about the project. His "no" was hardly a shock. He was complimentary about the writing and the story but beyond uninterested in participating.

During the time between our meetings, he had been evaluating what was happening career-wise, and came to an important, but relatively easy, conclusion. His latest song, Short People, was a surprising hit and he was enjoying both the popularity and the financial rewards. He had no interest in trying – or what would be more consequential – failing as an actor. Because I am such an astute listener, after a while, I began to get the feeling that he might not be the one who would take my script to the next level.

As it turned out, the decision to maintain focus on his music was a pretty good one. In addition to more successful albums, he wrote the score for many feature films, and several of his songs were nominated for Academy Awards. He also accepted handsome fees for songs that were used in commercials. While it is possible that he might have been a better actor than he imagined, he was unquestionably a huge hit as a composer and singer.

Randy Newman was my first significant rejection. Others - many others - would follow.

But don't feel too sorry for me. Well, at least not yet. There will be plenty of time for that later. Along the road to eventual failure, there actually were some "yeses". And some surprisingly good ones, too. None of them, however, arrived via a direct route. For example, this one:

Dick LaPalm was a friend who ran one of the major recording studios in Los Angles. Before that, when

Nat King Cole was a hugely popular singer, Dick had been his manager. He'd been in the music business his whole life and seemed to know just about everyone. We worked together in Chicago when he was the marketing chief of Chess Records, and I did their advertising. For many, reasons, we maintained our friendship long after he moved to Los Angeles.

There is no greater proof of our friendship than this: Dick possessed two highly coveted season tickets to the Chicago Bears. For Chicagoans, there are few items as precious. In divorces, determining which parent gets the children is more easily settled than which partner retains the Bears' seats. Instead of giving up the tickets when he moved to Los Angeles, he continued to pay for them, but sent them to me, wrapped in a package insured as if it contained rare gems. For years, I suffered through freezing temperatures in Soldiers Field watching the Bears sink to extraordinary levels of failure. The seats were good, the weather was bad, and the Bears were simply awful.

When I moved to Los Angeles, Dick and I continued our relationship – both as friends and business associates. The Village Recorder, the recording studio that he ran, was unquestionably one of the best in the city. It's where the Rolling Stones, Fleetwood Mac and a lot of other major stars recorded albums. Often, after leasing out a studio for an extended period and accepting an unconscionable amount of money, The Village Recorder ran an ad in Billboard and other trade magazines to let the music community know that another hit album had been recorded there. I did those ads.

Because he talked with them almost daily, Dick had lots of stories about rock stars. This is one he always found especially amusing.

When filming <u>The Last Waltz</u>, a documentary about the final performance of The Band, Martin Scorsese got to know all the players very well. While obviously a fan of the group, as the shooting progressed, he became especially impressed with the lead guitar player, Robbie Robertson.

In addition to being an exceptional musician and songwriter, Robbie also had a great sense of humor and a captivating personality. And it didn't hurt that he was also exceptionally handsome.

As the two got to be friendly Scorsese began to feel that Robbie's personality and talent would also serve him well as an actor. Eventually Scorsese acted on that belief and cast Robertson to play a significant role in his next film.

The Screen Actors Guild allows non-professionals to appear in a feature film without joining the union, but only one time. If they are in a second film, they need to become union members. Because Robbie had already on screen for much of <u>The Last Waltz,</u> if he was to be an actor in Scorsese's new film he was required to join.

That was not a particularly big deal. All he had to do was go to the union offices and fill out the necessary paperwork.

While there, Robbie met with a union representative whose job was to explain the benefits and responsibilities of SAG membership. Even more importantly, the representative offered some cautionary advice. Essentially his job was to warn all potential SAG members that being in the union was no guarantee of employment or, more importantly, earning a living wage as an actor.

He told Robbie that 90% of SAG members do not earn enough through their acting jobs to support themselves. Just to cover living expenses, most had to take on other jobs. He wanted to be positive that Robbie understood that reality and didn't continue until Robbie nodded in agreement.

Even then, he was not done. Because he'd been on the job for many years, he knew that actors who joined SAG often had unrealistic expectations. So he reiterated the financial issue and explained that the income for most SAG members was actually below poverty line. Averaged over the course of a full year, SAG members often earned less – much less – than $5,000. For many, that number was even lower.

Given that reality, he asked Robbie the same question he asked all new actors when they signed on as SAG members: how much do you think you'll earn?

Robbie didn't hesitate. "$500,000".

Hearing that outrageous number made the SAG rep almost speechless. He'd given his warning speech about income many times before and even the dullest listeners had grasped the message. Perhaps Robbie had misunderstood his question. So, he rephrased it. Slowly and methodically, he reminded Robbie that he was just joining SAG because of a single role. He had no previous acting experience and there was no assurance of ever being cast in another part. Once again, he reminded Robbie that 90% of SAG members earn less than $5,000 a year. So, slowly, carefully and with some trepidation, he asked again. What could possibly make Robbie think that he'd earn the staggering sum of a half million dollars as an actor?

Robbie considered the question carefully because he was having difficulty coming up with a good reason. But he did have an answer.

"I don't know. That's just what they're paying me."

Because of our friendship, I spent a lot of time with Dick at the Village Recorder - hanging out, meeting his friends, and eavesdropping as the biggest stars in the industry recorded and talked about music. I know this may be shocking to hear about people in the music business, but, on occasion, there was some partaking of non-pharmaceutical medications. My proximity to the participants meant that I sometimes enjoyed a contact high and, just as often, and without hesitation, happily shared in the consumption.

During one of our free-flowing conversations, I told Dick about my Scarlet Ribbons script, and he had an unexpected, but welcomed, response. Because of his many years in the music business and his extraordinary ability to maintain relationships, I probably should not have been surprised when Dick told me that he not only knew the guy who wrote the song but was happy to arrange for the two of us to meet.

Jack Segal and I first met at the Village Recorder and, afterwards, many other times in many other places. In his prime, Jack had written some songs that became classics, but by the time we got together he was no longer a hot young song writer. Which is another way of saying he was neither young nor in great demand. So, for relatively obvious reasons he was thrilled to learn that his lyrics had been the inspiration for a film script. Because his current involvement in the music industry consisted essentially of teaching a song writing course to fledgling composers of questionable talent, he had plenty of time on his hands and was excited about participating.

Once Jack was on board, it made sense for him to be responsible for all the music. So not only was Randy Newman no longer in the film, neither were his songs. They were out and Jack's were in.

As much as I loved Randy's music, I was more than willing to accept the change. Jack had some wonderful compositions to his credit. Two of them "When Sunny Gets Blue" and "When Joanna Loved Me" are unquestioned standards. Finding a place where both songs could fit into the script was relatively easy. Most of Jack's other songs were, at least in my opinion, not nearly as good as Randy's, but having him as an enthusiastic team member seemed to make the entire package stronger. In general, I was pleased to be working with him and adding his professional credibility to the project.

Because he was the person responsible for the "Scarlet Ribbons" lyrics, Jack, quite justifiably, had some comments about the screenplay. Those comments eventually led to script adjustments. Since

I was never fully comfortable with the plot, when his suggestions seemed reasonable, I was happy to make adjustments.

Some of that happiness began to fade as time went on. Here's one example: As an important part of the story, I thought it would be a good idea for the father to write a song as a Christmas gift for his daughter. That made sense. Because he had limited funds for a gift, a song written specially for her seemed like an appropriate present. So that song became an important piece of the film. And, because no such song existed, by default, it became Jack's responsibility to write it. The assignment was one he relished and couldn't wait to tackle.

While I continued to fine tune the script and talk about it to everyone who had even a peripheral relationship with the film industry, Jack worked diligently on his composition. It took a few weeks, but once he was certain he'd nailed it, we set up a date for him to come play it for me. He unfolded the sheet music, accompanied himself on the piano and proudly sang his heart out. There were almost tears in his eyes when he finished. He turned to me in anticipation of what he was certain would be unbridled appreciation.

I wanted to like it. I needed to like it. I wish I liked it. But I didn't. I'm certain I could have handled my rejection better. I know I could have been less than upfront about my disappointment. But some things are hard to fake.

For obvious and painful reasons, that meeting ended poorly. I think Jack might have been willing to do some work on the piece if I had been more careful about my critique or if I had offered something in the way of at least a helpful suggestion. The "what ifs" were plentiful, but the fact remained that he really liked what he had written, and I really didn't. Middle ground was non-existent. For the time being, we agreed to disagree.

But wait, there's more. There was another hurdle to overcome, and it, too, was a big one. Jack didn't like the way the film ended. He was proud of his lyrics and proudest of the mystery behind the appearance of the ribbons.

For me, that was more than a minor issue. The entire reason I conceived the film, developed the plot, and spent months writing the script, was because of the ending I had conceived. That's where I had begun. To me, the ending was everything.

But because Jack felt so strongly and because, after all, the film was inspired by his lyrics, I tried to find a way to reach a compromise. My solution was to retain at least some of the intrigue but also offer enough clues to indicate that the ribbons might have appeared through something other than the mysticism that Jack had always envisioned.

The new ending was, at best, satisfactory. But at least there was a conclusion that both of us were willing to accept. Sometimes compromises are inevitable. Sometimes they should be avoided at all costs. In retrospect, this was one of those times. What the ending now lacked was the enchantment Jack believed to be so important and the heart-warming explanation that had been the impetus for my script. I could have used Mr. Hindsight's advice at that moment but, as usual, he was apparently pre-occupied.

By that point, I had written and re-written the story many times. Characters had changed. Some were added and some removed. Plot points had been altered to a significant degree. Conflict was added, eliminated, and added again. And now, even the ending had been redone.

After months of work, I felt I that the ball had been advanced considerably.   Many friends had read various versions and offered suggestions. Some advice was rejected by politely pointing to the anatomical part of the body where useless suggestions could be shoved. Some of the ideas seemed like worthwhile improvements. Eventually, I felt comfortable with the plot. Although I didn't have a commitment from anyone to play the lead, I was comfortable that casting a singer/actor could be accomplished. Surely there were performers who could handle both assignments.   I knew I had a sweet story that had potential to become a Christmas classic. I had a partner who composed the well-known title song and offered the rights to his other, even more famous, hits. Music clearance was not going to be an issue.

I was ready to start checking off some other boxes. Instead of just talking about the film, it was time to start circulating the script.

First stop: Disney. In the land of G-rated movies, Disney was king. Even if I didn't know anyone there, Disney would have been an obvious place to begin. But I did know someone there and he was much more than a casual acquaintance.

Bob Levin and I had been partners in Chicago years before and remained close. We were the Bob and Howard of Bob, Pete & Howard, an advertising boutique that won a ton of awards. But for me, the awards were insufficient compensation for Chicago's brutal winters. After three years, we closed the business. I moved to California, Bob moved to Texas and Pete moved to New York.

Sometime later, Bob accepted a once-in-a-lifetime offer to become president of international marketing for Disney. His responsibilities included overseeing an advertising budget of several hundred million dollars and guiding the release of films that took Disney from last to first in box office receipts. Michael Eisner and Jeffrey Katzenberg got the credit and certainly deserved it, but Bob was an important cog at the very top of the wheel. Because of that, I felt confident he could get my script to the right people.

Following the well-established theory that there are better places to keep eggs than all together in the same potentially slippery basket, I looked for other paths to pursue, and then went down all of them. Disney would get the first look-see, but surely there were others who would find my script irresistible.

My writing agent in Hollywood was an obvious resource even though his experience was entirely limited to TV sit-coms. He wasn't optimistic about his ability to peddle a script for a feature film, but because I was a client, he was willing to shop it around.

As I recall, he explained it this way, "I'll make some calls." Probably not the wildly enthusiastic response I was hoping for.

I also had my own list. It included some professional acquaintances, some names given to me by friends, and some guys who either repaired my car or refinished my floors. Because, in Hollywood, well...you never know.

I made a lot of calls, had a lot of lunches in appropriate dining establishments and, as I should have expected, made very little progress. To be completely accurate: almost none. Some of the people I met had connections, but those connections seemed to have been poorly wired. A few believed they had secured an important place on the list of movers and shakers but didn't seem to realize that they were the ones who had been shaken and fallen by the wayside. Others listened attentively, offered encouragement and if I was really fortunate, split the cost of lunch.

Although I didn't realize it at the time, I was never more embroiled in the Hollywood experience than I was at that moment. I was having meetings with people who know little, talked a lot, and accomplished practically nothing. Those meetings are, if not the lifeblood of the entertainment industry, certainly the blood sucking part of the business. If a meeting is defined by the attendance of two or more people, then there are plenty of Hollywood meetings. But if meetings are defined as events during which something of consequence is determined, then my luncheon activities would be better described as social get-togethers. Despite the importance of the names bandied about and the earnestness of the discussions, the progress made was similar to a kaffeeklatsch chat during which the merits of oat and almond milk are examined in depth.

Almost immediately the "no's" began to trickle in. The first one came from Disney.

My friend had given the script to the Disney reading department where it promptly curled up and died. The reader didn't see much value to the script at all. For someone who is employed as a studio reader, that response is typical. At a major film studio – and Disney is most definitely major - readers occupy space at the lowest level of the pecking order. Almost by definition, they are the ones who get pecked.

The process works that way for good reason. Readers are the first ones to see almost any script (and certainly any script that comes without benefit of linkage to an important Hollywood name). That's because one of the most sacrosanct requirements of senior executives involved in film production is that they must, due to their jam-packed schedules of meetings, lunches, and phone calls, have scant time available to even glance at anything that hasn't been previously read, reviewed, or commented on. That's why readers exist.

A reader's job is to read (although some, in a burst of honesty, may admit that they only skim) and comment on the dozens of scripts that arrive at the studio on a daily basis. After spending as much as 10 or 15 minutes reviewing work that took months to write, the reader has an important decision to make. Either relegate the script to the ever-growing pile of rejects or send it on to someone who holds a slightly elevated position in the approval hierarchy. It's not a tough decision. For a reader, rejection is always safe. It's proof that their job is being done well. Although not specified in their job description when hired, it is their responsibility to keep unwanted, unacceptable material away from the ultra-busy higher ups. Nobody ever questions a "no". But a "yes" - even a qualified "yes" carries enormous risk. A "yes" requires follow-up. A "yes" means that someone in a much nicer office may need to re-arrange an important lunch meeting or arrive late for a session with a personal trainer in order to actually read the script. The danger could not be greater. Every time a "yes" from a reader eventually results in a "no" from a superior, unhappiness reigns.   A string of reader "yeses" that are ultimately rejected invariably leads to serious questions about the reader's taste, judgement and, more importantly, ability to spot potential hits. What is ultimately questioned, at that point, is the reader's job security.

My friend at Disney showed me the reader's comments. I felt some of the negative notes indicated that perhaps portions of the script had been read, but in many instances completely misinterpreted. It was clear that the reader was totally unfamiliar with the song "Scarlet Ribbons" and, out of laziness, boredom, or the impending need to quickly fetch an oat milk latte for someone with a window office, never finished reading. But the low-level rejection was more than sufficient to cement disinterest from Disney. No further "no's" from Walt or his minions were required.

My friend probably could have pushed a bit harder on my behalf but doing so would not have served him well. His job was to help the films that Disney produced become as successful as possible. His job was decidedly not to participate in determining what films should be made. Even at his very senior position, any suggestions he might make in that regard would almost surely have been met with a better phrased version of "Who asked you?"

So, OK, that door was shut. <u>Scarlet Ribbons</u> and Disney were destined to go their separate ways. It has yet to be determined if Disney ever recovered from that loss.

Because my script was for a Christmas film, I was confident that there would be, at the very least, a moderate level of interest. Studios, and especially TV networks, can always use something fresh for the holidays. And if the show does well, having a standard that can be aired year after year makes for a solid investment.

A lot of people were willing to meet with me. A lot of people read the script. Well at least they read a synopsis or maybe a few pages. They certainly read the title. It was only two words so even busy executives had sufficient time to do that. I was hardly overwhelmed with positive reactions but at least there was enough interest to keep me in the chase.

The first bit of definitive encouragement came from a producer who wasn't affiliated with a studio. He liked the script and wanted to option it. We negotiated a bit, but because he was the only one who seemed willing to put money on the line, I accepted the Writers Guild minimum and gave him 3 months to see what he could do. I know this is difficult to believe, but there were few times during those 3 months when I was overwhelmed with phone calls from him indicating that a major deal was in the offing.

Nevertheless, after those 3 months, he felt that there was sufficient enthusiasm for him to want more time.

Once again, I accepted minimum payment, and he pressed on. I realized, of course, that I was nowhere near having anything even approaching a deal, but I did have rent and groceries covered for the foreseeable future. And, because someone had been enthusiastic enough to put cash on the line not once, but twice, I was beginning to feel at least somewhat hopeful. The two paid options in my checking account were ample proof that I was in the game.

When the second deadline passed without a firm offer, he gave up. But all was not lost. While he had been busy accomplishing very little, I had been busy as well. Although I went down more than my share of blind alleys and turned over a lot of rocks that only revealed more rocks, I managed to uncover someone else who was interested. Actually, very interested.

I was offered Hollywood money for an option – in other words, much more than Writers Guild minimum. And the deal was for more than 3 months. The new guy wanted the script for a full year. There was no chance I'd turn down the offer. The money was great, but the enthusiasm and commitment were even better. I knew I was a long way from a green lighted production, but the time I'd spent writing was clearly beginning to pay off.

About halfway into the option year, the would-be producer wanted to meet. He wouldn't tell me the reason, but even though I knew that there was no deal in hand, he was very excited. He invited me to have lunch at one of the more important places to be seen – not too posh but well known and most definitely overpriced.

Because he'd been living with the script for some time, and had many conversations about it, he had some thoughts he felt were worth discussing. Based on some of the reactions he'd been getting from studios and independent producers, he strongly believed that a re-write would help. Essentially, the plot and the Christmas theme were all well received, but there seemed to be general agreement that more conflict and perhaps a more intense love story would amp up enthusiasm.

I agreed. I always felt that dialog was one of my strengths, but I struggled with plot development. There was no question that the script could be improved. But just because I agreed didn't mean I had a solution. I had just started a new job as the executive vice president of an advertising agency, so I didn't have time to do a re-write.

He had a ready response. He was willing to pay a writer to do the work if it was OK with me to eventually share screen credit. Again, I was totally on board. A good writer could certainly help overcome the script's weaknesses. Just as importantly, by hiring a writer, he was investing even more money in the project, so I knew he'd continue to be aggressive about trying to find a home for it.

About a month later he called with news. He'd been in discussions with a senior producer at a TV network and he assured me that there was genuine interest. In fact, there was more than interest – a meeting had been set up with the network executive and two of their senior producers. As the person who conceived and wrote the script, he felt it was important that I participate. Because this was, by far, the closest I'd come to meeting with anyone who could green light a production, I didn't need much persuasion. I was anxious to attend.

While the re-write was being done, I was busy at my advertising job. I knew that changes were being made but I had no idea what they were. That situation needed to be remedied before the meeting, so a revised script was delivered to my house. To say the least, it was quite a revision.

One of the concerns about my screenplay was that the story was perhaps too soft. Many people – and I was one of them - felt that more conflict would give the story more pace and more impact. I was prepared – and looking forward - to some new twists and turns. I was ready for something different. But I wasn't ready for what I read.

In my original version, the father's girlfriend worked in the film industry as a stylist. Her responsibility was to dress sets, arrange props and make sure that the scene looked the way the director and art director wanted. As a stylist, one of her responsibilities was finding needed props and making the arrangements to rent or purchase them. It was on one of those purchasing excursions that she met the father in his cab.

In the revised script, she was still in the film business but now worked as the script girl. The change in her job title wasn't especially important. What was important was the change in the film she was working on. In my script, the production was a G-rated, made-for-TV movie. In the revised version, it was a porno film – XXX rated.

In a typical film, the script person has important responsibilities - making sure that the correct lines are being read and that there is continuity between scenes. If a scene is being shot for a second time, she's responsible for making sure that the actor's hands are in similar positions, and that the wardrobe and hair look the way they did on previous takes. It's an important job because if the details don't match, editing becomes a problem.

In a porno film, the function of the script person is considerably diminished. Story, acting performance, and continuity are seldom more than minor considerations. What matters is the sex and what doesn't matter is pretty much everything else.

In the re-written version of <u>Scarlet Ribbons</u>, there was an issue with the lead actress. "Actress" is a rather generous way of describing the performing responsibilities for the female lead in an X-rated film. But this issue was a big one: she wasn't there. She may have been drunk; she may have missed her call time, or she may have been upset by something and walked off the set. I don't remember the explanation for her absence because it wasn't especially important. What mattered was that, without an actress or a willing, female naked body, the sex scenes were going to be far less erotic. So, to save the production, the script girl – the father's girlfriend – stepped out of her clothes and into the role. In so doing, she happily made herself – and her various body parts – both accessible and penetrable.

The conflict that was so appallingly missing in my version burst on the scene like a thunderclap when, unexpectedly, the father arrived on the set. For rather obvious reasons, he was less than pleased when he saw his girlfriend completely disrobed and performing some acts that even consenting adults do not always consent to.

When I read the new script, I had no trouble understanding that the tone had dramatically changed and that tension, conflict and energy had been added. But – and maybe it's just me - I was more than a bit surprised to see hard core pornography finding its place smack dab in the middle of a sweet Christmas story.

If I had bothered to ask about the writer's credits, I might have been better prepared for the new version. A few years earlier, after the unanticipated blockbuster success of <u>Deep Throat</u>, X- rated films became popular with mainstream audiences. One of them, <u>Behind the Green Door</u>, starred Marilyn Chambers. Like Linda Lovelace, she became a star even though her acting talents did not require memorizing or delivering any particularly difficult lines. The writer of that film was the guy who did the <u>Scarlet Ribbons</u> re-write. Apparently, the theory "write what you know" guided his hand.

I met the producer at his office about an hour before the network meeting we were scheduled to attend. I had decisions to make – none of them particularly appealing. I could have refused to participate in the meeting – citing my concern that, under normal circumstances, I don't consider fellatio to be a typical part of yuletide celebrations. Or I could assume the much more traditional Hollywood position by accepting the re-written version as pure poetic improvement and, if sold, accept my share of the writer's money. I knew, in the unlikely event that the script ever was made into a film, I could always have my name removed from the credits. Because, by this time, I was beyond ready to move on, I decided to go with the flow. Essentially the position I decided to take was this: pay me and I'll happily disappear.

Network meetings, I've come to realize are all relatively similar. They are held in either a conference room or an impressive office. The setting is usually casual, and the seats are often expensive, designer chairs. Everyone is cordial. Everyone is positive. But most of all, everyone is noncommittal. Even though no one said "no", when the meeting concluded, two things were clear: 1. we hadn't made a sale and 2. I was done.

The ease with which a made-for-TV Christmas movie could evolve into hardcore pornography was, for me, the final straw. At that moment, my energy for the project completely disintegrated.

I was somewhat surprised to realize that after so many hours of work, so many meetings, so many discussions, and so many possibilities I was able to close the book with such finality.

But that's what I did.

It was a few years before I worked up the energy to write another screenplay. And even longer after that for me to write a third.

In the true tradition of Hollywood, all three of my scripts made money for me. But none of them were ever made into films.

Beaver U.

A wonderful premise, a memorable title, and a guaranteed commitment from a major film studio.

What could possibly go wrong?

Some names are funny. They just are.

We've all grown up knowing people who have been less than fortunate because their parents have been overly creative or, what is more probable, entirely clueless.

Mrs. King certainly did her child no favor by giving him the first name of Nosmo because she was impressed by an important looking metal sign at her favorite restaurant: "No Smoking".

The unlucky twin daughters of a recent immigrant had to wait until adulthood before they were able to legally change their names from Modess and Modessa.

And, of course, there are limitless names that may or may not be attached to a real person, but are, nevertheless, a constant source of amusement:

I.P. Daley
Ophelia Bottom

Connie Lingues
Master Bates
Stella Virgin
Yuri Nator
Sal Ami
Heywood Jablomi
Ben Dover
Hugh Jass
Ivanna Kutchakokov
Jack Goff
Dick Burns
Mike Oxlong
Willie Dicker

There is the story, perhaps apocryphal, but nonetheless possible, about the substitute teacher who requested the students in her class write their names on the sheet of paper she circulated. When the list was returned, she read the names aloud and asked the students to identify themselves so she could associate faces with names. The process worked well until there was no response when she announced the name "Mike Hunt." After being greeted with silence and a few snickers, she tried again. "Is Mike Hunt here?". More silence and some choked-back laughter. But she wasn't done. "This isn't funny. I need to know what Mike Hunt looks like. Surely someone in this room has seen Mike Hunt." From that moment on, any chance of providing valuable instruction to the class evaporated completely.

Movie titles seldom offer the same potential for hilarity due to legal restrictions regarding off-color humor. But the film I was asked to write came close to skirting that line.

First, some background.

Among the many who read my Scarlet Ribbons script as I attempted to have it made into a feature film, there was a group that had recently enjoyed enormous success with their first film project: The Buddy Holly Story.

The Buddy Holly Story Story

There are many good story tellers.

Sometimes the story is the star – so fascinating all by itself that even a poor teller of tales can't ruin it.

There are some who spin yarns so effectively that the story is immaterial – just hearing the description of unfolding events is sufficiently enthralling.

My friend, Freddy Bauer, often provided a combination of both. I offer this example of a story he told many times to consistently amused audiences. Since he is no longer with us, I'll do my best to retell it, knowing full well that his embellishments will be sorely missing.

Fortunately, I have a lot to work with. This is a true Hollywood story with all the necessary elements: rags to riches, financial and critical success, drugs, and even tragedy. Undoubtedly sex was involved as well, but since Freddy was circumspect about some adventures, those escapades will have to be left to the imagination.

The story begins in Carversville, PA. a relatively small town about 2 hours from both Philadelphia and Manhattan. Because it is close to the Delaware River and all its natural beauty, many city folk have summer homes in the area. About 15 minutes away is the village of New Hope, not much more than a single street filled with an endless number of stores offering cuteness and scented candles. All year long it is busy on weekends. In the summer, there is a daily tourist infestation.

The area is quite lovely with its rolling hills, creeks, and woodlands. Although, like many other places that were once considered too far from the city to permit reasonable commutes, this part of the Pennsylvania riverside is now being developed. Much to the displeasure of longtime residents, clusters of new, similarly shaped, similarly painted, quickly constructed homes are springing up. There are now cul-de-sacs where trees and farmlands formerly co-existed.

Freddy lived in one of the oldest homes in the area and, in fact, one of the oldest homes in America. Built in the late 1700's, it has been somewhat updated, but the original stone exterior remains unchanged. The house was constructed over a creek with a trap door in the kitchen that reveals a staircase leading to the creek below. That unique feature was designed for very a practical reason. A few hundred years ago, it was where foodstuffs that needed to be kept cold were placed.

During his life, Freddy had a multitude of jobs – most of his own invention and mostly involved with radio, music, and entertainment. When this story begins, he was a consultant, or to be more accurate, unemployed.

Although he had stashed away enough money to keep food on the table and the wolf from the door, Freddy was not above accepting Uncle Sam's generous offer of unemployment funds. With a sense of justified pride, he became a regular visitor to the office where the checks were handed out.

That office was understandably busy because unemployed people who may be lax about other responsibilities are quite punctual about receiving their checks. Long lines were not uncommon. Freddy waited patiently in the longest line and, while there, struck up a conversation with someone else who had also willingly chosen the extra-long wait. Both shared the same reason – they liked the guy who handed out the checks at window #3.

With nothing more than that in common, they found reason to continue talking and, after gathering their monthly stipend, treated each other to lunch - a practice that they began to repeat with regularity. Because of their shared appreciation, it wasn't long before they invited the unemployment guy from Window #3 to join them. That is where the story picks up momentum.

Apparently, Mr. Unemployment's goal in life was not to be a minimum wage government worker handing out checks to people with dubious reasons for shirking employment. He considered himself a writer and, in fact, had written a screenplay. It turned out that Freddy's new acquaintance from the long line fancied himself a film director. And Freddy, firmly believing he had all the necessary tools to be a film producer, saw no reason why the three of them should not fulfill their destinies as Hollywood moguls.

Lunch concluded with a decision to start a film company. Project #1: make their new friend's screenplay into a feature film. The fact that none of them had experience, contacts or personal fortunes was considered only a minor impediment. They had two things firmly in place: a goal and self-confidence.

There are now some enormous gaps in the story. Big ones. I don't know how the process unfolded, but I do know the eventual result.

Somehow, a scene from the film was shot and edited. I don't know how much it cost, where the funding came from, who the actors were or how anyone involved was compensated. I don't know who paid for the camera, sound and lighting equipment or the wardrobe, props and set construction. I don't know how a crew was assembled, how an editor was hired or how a soundtrack was added.

What I do know is that, not only did all that happen but, at least in the minds of Freddy and his partners, the result was a total success. They firmly believed that if they showed the short film to others, raising the funds to complete the film would not be a problem.

Of course, that was a ludicrous belief. True, they had demonstrated a modicum of filmmaking ability, but they were in rural Pennsylvania, not a exactly a hotbed of film production or financial resources. It was hardly the best place to seek the million dollars of additional funding that was needed.

Because they had never lacked confidence and were now armed with something that proved their ability to make a film, they decided to skip the middleman. Instead of attempting to raise funds for an independent production, they opted to go straight to Hollywood where they could meet studio executives who would enthusiastically green light their project.

Once again, I'm short on details. I have no idea how they were able to arrange the hoped-for meetings. Major film studios have great regard for people with proven success, but minimal interest in anyone else. It is next to impossible to get wary studio executives to take time away from their important luncheons to see a short presentation film written, produced, and directed by people who have no previous credits, experience, or connections.

But somehow meetings those meetings took place. Even better, in what surely accounts for a Hollywood miracle, Freddy and his friends, after innumerable frustrating encounters with professional naysayers, were able to find a welcoming audience at a major studio. There, in a situation where the reasons for saying "no" always far outnumber the reasons for saying "yes", against an overwhelming stack of odds, their project received a positive reception and, even more astonishingly... funding.

How successful was that meeting? $1 million successful.

Although $1 million was a whole lot of money for Freddy and his friends, for the studio, it really wasn't much of a gamble. In the past, they had blown more on an actor who decided that honoring his contract was less important than over-dosing on heroin. They had spent more on a script from a famous writer who, instead of delivering it on time, had the temerity to die almost immediately on the way home from making the bank deposit.

The studio not only liked the script but were also impressed with the quality of the scene they saw and potential for a story about a real rock 'n roll star who died a famous and untimely death in an airplane crash. For a major Hollywood film studio, a $1 million investment in a project that had lots of upside was a mere pittance.

But for Freddy and his friends, a million dollars was a fortune.

They picked up the check on a Friday afternoon and then spent the weekend euphorically celebrating their success.

Had they been back home in Pennsylvania, that celebration might have included the purchase of several cases of beer, some burgers and buns for a backyard barbeque, and some rowdy participants who partied until sunset.

But they were in Los Angeles where celebratory options were ever present and the possibilities for extravagant entertainment were apparently unlimited. Champagne and over-eating at a restaurant frequented by A-listers was at the top of the list. A suite – better yet – several suites – at the Beverly Hills Hotel seemed appropriate. And, because Hollywood festivities are required to last well into the night, drugs needed to be added to their To Do List.

It didn't take them long to make the appropriate reservations and purchase a reasonable amount of cocaine. In other words: too much. Then they spent the duration of the weekend making sure every bit was consumed.

There are many tried and true ways to snort cocaine. All manner and sizes of plastic, paper and even metal straws function quite well. But as proof that the phrase "cocaine is God's way of letting you know that you have too much money" many feel it is preferable to roll up a $100 bill to accomplish the task.

Freddy and his friends had something even better: a $1 million check. From Friday evening until late Sunday night, that check got a workout as it was passed around, rolled, re-rolled, and put to the arduous task of vacuuming up every speck of the white, magical powder.

Early Monday morning, sleep deprived but still glowing with satisfaction over their weekend celebration, they went, as a group, to open an account at the bank.

After explaining that they wanted to start with a $1 million deposit, they were asked for the check. Unfortunately, no one could remember who was the last to use it, so a few moments elapsed while they fished around in pockets – only slightly embarrassed over the apparent misplacement of a million dollars. Eventually the check was found and proudly handed over. The vice president of the bank was more than a bit surprised to see that the check he held displayed the full effect of its weekend workout. It was well worn and frayed around the edges. After having been folded, unfolded, rolled, re-rolled, and shoved up multiple noses, multiple times, the condition of the mutilated piece of paper belied its extravagant value.

Freddy and his friends were justifiably pleased with their deposit but even more pleased that its condition was so disturbing to the bank executive.

In short order, the bank account was opened, the film was produced. and a few months later <u>The Buddy Holly Story</u> was released.

It was, by all measures, a resounding hit.

As promised, this story included rags to riches, commercial triumph, drugs, and a Hollywood ending. But I also promised critical success and tragedy.

How's this?

When the celebrity presenters on the nationally televised Academy Awards Show announced that <u>The Buddy Holly Story</u> was the winner for Best Original Screenplay, the recipient was not available to accept the award.

The night before he had committed suicide.

Enough about Buddy Holly. Back to me.

Even though my friends who were responsible for the film were brand new to the game, because they had demonstrated such complete command of the business (after all, they had hired the writer and then produced and directed a very successful film) they were instantly a hot Hollywood commodity. Not surprisingly, in short order, they secured a 3-picture deal with a major studio.

Although they had no interest in <u>Scarlet Ribbons</u>, they were interested in me. They liked the way I wrote but had no desire to make a sweet Christmas film. They were strictly focused on comedy – something I felt, if not right up my alley, was at least reasonably adjacent. So, we made a deal. I was hired to write a screenplay based on an idea that they – and I – thought had surefire potential.

When we met, they were already well into pre-production on their second film – a fictional story based on actual situations that had all the earmarks of a can't miss farce. The plot, while somewhat important, was, in many ways, incidental. The on-going humor was based almost entirely on the antics of the unusual cast that would be causing non-stop havoc behind the scenes.

More background:

In 1939, there were two blockbuster movies. <u>Gone With the Wind,</u> and <u>The Wizard of Oz</u>. Casting the leads for the first one was problematic because the options were overwhelming. Every major actor and actress in Hollywood actively vied for the roles and every day another A-lister expressed interest. <u>The Wizard of Oz</u> faced an entirely different casting dilemma. 150 little people were needed to portray the Munchkins. But at that time, it was rare to see even one little person in public. Finding 150 willing to be humiliated by appearing in a motion picture proved to be nearly impossible.

The difficulty was totally understandable. In 1939, Little People did their best to remain invisible. When seen in public, they carried the burden of being an embarrassment not only to themselves but their families as well. So they stayed out of sight as much as possible. Most of them lived lonely, solitary lives, completely cut off; hidden from the rest of society.

For obvious reasons, the search for actors to play the part of Munchkins was far-reaching and on-going.

Merely locating them was difficult but, once found, convincing them to appear in a film was even harder. Casting directors scoured the entire country and still fell far short of the needed number. In short order (pun intended) the nationwide search went worldwide.

Eventually – and the process took months – 150 Little People were brought to Hollywood and put up in a hotel situated near the shooting location.

What happened next should have been anticipated but came as a complete surprise to almost everyone. The Little People – the ones who had, for their entire lives never seen anyone who looked like them - were suddenly in a place where absolutely everyone looked like them. Instead of being outsiders, they were the in-group. After being secluded, made to feel different and unwanted, they were everywhere. A lifetime of pent-up emotions exploded in uncontainable joy. Their inner Shriner was released. From the moment they saw each other, they partied non-stop and consumed a seemingly endless supply of drugs and alcohol. Because for the first time in their lives they felt attractive, sexual inhibitions disappeared. By the second day after they arrived, the drunken orgy was running full blast and displayed no signs of diminishing.

For the Little People, it was a dream world. For the director and producer of The Wizard of Oz, it was a nightmare. Wrangling a cast of hung over, sleep deprived, non-professional actors – many of whom didn't even speak English - was a horror show. Understandably, the shooting schedule was continually extended – and the longer it took, the happier, drunker, and more unmanageable the Munchkins became.

The film my new friends were making, <u>Under the Rainbow</u>, was essentially an invented behind-the-scenes story that took place during the shooting of <u>The Wizard of Oz.</u> As such, it offered the assembled cast of Little People the same opportunity for merriment, bad behavior and over-indulgence that took place decades before. Although times had changed and assembling the cast of Munchkins was much easier, expecting them to behave any differently was pure folly. To the surprise of no one, the Little People partied like it was 1939 all over again.

Enough background. Time to move on.

Their idea for the film I was hired to write was inspired by an actual woman's college that was, to say the least, inappropriately named. If Beaver College had been a school for men, no one would have given the name a second thought. But for a woman's college …. well, the problem was obvious.

For years, even in America, there was a pervasive attitude about women and education. It began with the concept that a woman's place was in the home where her responsibilities were limited to cooking, cleaning, and churning out babies. Eventually women fought for – and earned – the right to attend school. But their attendance was followed by other concerns – especially when it came to higher learning. Educators worried that attractive women would be disconcerting to men who, instead of paying attention to their studies might have other, less appropriate, and more carnal desires in mind. Nevertheless, college for women gradually came into acceptance. For them, those same educators reasoned, studies could be re-adjusted and dulled down so that even the fairer sex could comprehend the information. But even that was deemed insufficient. Because competing with men and their obviously superior minds, would surely be a humiliating experience, many colleges were exclusively women-only.

But times were changing. Men's colleges, to the horror of many alumni, started allowing women to attend. The trend was happening slowly, but the direction was clear, and the end game seemed inevitable. All colleges and universities would eventually be co-ed. In time, even colleges that had been exclusively women-only, would eventually have to accept students with external genitalia.

The premise for the film I was hired to write was to explore what might happen when the rules for admission changed as the first male students arrived at a previously women-only college – one with a slightly fictionalized name, "Beaver U". Based on the obvious opportunities for comedy, nudity, and bad behavior, it was imagined that the initial men's class would be less interested in academic education and more interested in hands-on sex education. The basic idea for the yet unwritten Beaver U, was explained in a single phrase, "The Bowery Boys go to Vassar."

I got the joke immediately. And I was all-in from the get-go.

We had, I thought, an unquestionably great start. In addition to the title, Beaver U, there were plenty of ingredients that had the earmarks for a successful film. The introduction of a few unpolished men into a women's college that had no experience dealing with male libidos offered seemingly unlimited prospects for tasteless jokes, plenty of sex and a total disruption of academic rules and norms. If that sounds familiar, it's because a few years later, <u>Animal House</u>, a film with all those attributes, became a huge money maker.

We were confident that we had the important elements in place. We were, however, missing one thing: a plot.

The solution to that problem led to one of the very few positive experiences I can recall from my entire venture into the Hollywood scene. Instead of handing off the writing assignment to one person (me), it was determined that we'd make it a group effort – an incredibly foolish idea. Because too many people and too many egos would be involved, that idea should never have worked. But it did.

The process was straight-forward. A group of about 6 of us began meeting every week to talk about the plot and the way it might unfold. There was no structure to those meetings other than a strictly enforced starting point: before we did anything else, we shared a joint. And, because the effects of marijuana tend to wear off over time, there were occasions when we offered little resistance to sharing another one or two as the conversation rambled on.

The introduction of marijuana created 3 important and predicable outcomes: 1. A free flowing exploration of ideas, 2. A heightened readiness for uncontrollable laughter, and 3. An almost total inability to remember a single thing that was discussed.

In what was surely one of the few truly valuable contributions I made, I came up with a solution to the problem of memory lapses: I taped the entire meeting. In an act of pure brilliance, I was careful to turn on the tape recorder before taking my first hit, thereby ensuring that my lone technologic responsibility was successfully accomplished before I was too stoned to remember which button to push.

The sessions usually lasted an hour or two. We covered a lot of possibilities and gorged on a lot of less than healthful snacks. Ideas and convulsive laughter flowed freely. Everyone contributed. No one was in charge. No one was blamed for a stupid idea. In fact, those ideas were often the ones most appreciated.

The next step was all on me. I went home and listened to the tape – many times. Then I attempted to construct a story by putting the accumulated thoughts into something that resembled an actual script. A week later, when we gathered for the next meeting, we smoked some more dope, reviewed my suggestions, and let the sparks fly once again.

Under normal conditions, when a script is submitted, there is a strong sense of self-protected ownership. That's because, by then, the writer is heavily invested. The screenplay has been meticulously constructed. Criticism or suggested changes may be tolerated - and even reluctantly accepted - but are seldom welcomed or appreciated.

This situation was entirely different. I wasn't writing my own story; I was simply trying to organize the thoughts and ideas that all of us had tossed around. I was not married to anything I wrote. On the contrary, I was just as thrilled when one of my lines or thoughts was appreciated as I was when suggestions were made about something that should be changed, added, or eliminated.

The unwritten rule about comments was that there was only one goal: did the suggestion make the story funnier? Fortunately, there was an easy way to make that determination: whatever generated the biggest laughs was probably the way to go.

It's hard to imagine a more enjoyable activity than eating, laughing, and spending time with good friends. But, for me, there was a bonus. Because, based on the previous success of <u>The Buddy Holly Story</u>, and the 3-picture deal my friends had signed, the script we were working on was not only already green-lighted for production, but money had been allocated for the writer. Me.

So, for those keeping score, the full scope of our arrangement meant that, in addition to having a great time with my friends every week, I was being paid handsomely for my participation.

Even though I relished the process, I was also aware of potential roadblocks. I pointed out that there was a probability – more likely a certainty – that Beaver College (the actual school) would have some objections to the proposed title of our film: <u>Beaver U</u>. Legal issues are always a high priority in the entertainment business, and I knew this could be a difficult hurdle to clear. But it wasn't. My friend had anticipated the concern and had a ready answer. He didn't want to argue the point. He felt that if the film was a success, Beaver College would be entitled to compensation, and he was certain that a fair resolution could easily be determined.

So, we continued meeting, I continued writing, and the laughter and checks kept coming. Life was very, very good.

While <u>Beaver U</u> was gradually evolving from a concept into a very funny screenplay, my friends were busily involved in their second feature film, <u>Under the Rainbow</u>.

Their plate was very full. Interrupting the non-stop party of 150 Little People and encouraging them to arrive at the set on time, neither sleep-deprived nor hung over, required patience, resolve and the realization that such an objective would never be met. In addition, there were the normal, totally unpredictable production problems that always seem to occur when making a film.

After two weeks of shooting, one of the supporting actors stopped coming to work. He had a good excuse: he died. His absence required not only finding another actor to replace him, but also re-shooting every one of his scenes – a time consuming and expensive process.

Another actor determined that his consumption of cocaine was insufficient. As a consequence, he spent more energy fretting about his supplier's deliveries than learning his lines. On more than one occasion that concern was so great, he not only forgot his lines, he also forgot to come to the set.

Representatives from the studio, whose main responsibilities seem to be worrying and interfering, had concerns they felt needed to be expressed on an almost daily basis. Most of their issues were little more than annoyances and relatively easily allayed, but their frustration about the shooting schedule was, unfortunately, right on point. After the first week, the production was already a week behind. Even worse, that slow pace seemed likely to continue.

My friends had enjoyed a truly wonderful experience with their first film. They liked the cast, the screenplay, and the entire process. For them, every day of shooting had been an exciting adventure. As they viewed the dailies, their enthusiasm mounted. They wondered, because everything about <u>The Buddy Holly Story</u> was so positive, if they would ever feel unhappy or disappointed about any film they produced. Apparently, they could. For all of them, <u>Under the Rainbow</u>, was physically and mentally draining. The filming was slow, over-budget, and worst of all, not nearly as funny as they had imagined it would be. Nothing was going well and all of it was costing more money.

Despite ongoing threats from the studio to halt production, realizing that so much had already been invested made completing the film the lesser of two evils. Cutting bait would mean a total loss, but if the film was finished, at least some of the studio's money could be recouped.
Apparently, not enough. <u>Under the Rainbow</u> opened poorly and never gained momentum. The negative reviews from critics and lackluster enthusiasm from movie goers was hardly a surprise. Although not a total bomb, <u>Under the Rainbow</u> never came close breaking even.

For my friends, the fallout came quickly, but not unexpectedly. The studio decided not to honor their 3-picture deal and <u>Beaver U</u> became yet another in an endless line of screenplays that would never be made into an actual film.

When the dust settled, my friends left Hollywood and returned to their cats, dog, and their 1700's stone house on Fleecy Dale Road in Pennsylvania. I moved to Manhattan, resurrected my advertising career, and proceeded to fill the TV airways with mediocre commercials for a company that no longer exists. The studio retained the rights to <u>Beaver U</u> but, for both predictable and unexplainable reasons, kept it under wraps while other films about college life – and especially those involving tasteless jokes, nudity, and rebellious students – continued to be made, and continued to make millions.

There are two kinds of Hollywood endings. One is the self-satisfied, happy conclusion that most of the film-going public experiences: lovers reunite, the bad guy gets his come-uppance, or the mystery is solved. The other – and the one that occurs with far greater regularity – is far more melancholy. An idea that begins with great promise ends in disappointment and disillusion. No matter how much money may have been exchanged in the interim, for all those involved, little satisfaction is derived from their participation in an unsuccessful film.

A postscript.

153 years after it was founded, for very practical reasons (and certainly a few having to do with decades of embarrassment), Beaver College was re-named. Now known as Arcadia University, it is a fully co-educational institution.

Beaver U, on the other hand, continues to exist only in the minds of a few lifelong friends.

Goodbye, Goodbye Girl

Things were different in 1980.

Way back in the pre-millennium age, there were no cell phones, no personal computers, no social media, and no podcasts. There was no internet, no Facebook, no Amazon, and no Google. Apple was a brash, young upstart tentatively tiptoeing in areas so tightly controlled by mighty IBM that there was constant danger of being crushed into applesauce.

Although then, as now, we craved information, news arrived in less than real time increments. The least current information came from magazines that provided perspective on events that occurred a full week and often a month before. Newspapers that were delivered every morning contained news at least 24 hours behind the times. Radio provided important information about traffic along with hourly updates that essentially repeated the same information throughout the day. And at 6 and 11 p.m. the day's events were summed up in a few minutes on television along with much more detailed reports about the local sports team and valuable predictions about tomorrow's weather provided by bowtie clad professional meteorologists or extremely attractive women in skintight dresses.

All media flourished. None, however, did better than television. In most homes across America, the TV was turned on after dinner and provided the entire scope of entertainment for the remainder of the evening. Program choices were limited because there were only 3 networks. During prime time – from 7 until 10 p.m. - the battle for viewership was fierce because there were unprecedented – unconscionable - financial rewards for success. Every 1/10 of a rating point was worth at least $1 million. Loosely translated into real dollars, billions (with a "B") were at stake.

No question about it: the big money was in television.

Every year in early autumn, with great fanfare, all three networks announced their new lineups. Successful shows from the previous year returned – almost always with new guest stars, new plot twists and plenty of new bells and whistles. Programs that had achieved disappointing numbers were as welcome as yesterday's fish and were summarily replaced.

The new shows – the replacements – were chosen with great care because the rewards for high ratings were incalculable. Failure, however, could be devastating. Not only would the show's low viewership mean less income for its half or full hour of airtime, but just as importantly, a poor rating would also adversely affect the audience of the show that followed.

That's because, in addition to the other technologic marvels that 1980 citizenry had to survive without, there were no remote controls. Changing channels required putting forth the munificent effort of rising from the sofa, walking all the way across the living room and then – if you can even imagine this – manually turning a knob to switch channels in order to view another program.

Because, for great swaths of viewers, such strenuous activity was to be avoided at all costs, whatever show followed the one currently being watched had a definite leg up. So, for the networks, inertia alone was worth at least a rating point or two (as well as many millions of dollars).

All across America, the boob tube became the focal point for the evening. That was understandable because the benefits of TV viewing were unbeatable. Conversations were no longer necessary and, because dinnertime was now TV time, people could pride themselves on multi-tasking by simultaneously viewing and chewing. New terms like "couch potato" and "TV dinner" entered the lexicon.

It didn't require a financial whiz to realize the benefit of airing a successful show. Understandably, every network went to great lengths to make sure the new ones added to the lineup had the best possible opportunity to draw a crowd. But they were faced with an enormous problem: how could audience approval be determined until a program went on the air?

The answer came from the least creative department at the network: the research nerds. It fell to the guys with pocket protectors and calculators to devise a way of testing a show <u>before</u> the network was forced to make a very expensive commitment.

Suddenly, research was king, and the TV Pilot was born.

Instead of producing a full schedule (13 episodes) of a new show, the network went into test mode. For each potential program, a single "pilot episode" was produced. Those pilot shows were then shown to a carefully selected group of typical TV viewers. Based on the results of those showings, the network could make a better-informed decision about which programs were likely to do well and which were likely to find a secure resting place far down the toilet.

During pilot season, each network produced multiple shows – knowing full well that some of them would never make it on to their fall lineup. But, for the network, even knowing that the great majority of pilots would be unsuccessful, the process still made sound financial sense.

That's because if they produced a dozen pilots and then decided to go ahead with only 2 of them, the benefits would be significant. The primary benefit was that they'd have some assurance, based on test results, that the show would generate at least acceptable ratings. Additionally, by actual count, it cost less to produce 12 pilots than to produce a full slate of episodes for even as few as 2 or 3 programs – a total of 26-39 shows.

Not surprisingly, pilot season generated a frenzy of activity in Hollywood. Everyone had an idea for a show. Absolutely everyone. Sometimes the concept came from network executives. Sometimes it came from producers of shows that were already successful. Sometimes the network had existing commitments to stars. Sometimes film studios like Columbia, MGM or 20th Century Fox offered suggestions. And every waitress, car parker and pool boy in Beverly Hills had a personal treasure trove of surefire ideas.

Each network considered the proposals carefully. Discussions – pro and con – occurred daily. Everyone who participated had a comment – some of them, surprisingly, worthwhile. Most participants just enjoyed hearing the sound of their own voices and did their best to be simultaneously opinionated and noncommittal. But deadlines are real, so eventually decisions were reached, deals were made, and some proposed pilots moved forward into production.

The process may seem orderly and carefully orchestrated. It is not. In addition to research results, the reasons for selection are often highly arbitrary and based on nothing more than hunches, friendship, a desire to hang out with a certain celebrity or, if all else fails, the flip of a coin.

Network executives, like many executives scattered throughout the corporate world, are not always deserving of their lofty salaries. They are loath to take risks. They fear loss of face infinitely more than they relish success. Like the donkey that starved to death standing between two piles of hay, there is little that confounds network executives more than taking a firm stand and making a decision. What they do best is offer thoughtful reasons for going both left and right. Even those on the higher rings of the corporate ladder end up bumping into each other more often than leading the way.

While there are many who have the authority to say "no", a "yes" requires considerable courage. That's because if the decision to move forward turns out to be incorrect – and expensive – the underlings who had previously offered wholehearted support are quick to abandon ship. They justify their abrupt about face by pointing out that somewhere, somehow, their misgivings were previously noted and have now been unearthed in a desperate attempt to save their own jobs.

Pilots that test well and have the blessing of an executive who possesses both testicles and a magical gut that has previously predicted winners, now become programs that are produced and then promoted heavily. More often than not those shows eventually meet with ambivalent audience interest that is soon followed by the humiliating removal from the network's schedule. Research, it turns out, can be flawed.

Pilots that test poorly, because they are already paid for in full, are sometimes slipped into an opening during the summer schedule. Ad revenue for shows during warm weather months is lower because viewership goes down when temperatures rise, and people spend more time outdoors. The theory is that no one is watching anyway, so it doesn't matter what is on the air.

Poor test results are the surest way for a pilot to be discarded, but there are many other reasons for an abrupt ending.

An unlikable star, less than brilliant writing, a poorly produced plot, unappealing situations, mediocre acting, competition from similar shows, a genre past its time, and a plethora of other issues can all play a part. Even a single, relatively minor problem can be more than enough to bring a show down. But for success, everything – absolutely everything – needs to fall into place. Not surprisingly, that seldom happens.

Every year during pilot season, there are one or two shows that test audiences absolutely love. With off-the-chart research results in hand, networks confidently green light these few sure-fire winners for a full slate of episodes. It happens every year. Unless it doesn't.

Apparently, 1980 was one of those years and I was involved in one of those shows.

It took a confluence of bad timing, poor judgement, and inflated egos to wrest failure from the jaws of inevitable success. Here's how that sad saga unfolded.

At the time, MGM was slumping badly. Their feature films were not doing well at the box office, and the studio hadn't produced an on-air TV series for several years. To save the sinking ship that was their film division, MGM made a dramatic and somewhat questionable move. They hired David Begelman, an executive who had led Columbia on a run of major hits, but who also joined them with heavy baggage. He had been accused of embezzlement. The accusation turned out to be deeply embedded in truth and although he admitted guilt, Columbia didn't press charges. They reasoned that having him resign in disgrace was, at least for a big-time movie exec, punishment enough.

But apparently in Hollywood, respect for box office success clearly trumps immoral, dishonest, and blatantly illegal activities. So Begelman was handed the keys, a substantial salary, and the challenge of reinventing both himself and MGM.

Although MGM had offered several pilot proposals to the networks for the coming season, the responses had been almost entirely negative. Only one attracted interest. The studio owned the TV rights to Neil Simon's film, <u>The Goodbye Girl,</u> and NBC had already indicated enthusiasm about its potential. Even though getting a green light to produce a pilot was a long way from having a hit show, it was, at the very least, a first step towards establishing a functioning television division at the studio.

The Goodbye Girl was one of very few pilot concepts that had all the positives in place. It was a spinoff of a highly successful feature film that was written by the acknowledged comedy master, Neil Simon. Another TV spin off from one of his plays, (and also a feature film) The Odd Couple, was already one of television's legendary successes. So, for The Goodbye Girl, the stars were in alignment. Success, if not inevitable, was at least plausible.

To keep the ball rolling in the right direction, MGM needed someone to helm the project. Because the show was so important to the studio and because it was their only shot for the coming season, they took no chances. Allan Katz was hired as writer and executive producer of the pilot. He'd begun as a writer on Laugh-In and quickly stepped up to producer and executive producer responsibilities on many other successful shows. Most recently he had been the executive producer of MASH, the number one rated TV sit-com for several years. With Allan on board, the quality of the writing – and humor - was never in doubt.

Jimmy Burrows agreed to direct the pilot. His father, Abe Burrows, had been a well-recognized Broadway actor for years, so Jimmy had been around comedy his whole life.   While most directors only had eyes for film, Jimmy was laser focused on television. His talent proved to be ideally suited for situation comedies and in a relatively short time he became a Hollywood favorite. He directed many episodes of popular sit coms and was the director of choice for most of the episodes of "The Mary Tyler Moore Show". A few years later, along with the Charles brothers, Jimmy created "Cheers", another long-running hit show.

During pilot season, Jimmy was unquestionably the busiest and most expensive of all the directors. But having him on board was an important early addition, and yet another security blanket for MGM.

The most critical member of the production team was, quite obviously, me. My job was as ill-defined as my crushing lack of experience or credentials. Allan wanted me on the team because, as a veteran of TV wars, he knew that having someone on his side at all times – someone he could count on for honesty and perhaps even a bit of protection when needed – would at least buffer some of the animus that would surely be coming his way.

Allan and I had a long history together. We worked at the same advertising agency in Chicago where we wrote and produced radio and TV campaigns that were outrageous, memorable, and occasionally even effective. Most noteworthy of our efforts was Screaming Yellow Zonkers, the first – and possibly still – the only food product sold in a black box. The illustrations were done by Push Pin Studios in New York and Allan provided almost all of the hysterical copy. I deserve significant credit for the writing on the package too because I made important contributions. Allan showed me his copy and if I laughed, it went on the box. We have remained friends ever since.

Although studio executives usually have formal offices – and, depending on their title, quite often very imposing ones with sitting rooms, private bathrooms and desks the size of a family sedan - producers, writers and assorted "creatives" usually do not. Their workspaces are often in bungalows furnished with whatever the previous tenant didn't want to keep.

The bungalow assigned to Allan was typical. There was an area set up as a poorly furnished living room and two much smaller rooms – one with a desk for him and another, hidden around a corner, where his secretary sat. Sitting was pretty much her main assignment and she took it very seriously. She left her appointed spot only for lunch and union-mandated coffee breaks.

The main room was where everything happened. It's where the two of us had coffee every morning, where we planned the day, made script revisions, and discussed important issues like whether there would be time for tennis later in the afternoon. Amazingly, there always was.

It's also where everyone came to meet with Allan. There was a steady stream of set designers, cameramen, assistants and, pretty much, everyone else on the production team.

Casting was a primary function of the room. The fact that it didn't feel very formal made the always uncomfortable process of casting a little less intimidating.

For most actors, casting is a nerve-wracking experience. They know they have a very limited amount of time to make a good impression, so their anxiety level is usually high. They know there is competition because the waiting area is filled with actors who are auditioning for the same part. And, although their agents have probably offered some notes to prepare them for the session, they really have no idea how a choice will be made.

Casting sessions usually begin with a brief introduction and some chit chat. But, in a manner of minutes, the actual audition begins. Often the scene that has been chosen involves another actor, so someone is assigned the task of reading with the actor who is auditioning. Usually that someone is the casting director or an assistant. Very seldom is that person a seasoned professional – which hardly enhances the opportunity for the actor to deliver a good performance. There could be any number of people who participate in the final judgement but not all of them are in the room when the audition takes place. Senior executives are far too busy having important lunches to attend casting sessions. They comment on the performances later after viewing them on videotape. Even in the best of situations, the experience is awkward, uncomfortable and provides the actors with severely limited opportunity to demonstrate their talent.

And yet, there are some who thrive in auditions. They enter with confidence, perform with assurance, and leave feeling good about themselves.

The other 99 out of 100 depart with full bloomed insecurity. Whether or not their beliefs are based on fact, they firmly believe they could have done better, should have done better, and will not be invited to return for a call back.

Because the process of auditioning is so awkward, it is an opportunity made to order for Allan. The more uncomfortable the situation, the funnier he gets. He was consistently able to diffuse the tension almost as soon as the actor walked into the room. He views that as his responsibility, and he handles it better than almost anyone. Although it may be difficult for actors to relax during an audition, Allan at least gave them a running start.

During the get-to-know-you moments before the reading takes place, the actors are often – understandably – ill at ease. Some are skilled at the art of making small talk with total strangers, but most are not.

One actress struggled for something positive to say, so she commented on the room. She told Allan that she appreciated the way it was decorated and even mentioned that she particularly liked one of the paintings. I have no idea if she really liked it or if that was just the first positive thing she could think of. In truth, the painting was not good – it was a reproduction of a terribly executed outdoor scene that had been printed poorly and framed even worse.

It was impossible for Allan to let her comment slide. "Really, you like that painting? I think it's awful. In fact, let me show you how awful I think it is." With that, he got up, walked to the painting, jammed his pen into the middle of it, and ripped downward, leaving a gaping hole in the middle. Then he calmly walked back to his seat on the couch, ready for the audition to begin.

I was hysterical. She was aghast. I'm not sure how she recovered – or even if she did. I do know for certain that she didn't get the part.

The painting remained in its relatively destroyed state for a long time and curiously, no one mentioned it. But, at a later casting session, another actress felt compelled to ask.

Allan was quick to explain. He walked to the painting, jammed his pen next to the original hole and ripped downward. Then he took a scissor and removed a strip from the center of the picture, showed the strip to the actress and told her "I'm going to keep this swatch so I can match it with the new carpet."

Somehow that explanation made sense to her. But she didn't get the part either.

Even though I spent all my time with Allan in his office, because of my exalted position, I had a private office of my own. It was inconveniently located in another building but, what it lacked in accessibility, it made up for in other ways. Years before, it had been Lana Turner's dressing room and had been attractively decorated in my favorite colors – baby blue and pink. There was no desk, but there was a small living room, a very large closet, and a private bathroom. All of that was totally unusable because none of the lights worked. The darkness wasn't much of a problem because I was almost never there.

One afternoon, for reasons that will forever remain a mystery, I went to my office and discovered the source of the lighting problem. There were no bulbs in any of the lamps. I called Allan's secretary and explained that, entirely on my own, I had solved the darkness issue. She was unimpressed by my discovery but was willing to provide a solution. Her response: "I'll have an electrician sent over".

Within minutes, an electrician arrived. Because the job was not one that could be easily handled, he brought two helpers. Between the three of them, in only a matter of a half hour or so, they were able to replace the bulbs in all 4 lamps. I never saw the bill for their professional service, but my guess is that, in addition to the new light bulbs, the union electricians were well compensated for the expertise, efforts and screwing dexterity.

Casting <u>The Goodbye Girl</u> went slowly because the stakes were so high. After meeting a lot of big-name talents and screen testing many of them, Karen Valentine was cast as the lead. Her performance in <u>Room 222,</u> a show that was originally created as an ensemble production with a cast of equals, eventually became a break-out, star-making role for her. Karen was the unanimous choice of not only Allan and Jimmy, but the NBC executives as well. She had legitimate acting chops and showed excellent comic timing. She was also unquestionably adorable.

The search for an actor to play the Richard Dreyfus role took a while. At one point, Jimmy and I went to New York to meet with some of the actors currently starring in Broadway shows. While none of them ended up in the cast, there were obvious benefits to being in Manhattan on MGM's dime.

We stayed at the Plaza Hotel where, for reasons having to do with confusion or ineptness; I ended up in the room that Jimmy had specifically requested. Although it was considerably nicer than the one he was forced to endure, just between us girls, he didn't exactly suffer. On our first morning there, because of schedule issues, we had a quick breakfast at the hotel, where for slightly less than $100 each we enjoyed a lavish breakfast of coffee, toast, and scrambled eggs. Today, that would still be considered expensive. But in 1980, it was beyond ridiculous.

After striking out in New York, the search for a leading man continued in LA for another few weeks. Michael Lembeck, son of one of the main supporting actors in <u>Time Out for Sergeants</u> (The Sergeant Bilko Show), and later a very successful TV director himself, eventually outdistanced the other contenders.

Lily Haydn was cast as the daughter. She had never acted before but had amazing bloodlines. Her mother, Lotus Weinstock, had done stand-up at almost every comedy club in NY and LA and had at one time been the girlfriend of Lenny Bruce. Because of her limited experience, Lily was a more difficult sell to the network, but her natural ability and disarming style ultimately won them over.

From the first table reading, everything about the show felt right. The fact that I had nothing to compare it to seemed unimportant. I understood funny and I understood good acting and, along with Allan and Jimmy, treated the useless suggestions from the network execs with the lack of respect they thoroughly deserved.

As we moved further and further into rehearsal, the notes from the network continued to reveal a complete misunderstanding of anything to do with comedy. Issues were raised about wardrobe, hairstyles, and other trifles. Their suggestions were offered with a sense of seriousness that might normally accompany the eulogy of a fallen national leader. The depth of their concern knew no bounds, yet the reasons for their comments seldom made any sense.

Observing the network suits in action was only amusing up to a point. There was obviously an unwritten mandate requiring each of them to make comments for fear that a lack of expressed concerns might indicate a lack of devotion to the project. But their comments were always balanced by the realization that nothing they said should ever be deemed controversial or, even worse, actionable. They fretted and offered notes with proper obsequiousness but were careful not to offend and nodded knowingly and appreciatively when their requests were either ignored or denied. I was continually impressed by their ability to display a strong combination of positivity combined with apprehension about infinitely unimportant topics. Their goal was opaque: at any time in the future, they could refer to a previous conversation and prove that their doubts were well deserved. Every one of them mastered the art of sounding intelligent, communicating little, and all the while making certain that their tastefully knotted ties never loosened.

While conversations with the network execs continued unabated,
sets were constructed, wardrobe decisions were made, and rehearsals continued in earnest. At the same time, the main production was honing into shape I was busy working on the opening credits. I had some interesting ideas about songs that would be applicable and did my best to secure the music rights.

My first choice was the Groucho Marx song, "Hello, I must be going." With its comic tone and message – and especially with Groucho's performance - it seemed just about perfect to set the mood for a show called <u>The Goodbye Girl.</u> And it surely would have been except for a minor issue: Groucho's estate didn't share my enthusiasm. Their first suggested price was outrageous and when I made a counter offer, they raised it.

My second choice would also have been wonderful but was equally problematic. I knew it would be. The Beatles performance of "Hello" ("You say goodbye, I say hello") was more than an acceptable back-up. Although in later years the rights to several Beatles songs were granted for TV commercials, we had no such luck. I didn't even get to negotiate price. I just nodded knowingly to myself when I heard "no way" over the phone.

The more we rehearsed, the more the show kept improving. Allan re-wrote on a daily basis. Funny became funnier. Jimmy encouraged the actors to try variations of their performances to find the perfect combination of believability and hilarity. Everyone was open to everything. No one was afraid to try even the most outrageous idea. By the time we were ready to shoot, the show was tight. And very, very funny.

As a general rule, sit-coms are filmed twice - both times in front of a live audience. There are significant benefits to a second filming. In between the two performances the cast gathers and, along with the writer, director, and a few well-dressed network execs, discusses what worked, what didn't and what should be changed. Sometimes lines that felt perfect in rehearsal fall completely flat in front of an actual audience. And, often, there are surprising laughs where none had been anticipated. As the first show is being filmed, notes are taken. Then, during the break, the entire performance is discussed, suggestions are made, and lines are rewritten. The second show, even though it is essentially the same, feels quite different in many ways.

What happens during the break between performances is quite revealing. If the first show went poorly, everyone feels the weight of failure. The air in the room is heavy with gloom. There is no escaping reality. If the show didn't work the first time, everyone knows that the problem is not going to be solved by anything that can be quickly changed during a brief intermission. Improvements are possible, but a better failure is still a total flop.

The meeting between the two performances of The Goodbye Girl was unusually brief and extraordinarily upbeat. That's because everything we thought would work, actually did. Even parts that we hoped might draw an appreciative giggle or two brought long and loud belly laughs.

We went through the motions of suggesting improvements. Just because the show was good didn't mean it couldn't be better. We even listened to the long-winded, empty-headed chatter from the network suits. Everyone was willing to try something new but only because everyone felt certain that, based on what was already in the can, we had a hit on our hands.

Surprisingly, the second show went even better. There was no nervousness or concern. The actors exuded confidence. Their obvious enjoyment was contagious. The audience – the very same people who had seen the show before – responded even more joyfully. For many of them, hearing the same joke a second time made it even funnier.

The wrap party was definitely a party. It's possible, although I can't be certain, that one of the network executives even loosened his tie. Confidence reigned supreme. A good time was had by all.

Even though editing, mixing and color correcting wouldn't be completed for a week or more, already the buzz was beginning to mount. The network suits who attended the filming dutifully reported back to the network suits who hadn't. Even though they wanted to be cautious, their giddiness about being associated with what seemed destined to be a legitimate hit was hard for them to keep under wraps.

Good vibes notwithstanding, <u>The Goodbye Girl</u> was hardly out of the woods. The show still faced the daunting testing gauntlet – the place where TV pilots go to die. Test audiences are a fickle bunch. It seems that every person recruited as a research participant no longer considers him or herself to be a typical TV viewer. Instantly they transform into film critics. As, such, during the testing process, cynicism prevails.

Determining the future success of a film or TV show based on the opinions of a panel of "regular people" is, at best, a dicey endeavor. No one in the industry likes testing. Everyone concedes that it is an imperfect process. And yet every film studio and every TV network participates. Audience comments are studied intently, numbers are scrutinized, inferences are drawn, concerns are raised and inflated. Cons are carefully evaluated. Calculations are checked and re-checked. Assumptions are made and re-made. And then the head of the network (the only one who actually has the ability and authority to say "yes") issues an official pronouncement.

The decision from on high mirrored the reaction of the audience that saw the live performance. And it was fully supported by research. The test results were off the chart. In fact, <u>The Goodbye Girl</u> was the highest rated of all the pilots tested that season.

<u>The Goodbye Girl</u> was a "go."

MGM was thrilled. NBC was thrilled. And the happiness trickled down. Everyone who participated in the show, no matter how minor their involvement, experienced the glow of success. There is nothing quite like the glorious feeling of being a player on a winning team.

Because there were so many positives, even before NBC officially ordered episodes of the show, we set about the business of taking care of the details that needed attending.

One of our tasks was getting network clearance from Standards and Practices - the legal group that grants approval, demands change or sometimes removal of just about anything in the show that might be of concern. They do their work with almost fiendish care. Nothing makes the worker bees in this department happier than the opportunity to tell a high-priced Hollywood writer or director that something they love is simply unacceptable.

Under the watchful eyes of Standards and Practices, there are no uncomely sightings of cleavage and no implication of deviant or even normal sexual activity. Equally unacceptable is an indication that a woman possesses something as wantonly alluring as a nipple. They are as careful about words as they are about visuals. In evaluating the show, they expressed many concerns about jokes that they found in less than appropriate taste, but there was one line they found to be beyond the pale.

Before revealing the offensive line, allow me to explain:

The Goodbye Girl revolves around an unusual threesome. They are: a mother, a daughter, and an aspiring actor who has somehow been given the keys and believes he has the right to live in their subletted apartment. Although no one is particularly pleased with the living arrangement, for financial reasons they agree try to live together until more suitable accommodations can be found.

The actor may or may not have talent, but he has unquestionably enjoyed little success. At one point, to earn some money, he is reduced to appearing in a play for young children, dressed head to toe in a squirrel costume. To complete the outfit, he carries a large burlap sack filled with Styrofoam acorns. He returns home from the show earlier than expected, still wearing the ridiculous costume. It's a sure-fire sight gag and the audience loves it. They also love his response when the mother reasonably asks, "What happened?"

He explains, "The director asked me to speak like a squirrel and, in his opinion, all squirrels have a speech impediment. It was too embarrassing. So, I quit on the spot. I threw my nuts over my shoulder and walked out."

Not unexpectedly, the line got big laughs during the performance. That amusement, however, was not shared by Standard and Practices. They returned the script to us with a thick red line crossing out the words "...threw my nuts over my shoulder..."

Allan was not surprised that the line had been rejected. I also understood the concern but wasn't willing to give up easily. I was determined - even knowing that the battle was already lost – to at least get some satisfaction by furthering the discussion.

I called Standards and Practices and explained to the woman in charge that I was completely baffled. I told her I couldn't fathom the reason for the red line.

At first there was only incredulous resistance. "Well, it's pretty obvious why the line is offensive."

I told her that it wasn't obvious to me. What could possibly be offensive?

That's when the uncomfortable stuttering began. "Well...you know. It's just... I'm sure you understand the implication."

I feigned ignorance once again. "Honestly, I'm totally lost. What implication?"

"Well, he's talking about his nuts..."

"Yes. Of course. He's a squirrel. They're not great conversationalists. Nuts and acorns are pretty much all squirrels talk about."

"But... you know. It's a different kind of nuts."

That's the opening I was waiting for. "You mean the problem you have is that you think he's talking about his testicles? You think that's what he means when he says he threw his nuts over his shoulder?"

The response was reluctant. "Yes."

I was on fire. "He's an actor, not a contortionist. And even if he was, how could he possibly flip his testicles over his shoulder? What kind of a ridiculous, filthy mind could conceive of that?"

"Well, I'm sorry you feel that way. But the line has to go."

"We can live without the line. We have lots of alternatives. But I don't know how you can live with yourself – finding an absurd, sexual reference in the most innocent situation. You certainly have a healthy imagination but I'm very happy that I don't have to live inside your head."

I had no illusions about how the situation would eventually resolve. But I felt quite pleased with myself for at least getting some satisfaction out of the conversation.

The "nuts" line disappeared, as did some other excellent jokes. But there was little that even the smallest minds at Standards and Practices could do to ruin the show. The Goodbye Girl flat out worked, and everyone who saw it agreed that it did.

The only disappointment came when the show order came in from NBC. They committed for 4 – much less than the full schedule of 13 episodes that had been anticipated.

Begelman was outraged. How could the highest testing pilot not get the same order that many lesser shows had been given by other networks?

NBC had the answer to his question. Unfortunately, it was a very good answer.

A lot was happening in 1980. For starters, it was an Olympic year and NBC had the rights to broadcast the highly anticipated summer event. A lot of their regularly scheduled programs would be pre-empted because viewership of the worldwide competition often shattered records. NBC paid handsomely for the rights to broadcast the Olympics and they intended to get their money's worth by showing as many events as possible.   It wasn't only The Goodbye Girl that would face reduced airings, the same would be true for all of NBC's regular programs – even their current top- rated shows.

In addition, 1980 was an election year. Quite often candidates purchase time to tell their story to the American people in something longer than 30 second increments. That meant even more shows would be pre-empted. As the election nears, public interest increases, so all networks extend their news coverage and produce programs specifically devoted to the latest developments.

NBC did the math. In 1980, there would simply be less available openings for any of their regular scheduled programs. Brand new shows that were just beginning to develop audiences would be among the first to be pre-empted.

The fact that the decision to order only 4 shows was rational, thoughtful and beyond reasonable, didn't sit well with Begelman. After the fiasco about his embezzlement and subsequent firing from Columbia, he was in desperate need of a success. Landing a TV show – the first for the studio in many years - would be a major feather in his cap. But being offered only a token commitment was, at least in his opinion, a major slap in the face.

Begelman decided to play hardball. His position was clear: if NBC didn't commit to a full schedule of 13 shows, he wouldn't let them have any. After all, he was offering them a guaranteed money-making hit and he certainly wasn't going to let them have it at a bargain basement price. There would be no compromising. He gave NBC an ultimatum: order a full schedule of 13 episodes or get nothing.

The dick measuring contest was on.

Begelman's dick was pretty good sized. No one had doubts about <u>The Goodbye Girl</u>. While everyone recognized that it was impossible to guarantee a hit, the show did have everything going for it: a well-known title, a proven TV personality, and a pilot that was, by all accounts, very funny and very well received. Begelman also knew that historically, after pilot season ended, the show that tested best had always received a full order for 13 shows. Many of those programs had gone on to become huge hits. It was unprecedented that the #1 tested pilot receive such a minimal order. Begelman felt his position – and dick size – was more than sufficient.

NBC's dick was of significant proportion as well. In 1980, there were, by actual count, only 3 networks. If they refused Begelman's demand, there were only two other potential buyers for the show. And both ABC and CBS had already made their commitments for the coming season. Replacing one of their scheduled shows with The Goodbye Girl would be extremely expensive. Not only would they be paying for The Goodbye Girl, they'd also have to honor their existing contracts and pay full price for the 13 episodes of the show it would replace. They'd be paying twice as much for a show that had never been seen by a national audience. The financial risk was enormous. And every network executive knew, based on years of experience, that even pilots that tested very well and seemed like sure fire hits occasionally ended up failing miserably.

The stand-off didn't last long. NBC politely, but firmly, said "no thank you" and withdrew their offer. It is also possible, given the personalities of the people involved, there may also have been some less than gentlemanly language expressed by the participants.

Undaunted, Begelman immediately approached ABC and CBS. He made his case, explained his outrage, and told them why he'd be thrilled for them to have the hit show that NBC turned down. He – along with either ABC or CBS - would take enormous pleasure in spending the next years not only reveling in the success of The Goodbye Girl, but also being delighted at humiliating NBC for their dire mistake.

The heads of both networks listened and nodded. But the discussions were short. Both were willing to pass.

Very quickly, despite rave reviews and the most promising future of any new show that year, it was goodbye for <u>The Goodbye Girl</u>.

Begelman continued to helm MGM for a short while. But his lack of success with that year's slate of feature films combined with his complete failure to resurrect the television division assured his early demise.

NBC had a rough year as well. When President Carter pulled the United States out of the Olympics, viewership of the event plummeted. It turned out that they really could have used a hit comedy to boost ratings. But that door had been slammed shut and permanently locked.

Of course, the real tragedy was that my short-lived career in television came to a crashing halt. And all I had to show for the experience was a peek under the TV industry tent, and yet another Hollywood story with a less than perfect ending.

Brushing with Fame

Brace yourself, this will come as a shock: Actors who appear in commercials do it for money. Even the dullest among them (and there are a few who fit comfortably into that category) realize their appearance in a commercial will not boost their acting careers. Being branded as a Sell Out – even a well-paid one – is considered disrespectful of their craft.

So, as a general rule (although it's more like an actual, albeit unwritten, rule) actors in commercials are either on their way up or on their way down. If they're flying high, even for astronomical fees, any offer to be an advertising shill, is almost always turned down. There are, of course, exceptions. Some very well-known stars have appeared in commercials that only aired in another country. And, of course, everyone has a price. If there are sufficient digits before the decimal point, well… maybe.
It's hardly surprising that, even though I worked with some famous actors, it was usually before or after their notoriety was in full bloom.

If you're expecting a "tell all expose", prepare for disappointment. Even if I wanted to write one, my interactions were too limited. The best I could offer would be a "tell some."

I don't claim to really know any of these people. Our status was never anything close to equal. We didn't casually meet at a party, we weren't together so I could interview them, and I was hardly seeking an autograph. We were together for only one reason – to do the best possible job of bringing to life the commercial that I wrote or was directing. Even though we both knew who was earning the big bucks, I still had a reasonable amount of authority about what happened during the day.

That meant the basis of our relationship was, at least to some extent, balanced. For a few brief moments in time, the actor knew I could be helpful or, depending on my competency or lack thereof, I could also be a problem.

Understandably, quite often, we had a conversation. Questions were asked of me, and I did my best to answer. Those questions were unlikely to be "what is your technique for avoiding paparazzi or "what Hollywood star are you dating now?". While, happily, sometimes the conversation was just that – a conversation – usually the exchange had something to do with the commercial. Often the actor had thoughts – and sometimes issues - with the script or some aspect of the production. Because I was supposedly in position to at least attempt a remedy, I was often asked to do just that.

Sometimes the concern was about a specific phrase in the script. The actor understood that a message needed to be conveyed, but the precise wording was often something that felt a bit awkward. Ergo the request: is there another way to make the point?

Often that was something I could handle. Based on the conversation, I'd edit the script. And because I was usually the senior representative from the agency, I was able to approve my own changes.

Once that happened, my stock rose considerably. I was never invited for dinner or asked to sit next to them courtside at a Laker game, but for the rest of the day I was The Man.

Because they understood that I had at least some potential to be helpful, on the day of the shoot, the actors were almost always nice to me. But I was more interested in the way they treated everyone else.

Results, not unexpectedly, were mixed.

Many, for understandable and completely anticipated reasons, expected to be treated like celebrities. Requests from them often felt more like demands. Those requests generally involved personal comfort. Some had read the "no black jellybeans" textbook and memorized the important parts.

One actor (part of the ensemble cast of a formerly highly rated sitcom, but now essentially unemployed) was outraged that, among the selection of shoes shown to him was a pair of brown ones. He was furious. "I specifically said no brown. What about that didn't you understand?" The wardrobe woman defensively pointed to the 5 pairs of shoes that were definitely not brown. But, for him that hardly sufficed. "I hate brown. Hate it, hate it, hate it. I hope the rest of the day doesn't continue like this."

We hoped so too. But the tone was set And, since it only takes one asshole to ruin everything, he successfully accomplished that task.

But even though his complaints kept on coming, most went unheeded. I didn't make any of the script changes he adamantly demanded and didn't even attempt a compromise. Because of his attitude, I had no interest in making his life any easier. I just told him that the script had been approved, and for legal reasons, no changes could be made.

That shoot day was uncomfortable from beginning to end. But it stands out because it wasn't the norm. Most of the actors – and especially the more successful ones – were not only professional in their approach to the work, but also in the way they interacted with everyone on set.

Because this was always intended to be a "Tell Some" and not a "Tell All" book, the actor will remain unnamed. If, however, you happen to catch me in an unguarded moment after a drink or two, there's a good chance that I will fess up.

Discovering John Belushi

I discovered John Belushi pretty much the same way Christopher Columbus discovered America. Unquestionably, both already existed, even though neither was known to the great nations of Europe. That wasn't surprising. John was also essentially unknown in the U.S. and even in Chicago, his hometown.

Taking credit for discovering someone who was obviously already there may be a bit of a push, but in my defense, I was among the very few who were present at Belushi's coming out party – his first Second City performance. So, there is that.

My presence at the show was not just a lucky coincidence. I was there in anticipation of some special comedy performances. But none of the performers I had come to see was John Belushi.

Two of the cast members I knew were participating in what they hoped would be their farewell performance. Both were taking a leave of absence, a peculiarly business-like explanation for what they were doing - pausing their Chicago gig to seek fame and fortune in LA.

For both, it turned out to be a propitious move.

Harold Ramus did not strike gold as a performer but became one of the most successful comedy writers and directors in Hollywood. While hardly creating fine art, many of his films (among them, <u>Ghostbusters</u>,

<u>Caddyshack</u>, <u>Analyze This</u>, and <u>Animal House</u>) were huge hits.

Brian Doyle Murray flew under the radar as an actor, writer, and stand-up comedian but, nevertheless, worked often enough to cover his rent and allow him to mingle with B, and occasionally, A-listers. His younger brother, Bill, however, achieved stardom on the TV show "Saturday Night Live", and then went on to greater success as an actor. In addition to his many other starring roles, Bill Murray made 6 films with Harold Ramus – some were blockbusters, and many are classics.

Because our ad agency often wrote and produced radio commercials that were at least intended to be humorous, we were always on the lookout for potential talent. Second City was - and continues to be - the logical place to start.

It didn't take long for the performers there to form the nucleus of our "go-to" group. Although all members of the Second City Troupe had hopes of future success, at the time none were living the lifestyle of the rich and famous. So, when given an opportunity to make extra money – and because getting a check for being in a radio commercial was proof of their membership in the unofficial Society of Professional Comics - they were always pleased to get a call from us. In addition, getting paid for being funny felt a lot better than getting paid to ask, "do you want fries with that?"

Partly because they saw us as golden egg-laying geese, and partly because working together was usually a positive experience, we developed a comradery bordering on friendship. That's why we were invited to attend Harold and Brian's farewell performance.

The absence created by their leaving, meant there were holes in the cast that needed to be filled. So that night, several newcomers were introduced. One of them, making his first appearance in front of a live, paying audience, was John Belushi.

After the show, we congratulated the departing comics and wished the well in Hollywood. We also posed a question: who's the new guy? Clearly, he had made an impression.

During the next few months, we continued to return to Second City – often specifically to see John. His talent was undeniable, and because of that, we cast him in a few television commercials.

Those 3 commercials turned out to be the only ones he ever made.

The first was for a local Milwaukee bank. He played the part of a bank officer who tried to convince Jesse James that stealing money was so last year because, with one of the bank's credit cards, he could have access to money whenever he wanted. It was a relatively straight-forward acting role and one that John carried off effortlessly. The horned rim glasses with clear, windowpane glass lenses that he wore in that commercial remain in my possession as a reminder of my ability to recognize – and occasionally even reward – emerging talent.

In the second commercial John's remarkable comic improvisational ability had the opportunity to shine. Northwestern Mutual, a major insurance company based in Milwaukee wanted to do a Milwaukee-centric commercial. A jingle had been written and recorded. We were given the assignment of using that music as a soundtrack for a yet-to-be-conceived TV commercial. Because simply showing scenes of the city's best-known landmarks seemed woefully insufficient, we thought adding some humanity would be helpful. We envisioned a young couple – a man and his very pregnant wife – spending the day touring Milwaukee. The soundtrack was packed with lyrics, leaving little room for dialog, so we created a story line that didn't require much conversation. Our idea was that the pregnant woman, concerned about her enlarged belly, questioned her attractiveness.   It became the responsibility of her husband to ease that concern.

We spent the day setting up shots in some of Milwaukee's most recognized locations and, in each of them, asked John to do something to put his wife's concerns to rest. What he continued to do, in set-up after set-up and location after location, was nothing short of remarkable. He made her laugh every single time – always by doing something totally unexpected. Her spontaneous laughter had nothing to do with her acting ability – her reaction was the same as ours. It was impossible not to laugh at John's consistently inventive performances.

The commercial was hardly brilliantly conceived but, because of John, it worked beyond expectations. The top brass at Northwestern Mutual loved it. Little did they know that they had a classic on their hands. Once John became a star, deciding to rerun it – as often as possible - was a no-brainer.

The last commercial he did was for a hotel. Owners of The Pfister, Milwaukee's premier hotel, had recently purchased a rival. Although the rooms were sorely in need of updating, the classically designed ballroom required no transformation. So, while the rest of the hotel was being renovated, there was still an opportunity for the hotel to increase their event business.

Two concurrent situations led to the commercial we conceived. First was the enormous success of the film, <u>The Godfather</u>. Second was John's uncanny ability to impersonate the Marlon Brandon character from the film. We'd seen him perform that character several times in Second City shows, and, like the rest of the audience, found it to be spot on.

For the commercial, we re-created the wedding scene from <u>The Godfather</u> in the ballroom of the hotel. Although the scope of the production was huge, the budget was miniscule. So instead of hiring actors, the entire cast was made up of hotel employees – housekeepers, desk clerks and the kitchen staff. We told them that they were going to be in a commercial with Marlon Brando, so their excitement was palpable. John remained off camera – in heavy make-up - until he was brought to the set. Then, in a perfect Brando imitation, he parodied the most famous line of the film, "I want to make you an offer you cannot possibly refuse. On the day of your daughter's wedding, take her to a place where she'll have a nice reception."

Not surprisingly the commercial was a hit, the hotel's business event skyrocketed, and we won a bunch of awards. But, after a promising start, John's career in TV commercials came to a halt as he focused on building his comedy career.

Although we were keenly aware of John's extraordinary talent and convinced that his star was going to ascend, we knew others were less certain. His high school football coach was disappointed that John didn't want to continue honing his promising athletic skills. His father couldn't believe he wanted to skip college in hopes of earning a living by attempting to make people laugh. Even his high school drama teacher felt that with his physical limitations (he was hardly tall, dark, and handsome), embarking on an acting career was an extremely risky endeavor.

Of course, we realized that if he did become a star, no one would admit to any of those negative thoughts. Once he was famous, anyone who had been in contact with him would be only too pleased to say that they always knew he was someone special; someone clearly destined for stardom.

That's why we thought it would be worthwhile to start doing some interviews immediately and begin putting together documentary pieces for a film that would eventually become <u>The John Belushi Story.</u>

Sadly, although the idea made sense to us and would likely have been a valuable commodity, <u>The John Belushi Story</u> never got much further than a written proposal and a few unsuccessful meetings with potential funders. Even so, for John, just seeing how highly we thought of him was a terrific ego boost.

After Second City, John's next job was performing in "Lemmings", an off-Broadway show that quickly generated positive buzz. Chevy Chase, a comedian who already had a following was the big draw. Another cast member, Alice Playton, had become somewhat well-known for her performance in the "Poached Oysters" TV commercial for Alka Seltzer. John, although initially unheralded, ended up as the star. His imitation of Joe Cocker eventually became the closing act – and one that never failed to prompt standing ovations.

While he was appearing in "Lemmings", we were shooting a commercial in New York, so we arranged to meet up with him after the show and take him on his first limousine ride in Manhattan. Because, as a still struggling performer he was living in semi-survival mode, he was impressed by the chauffer and the all-star treatment. It was a style to which he would like to have become accustomed. It was not long before he did.

Years later, John and I re-connected very briefly. It was well after his appearances on Saturday Night Live had made him a popular comic and after his performance in <u>Animal House</u> made him a household name. Starring roles in other films followed. While <u>1941</u> was in production, a friend who was now assistant to the director of the film found out that I knew John and arranged a phone call.

On that call, I told him that, as he surely knew, I was hardly surprised by his success, but was happy to see how much he had achieved. Even though I felt certain his talent would be recognized, I'd never anticipated that he'd become a star in two fields – TV and film. I was a bit taken back by his response. He was offended because my number was wrong. He took pride in pointing out that he was not just a success twice over; he was a legitimate 3-way star. Of course, he was correct. In addition to his film and TV credits, he and Dan Ackroyd – as the Blues Brothers - had a top selling record.

It was not long after that I learned of his death. It was hardly a shock. Rumors about his drug use were rampant. Fame, money, adulation, and solicitous invitations to events where only the rich and famous are granted access, put him on the well-worn path to hedonism and self-destruction.

John was unquestionably a very funny guy. For a while, he was arguably the funniest person in America. But as is the case with shooting stars, the brightest flames often burn out quickly.

How Jeffrey Katzenberg got to be Jeffrey Katzenberg

Jeffrey Katzenberg is readily and appropriately acknowledged as one of the most powerful people in Hollywood. For years he headed the film division of Disney Studios, and under his guidance, the company not only rebounded from years of losses but was able to claim industry leadership by producing mega hit after mega hit. Later, he partnered with Stephen Spielberg and David Geffen to form DreamWorks, quite possibly the most prestigious film, television, and animation company in America.

His accomplishments and status are well known. So, too, is his intelligence and ambition. But there are plenty of smart, highly motivated people in the film business. So how was he able to forge his way past them all so quickly?

These days, wearing bespoke suits and designer glasses, Jeffry Katzenberg looks very much the part of an extremely wealthy corporate executive. But that was not always the case.

The younger version was thin (probably for many years the word "skinny" was more appropriate), short and, to be kind, not possessed of leading man looks. Any one of those features – had it been significantly upgraded - might have been helpful in gaining some sort of respect in a glamor industry that seems to admire appearance above all else. But, completely devoid of even a single positive visual attribute, he began his Hollywood ascent with 2 strikes against him. However, much to the surprise of others, although certainly not to himself, in continuation of the analogy, he immediately began to hit it out of the park on a consistent basis.

When I met him, Jeffrey was at the top of his game at Disney. His private office was enormous and imposing. So too was his outer office where two executive two secretaries worked feverishly to keep him on schedule and do their best to fulfill his continuous requests.

Our meeting was hardly a gathering of equals, but it was one I looked forward to because I was more than a little curious to witness firsthand what made him so remarkably successful.

It was beyond obvious to me that he had reached his lofty position by, at the very least, a combination of intelligence and relentlessness. But attributing his success to brains and aggressiveness is like explaining a basketball victory by saying that the winning team made more baskets. The question should be: how did they make those baskets and how did they prevent the other team from scoring more? I was hoping to see for myself what made Jeffery Katzenberg so special; so unique.

The meeting would be my opportunity to at least get a glimpse into the way he operated and possibly even gain some inkling into what made him such an unstoppable force.

It didn't take long to find out. I got the answer in the one minute we spent together.

The purpose of the meeting was to show him the commercial I made for the videocassette release of the film, <u>Ruthless People</u>, starring Bette Midler and

Danny DeVito. I watched the film several times, consulted with the woman at Disney in charge of the project, and edited a 30-second commercial that utilized what we both felt were the strongest clips from the film. I wrote - and an announcer recorded - a Voice Over that essentially explained that this great film was now be available on videocassette for the remarkably low price of $29.95.

Our meeting with Jeffrey was scheduled for a very specific time. Because his day was, as usual, completely packed, there were, apparently, few openings. We were told to be there precisely at 12:15. We arrived about 10 minutes early, were met by one of his secretaries and told to wait until he was ready for us. We knew that our time had come when he appeared in the doorway and made a gesture with his head indicating that we should enter.

There was good reason for his less than cordial welcome. Although we had prepped ourselves for an important meeting with the guy who ran Disney Films, for him, our visit was not much more than an unwelcomed interruption. As we walked in, he was thoroughly engaged in serious discussions. Neither of his hands were available because each one was holding a phone. He was actively participating in two simultaneous, but completely separate, phone conversations. Without taking a break from either call, he indicated – by pointing to the TV with his elbow – that we should get the commercial ready to show him. Once it was placed in the machine, he used the "waiter, please bring us the check now" gesture to let us know that he wanted us to run the tape.

We showed the commercial and he watched it while continuing to be fully engaged in both phone calls.

The commercial ended and, in short order, so did his calls. The instant he hung up, he gave us his comments.

What we had done was, wrong, wrong, wrong. He was quite specific about the scenes that should have been used in the commercial – and none of them had been selected. After completing his instructions, without pausing for a breath, he indicated that we were dismissed, picked up a phone, and immediately joined another conversation.

All told, we had been in the room with him for about a minute – half of which was spent viewing the 30 second commercial.

What fascinated me was more than just his ability to participate in two separate phone calls at the same time he viewed the proposed commercial. What impressed me even more was the decisiveness with which he articulated what was wrong and how, specifically, to fix it.

Under normal circumstances I would have attempted to at least explain the choices I made and the reasons I felt my proposed commercial would be successful. I didn't do that for two reasons. 1. There was no opportunity. The meeting was clearly over and, as far as Jeffrey was concerned, there was nothing to discuss. Our marching orders had been given. 2. He was absolutely right.

Instead of being upset because my efforts were neither appreciated nor even acknowledged, I realized his perspective on the film and the commercial was considerably more accurate than mine could possibly be. I had seen the film twice. He had been living with it for well over a year. He had greenlighted the script, hand- picked the stars and the director, watched the results of every day's production, was insistent about editing decisions, analyzed the research, and knew – with absolute certainty – what parts of the film audiences loved and what parts they felt were less than wonderful.

He wasn't shooting from the hip with his comments. He wasn't offering a personal opinion. He knew – and probably should have told the woman in charge of the project – precisely which scenes would be most effective in the commercial.

For him, the meeting was business as usual. But for me, witnessing someone handle two phone calls at the same time that he watched and critiqued a commercial was more than impressive. Even though his dismissal of my effort was done in record time, I understood that his rejection was not based on an emotional reaction, but on total understanding of the film and its appeal.

The man could obviously walk and chew gum at the same time. And, if he felt like it, probably juggle and solve calculus problems in his head.

Epilogue

A few years later, I mentioned my 60 second Jeffrey Katzenberg meeting to someone who proudly told me that, at one time, Jeffery had not only worked for him, but had even carried his bags.

The purpose of that remark, I suppose, was to impress. After all, he wanted me to know that at one time he had been more important than the person who was now running Disney Films. Frankly, I wasn't impressed in the slightest. All he did was confirm that he had he failed miserably in recognizing Jeffery's intelligence, work ethic, and trajectory for success.

Unquestionably, along his ascendence to the top, Jeffery encountered many people who he liked, some who impressed him, and a few whose relationships he regarded as being so important that he found a place for them as advisers and co-workers. Those few, he surely rewarded with handsome positions and equally handsome salaries.

I was hardly surprised to realize that Jeffery Katzenberg felt no compulsion to stay in contact with the guy I had recently met – a guy who never recognized the extraordinary capabilities of someone on a clear path to becoming a titan in the film industry.

Instead, he had judged Jeffrey Katzenberg to be someone whose skills would be most appropriately used for carrying suitcases.

I can say with total assurance, it wouldn't have taken me a minute to avoid making that mistake.

The Nobel Prize for Kindness goes to ...

Dinah Shore was, unquestionably, a major celebrity. The reasons for her substantial fame, however, are both completely obvious and yet somehow, surprisingly elusive.

Although I was surely aware of her popularity, it wasn't until I witnessed the Dinah magic first-hand that I truly understood the extraordinary talent that was the at the core of her success.

It is worth noting that the two most common attributes for Hollywood stardom are well acknowledged. Anyone possessed of exemplary good looks or staggering talent has a clear path to the top. Neither characteristic, however, is appropriately descriptive of Dinah Shore.

She was certainly attractive, but hardly a show-stopping beauty. And, although she was an excellent singer (in the 1940's she had several recordings that did quite well) her musical ability alone would never have been sufficient to take her to the heights she ultimately reached – and continued to sustain for years and years.

While obviously bright and clearly ambitious, those qualities were only marginally responsible for her fame. But anyone who watched her top-rated TV show could pinpoint with absolute accuracy her unique gift: she charmed everyone who was with her and made them feel good about being there.

By any measure, Dinah was the consummate hostess. Although surely aware of the rules of etiquette and unlikely to commit the sin of placing the dessert fork next to the soup spoon, it was never her intention to be known as the white gloves and pearls princess. Instead, she created a welcoming environment in her own, totally individual, way.

Her goal was quite simple: She wanted everyone in her presence to feel comfortable. And "everyone" really included everyone – the most famous Hollywood stars, the most powerful political leaders, the wealthiest business tycoons, and anyone who, accidentally or on purpose, happened to be in her immediate vicinity.

When I met her, she was essentially retired from show business after having starred in her own TV show for years. She was, however, still actively involved. The golf tournament, played annually in Palm Springs and a major event on the Women's professional golf circuit carried her name. The tournament had several different sponsors (Colgate, Nabisco and, later Kraft Nabisco) but the name Dinah Shore was always prominently displayed first. Her credibility as both a luminary and golf enthusiast was critical to the establishment of the WPGA. It was her enormous popularity, and not so much the quality of her game, that forever established her as the First Woman of Golf.

Our advertising agency arranged for her to be the spokesperson for one of the major California banks. I wasn't involved in the negotiations, but I'm quite certain that she was more than acceptably compensated for her participation. She may have been a kind and generous person, but her financial representatives felt no need to duplicate her personality traits. Their only goal was to make her fee as financially rewarding as possible and, in the process, do the same for their 10% cut of the action.

Our first in-person meeting, as well as all our other business meetings, took place in her Beverly Hills home. She had been one of the most recognized and well-loved people in America for decades, but she never carried herself as someone intimidating. Quite the opposite. She always made any meeting with her tension-free and completely pleasurable for everyone – even the junior representatives from the agency who felt beyond privileged just to be in her home.

For those of us who were used to regularly attending meetings in board rooms or executive offices, her living room was an unaccustomed destination. And it was much more than the tastefully decorated room in her beautiful house that made the meeting feel so special. It was because she never treated us as business associates, but always as welcomed guests. In preparation for our arrival, she usually baked something– often a cake. Her housekeeper brought in the trays from the kitchen, but Dinah did the serving. She cut the cake, poured the tea, and made sure that everyone was well taken care of.

It was based on those meetings that I was able to understand, first-hand, the Dinah magic. She listened intently, participated fully, and was never anything other than totally and enthusiastically agreeable. Her positivity was contagious. She liked everything, and had kind, encouraging words for everyone. The meetings could not possibly have gone better.

Or so we thought.

Apparently, although we never heard the word "no" or anything even remotely negative, clearly there were at least some things that Dinah did not feel were completely appropriate. Changes in the script or the location or her wardrobe would have to be addressed.

We learned about those needed adjustments later, not long after our meetings at her house had been warm, pleasant, and totally without friction. A phone call from one of her representatives usually began with a phrase along the lines of, "Dinah is not happy about ...."

Based on whatever seemed to need fine tuning, the requested alterations were made, and at the next meeting in her living room, while enjoying tea and cake, the revisions were presented. Her response was always the same. She never acknowledged her previous displeasure but always expressed delight about what she deemed to be significant – albeit unrequested - improvements.

Amazingly, without ever being negative even once, but with a desire to have things changed in accordance with her own very specific needs (and those changes were often significant) Dinah always managed to get her way. I watched it happen every time we discussed a proposed commercial and was always awed by her seemingly effortless ability to exert total control in the surest, gentlest, and kindest way possible.

Producing the commercials that we shot with her took us all over California. Travel arrangements were made with her celebrity status in mind. When we shot in the Sequoia National Park, even first-class air travel was deemed insufficient. So we flew between private airports on a Lear jet. But, although she appreciated the gesture, she was just as pleased to have lunch with me at a diner that I had been to before and thought she'd enjoy because it was so peculiarly All-American corny. She did. She was also totally comfortable with the two complete strangers who recognized her and sat down to join us at our booth. They weren't autograph seekers. To them, Dinah was not a celebrity. She was someone they felt they knew personally. They talked with her as if she was a good friend. And, unlike almost any other Hollywood A-lister, instead of being affronted by their intrusion, she not only made them feel welcomed but seemed beyond fascinated that they were able to find baby-sitters so they could get away for a mid-day break at their favorite restaurant. In true Dinah style, she made them feel welcomed, but was able to encourage their departure so kindly that the conclusion didn't feel abrupt.

Being warm, open, approachable, and terminally kind, may seem to be curious abilities for catapulting someone to the extraordinary level of success that Dinah achieved. But for anyone who ever spent time with her or who watched her TV show, her genuine sense of joy, friendship and humor existed on an almost unworldly level. Even better, it never for a single moment felt like an act. No matter the situation, she always seemed to genuinely enjoy whoever was with her and, just as importantly, made sure that they knew it.

My last interaction with Dinah came a year or two after her contract with the bank was up and we were no longer working together.

I was directing a TV commercial for the Los Angeles Open Golf Tournament. Lanny Wadkins, who won the championship the year before, was the spokesperson. Because the Riviera Country Club, where the tournament was to take place, was being readied for the competition, we shot the commercial on a golf course in Palm Springs.

The manager of the course was not at all pleased to have us there. He took great pride in the condition of the course and was fearful that our crew of about 15 might not only cause some damage but also interfere with the important members who were likely to be playing at the same time we were shooting.

Because I was the director, he pulled me aside and went to great lengths to explain the very limited parameters within which I had to work. Our crew was not to step on any fairway or green and we needed to make sure that our presence would not disturb anything or anyone. He pointed with enormous pride to the meticulous quality of the course and was almost breathless when noting the prominence of the club members. Because of the exclusiveness of the club, all members were wealthy, many were well-known, and none would appreciate even the slightest interruption to their game.

While ramping up to an even greater list of rules that could not be violated, he noticed something at the same time I did. The most recognizable member of the golf club was on the fairway and in a cart coming towards us.

As he was about to point out the obvious reasons for his concerns by indicating that one of the very celebrities he had been talking about – no less a luminary than Dinah Shore herself - was now approaching. What I did next horrified him. Instead of nodding my head in complicit understanding, I ran directly into the middle of the fairway, wildly waving my hands to stop the approaching golf cart and began shouting. "You can't play here … we're shooting a television commercial."

Ashen faced and totally aghast, the manager did his best to catch up with me in a futile attempt to make me to stop. I was not only breaking almost every one of his rules; I was directly disrupting the play of the single most influential golfer in the entire club.

What happened then, stopped him cold. Dinah, of course, recognized me, jumped out of her cart, ran over, and gave me an enormous hug. I told her why I was there and called Lanny over to make the introductions. Although they both surely knew of each other, they had never met. We chatted happily for a few moments and then Dinah got back in her cart and continued her round.

The manager of the golf course did his best to slink away and make himself invisible. Realizing that I knew Dinah – and even more importantly that she knew me – was far more information than he had been prepared for.

Clearly, the tables had turned. Instead of telling me in no uncertain terms what I would not be allowed to do, if I had requested a cup of coffee, he probably would have asked if I preferred a latte.

The Easiest Gig in the World

The technical term is "Voice Over". But the job is more commonly known as "Announcer" – and it belongs to the unseen voice heard in just about every commercial.

The qualifications for the job are relatively limited. Those qualifications often include an inordinate fascination with one's own voice and the ability to read out loud. That's about it.

Announcers show up and read a few words off a printed page. Although not a requirement, some feel obligated to feign some appreciation for being requested to participate (and be paid handsomely) before hastily making their exit.

Essentially that's all there is to it. Correction ... that's not quite accurate. That's <u>precisely</u> all there is to it.

Even more remarkably, although any compensation for such minimal effort might seem generous, the truth is that the money can be quite significant.

Announcers for TV commercials, receive exactly the same payment as the actors who are featured in the commercial. But their involvement in terms of time and effort is considerably different.

The difference begins with casting.

Professional announcers have readily accessible demo reels. Quite often, they are chosen directly from those demo reels without fuss or effort on their part.

When that happens, until they get the call, they don't even know they are being considered for the job. More often, however, the decision makers like to hear their carefully written lines being read by several potential candidates. In the pre-historic days before the internet, that used to be a big deal, but today, it's something easily accomplished from the comfort of home.

Actors, on the other hand, participate in a decidedly more time-consuming process. After being prepped by their agent about what to wear, they report to an initial casting session held in a location that is almost certain to be inconvenient. Parking is likely to be problematic and almost assuredly not validated. After waiting in a room and attempting uncomfortable chit chat with others vying for the same role, they are ushered into a relatively sterile room. There, without props, but with the assistance of someone who is not an actor, they are given the opportunity to demonstrate their skill. Often, they are granted a second reading, but seldom more than that. Even though they have allocated a significant portion of their day for their effort, in a matter of minutes, they are done. Their performance is videoed and if it passes muster by others who were too important and too busy to attend the session, the actor is invited to a Call Back. Another day is set aside and, along with others who have been culled from the first session, they are invited to the same inconvenient location and given the opportunity to repeat or, hopefully, improve their performance.

Upon receiving the happy news that he or she has been chosen, a return visit is often required so that wardrobe choices can be discussed. Often decisions and fittings can be finalized at that time, but on occasion, an additional visit may be needed to be certain that the selection was correct, and any required alterations are noted. i

By then, the actor has invested at least 3 days and possibly more. And that's just to get the job. The real work is yet to come.

On the day of production, the actor is usually requested to be among the first to arrive because prep time is needed. In addition to any last-minute wardrobe adjustments, the hair and make-up specialists need time to work their magic. The remainder of the long day is mostly spent waiting. Setting the lights, positioning and re-positioning the camera, arranging and re-arranging the set all seem to require endless discussion and minute adjustment. When all that has been accomplished, the actor is called upon to perform. After a few takes, it's back to waiting while everything is re-set for the next shot.

A typical production day lasts 10 hours. Actors are expected to
be present and readily available the entire time. Even if all their scenes have been shot, they are often asked to wait until "Wrap" is called before they are free to leave.

In contrast, the announcer is asked to show up at a relatively convenient recording studio at a time that fits his schedule. After reading out loud for about an hour - or usually less - the day's work is done. After a quick good-bye and an ingenuous thank you, he (or she) is on their way.

Almost astonishingly, compensation for both the actor and the announcer is precisely the same. In most situations, as union members, they each receive the specified minimum. Although that amount is considerably higher than most state sanctioned minimum wages, it's still insufficient for a move to Easy Street.

But for both actors and announcers, the word "minimum" is not always applicable. Some, having established their worthiness is any number of ways - even if only in their own minds - request double or even triple scale for their efforts.

Although triple scale announcers, quite obviously, make more money than those who work for scale, they are pikers in the world of "how high is up?" The answer to that question is: almost inconceivably high.

"A" level actors may be loath to appear in anything as career-damning as a television commercial, but for a price, many are more than willing to be the invisible off-camera voice.

It might be reasonable to ask why the unidentified voice of a movie star would be more valued than the voice of someone else. Not surprisingly, there are answers.

The voices of some actors are highly recognizable. For that reason alone, there are advertising executives who believe such a voice brings extra attention to the commercial – thereby making it more memorable and theoretically more effective.

There is reason to question that theory. It is difficult to conceive of someone watching TV, enjoying a snack during a commercial break, and pausing for a moment to exclaim "Hey, why that's George Clooney's voice, isn't it"? Then, based on that realization, immediately putting down the half-consumed slice of pizza, picking up the phone and making a call to switch insurance carriers. If that seems a bit extreme it's only because it is.

There are, however, valid reasons to pay handsomely for a well-known actor's voice. That hefty paycheck assures the opportunity to hang out with an A-level celebrity. Because of the money involved, after the recording session, there is almost certain to be an informal get together, quite possibly involving dinner. And, depending on the robustness of the negotiated contract, even the star's attendance at the company's annual stockholder's meeting is certainly possible. And impressing others with tales about socializing with celebrities certainly has a value.

So, how much? A million dollars?

Please. We're talking about a highly recognizable, very famous person. We're talking about one of the best-known names and faces in the entire world. So please re-think the offer and up the ante. For someone this special, it will take multiple millions at the very least.

Although only true superstars are paid such astronomical amounts, even unknown, working-for-scale, union announcers can do pretty well. That's because they make additional money through residuals. While getting paid for no further effort may seem peculiar, the concept of residuals makes sense. Instead of going through the time, effort, and expense of re-creating the original production, everybody wins by simply re-using what's already there.

Residuals work this way: In 13-week cycles, actors and announcers receive compensation based on where and how often the commercials air. If shown only in a small city, the residuals are relatively low. When the commercials run in major cities like New York and Los Angeles, the residual payments increase substantially. When aired nationally and often, there is unbridled joy because payments are maximized.

How much can a Voice Over announcer earn for a single recording session? A lot. I personally know of one who made close to a million dollars in a few minutes for almost no effort at all.

Allan Barzman was the announcer for the EverReady Battery commercials. There were lots of them and they ran – nationally and often – for years. The concept was always the same: a toy bunny powered by EverReady batteries outlasted all competitors time after time. While the others slow and eventually stop completely, the EverReady Bunny continues. Allan's voice at the end of the commercial sums up the benefit in two words: "still going."

Allan was a partner in Bert & Barz, a company that specialized in radio commercials. Allan and his partner, Bert Berdis, wrote, performed, and recorded those commercials in their own studios. One afternoon, during a break between other work, Allan went into one of his own studios, had his own engineer record the session, and spent several minutes repeating the words," still going". The ad agency people chose one of those takes and, for the next decade, used it at the end of every commercial. After airing for months, Allan offered to do additional versions so the company would have more options.

There was no interest. They liked what they had and wanted to continue using it. So they did.

The commercials ran nationally for years and years and years. During that time, Allan was able to pocket something in the range of a million dollars - a respectable return for 10 minutes of effort.

Playing with the Big Kids

My personal experience with celebrity announcers has been relatively limited, but each occurrence was amusing, at least mildly educational, and certainly unique.

Paul Winchell

Everything about the commercial I did with Paul Winchell was peculiar, but in a good way. Although the words to be recorded were intended to be at least somewhat humorous, that was hardly the part of the session I found most amusing.

Unquestionably, Paul Winchell had a distinctive voice. But, unlike most traditional announcers, his did not carry the weight of authority. In its stead, any words coming out of his mouth seemed to convey a sense of levity and bemusement.

The commercial was for a product the Ft. Howard Paper Company was introducing. Our advertising agency had done the package design and come up with the name – Dimples.

Paul was certainly an appropriate choice. If there is any category where a serious statement about quality or efficacy is inappropriate, that category would be toilet paper.

I was looking forward to the recording session. I was confident that getting to meet Paul Winchell would be a treat, and having the opportunity to direct him would be even better. But even that enthusiasm could not keep me from thinking about the peculiarity of the situation.

Years before, Paul Winchell had carved out a successful career in radio. His skill was unique: he was a ventriloquist, albeit a flawed one. Although his writing skill and sense of humor were excellent and his ability to create unique voices for each of his characters was impressive, he lacked perhaps the most important skill for a ventriloquist: he moved his lips.

Because radio is a poor visual medium, that limitation was not an impediment to his success. Paul Winchell and his main puppet, Jerry Mahoney, were an instant hit and remained popular for years. However, when the show moved to television, the moving-the-lips issue was difficult to hide. Clever editing and close-up shots of the puppets helped a little. But even his most ardent fans had difficulty overlooking the fatal shortcoming, and it was only a matter of time before the show was cancelled. Paul Winchell and his cast of dummies essentially disappeared.

But here I was anyway, about to do a recording session with a guy who had become a very big star by pretending to be a ventriloquist even though he lacked the most important skill that job required.

No matter. Now he had come full circle. As the unseen voice for a TV commercial, he was back to his roots and back where he was most comfortable. Not surprisingly, he did a terrific job. My desire to participate by offering directing advice proved to be beyond unnecessary. I wisely demurred. Paul was in his element and, completely unaided by me, delivered a wonderful performance.

Success for Dimples, however, was not to be. Charmin, backed by Proctor & Gamble's multi-million-dollar marketing budget, continued to dominate the category. Competing was futile.

Recognizing a loser when they saw it, the Ft. Howard Paper Company, quickly made the correct decision, and flushed the brand down the toilet.

Tony Randall

Tony Randall co-starred in "The Odd Couple," one of the best-loved and most successful TV sitcoms of all time. Even before then, he had made a name for himself and was certainly a ranking member of show business royalty. But once The Odd Couple began, his place at the top of the pecking order was assured.

When I worked with him, the show was in re-runs and had been for years. That meant he was receiving significant residual checks every month just for getting out of bed. But, other than the arduous task of endorsing those checks, his involvement with the entertainment industry was limited and had been for some time. So, although hardly in need of the money, the feeling of being wanted was hard for him to resist.

He approached the job with the same air of professionalism I assume he brought to all his previous film and television work. He arrived on time, carefully assessed the surroundings, and registered his appreciation for the quality of the room and the preparedness of the recording engineer. There were even some kind words for the script.

Then to ready himself for the session, he warmed up by running through a series of vocal exercises, concluding with an aria from a well-known opera. None of us applauded, but we were all impressed.

Once in the booth, he got down to business. He did a few straight-forward takes and then offered a series of variations. When it was obvious that we had an abundance of choices, we asked him to join us in the control room so we could listen to the playbacks together. We were all quite pleased with several takes, but he insisted that he could do better. So, he went back into the booth and did more.

Then, although his work was completed, instead of leaving, he remained in the studio, stayed with us during the entire mixing process, and happily offered suggestions until the final version was finished.

It was, admittedly, just a commercial and hardly approached anything as consequential as the major productions in which he had starring roles. But the respect he showed for the work, the process, and everyone involved – including himself – elevated the experience.

It was clear that he enjoyed being back in action. And so did we.

Herschel Bernardi

One of the trickiest aspects of being a big star is facing the realization that stardom often has an expiration date. It is surely exhilarating to bask in almost unimaginable sunshine, but once the light begins to diminish - even if the realization comes slowly - the darkness becomes pervasive.

After experiencing the highs of constant adoration, a faded star is often an unhappy one.

Such was the case when I did a recording session with Herschel Bernardi.

After years of receiving nightly standing ovations for his performance as Tevye in Fiddler on the Roof, Bernardi felt it was time for him to move on. He was unprepared when the rest of show business moved on as well. With the thunderous applause that had nourished him now missing, his was not a happy retirement and he seemed determined to inflict that unhappiness on everyone he encountered.

On the day of the recording session, I was the first to be greeted by his negativity. He didn't have to utter a single word – the aura of unhappiness engulfed him.

Even though the requirements for Voice Over performers are minimal, Bernardi determined that the concessions he had to endure were too many and too annoying.

Everything was bothersome. The driver who was supposed to pick him up at 10:30 a.m. arrived 10 minutes early. The presence of a stretch limousine waiting outside his home made him feel rushed. He barely had time to enjoy his morning coffee. The poor street repair in Manhattan made reading the paper in the car problematic, and the 11:30 a.m. call time for the recording session was ridiculously early. That's why he arrived at the session in robe and slippers.

But when it came time to work, he couldn't help himself. He stopped complaining, read his lines with assurance, and realized in less than 15 minutes he had earned an unconscionable amount of money and was free to be driven home.

He had arrived annoyed, but for reasons that seemed inexplainable, managed to leave in an excellent mood.

Proof of that positivity came in the form of something I have never witnessed before or since. He wanted to demonstrate his ability to record his name backwards so, when played in reverse, it would sound normal. It is an almost impossible – and totally useless feat.
But it amused him enormously and the rest of us did our best to feign amazement.

I would have invited him to lunch, but he was dressed for breakfast.

Burgess Meredith

Today, having access to pretty much any film you want to see whenever you want to see it has become as commonplace as flush toilets and electricity. But there was a time when that was very much not the case.

Sometime around 1985, based on the burgeoning popularity of video cassette players, the Walt Disney Company began to investigate a new concept: letting people own copies of their films. Understandably, they started small. Disney's entire VHS division consisted of a half dozen workers who occupied a few offices in one of their least desirable buildings.

Two years later, that division had an entire high rise all its own.

There was good reason for the speedy success. Many Disney films were made to order for families. Not only were the story lines suitable for children, but busy mothers instantly realized that the videos were excellent, easily accessible, and surprisingly competent, babysitters.

We were asked to make a TV commercial for one of the first films Disney offered for sale on video cassette - the animated classic, <u>Beauty and the Beast</u>. What we conceived was simplicity itself. Interspersed between cuts of the most memorable scenes from the film we wanted to show close-ups of children delighted by what they were viewing.

To ensure that we'd have responsive children, we hired specialists - a husband and wife team known for casting children. They took no chances and brought in what seemed to be an entire nursery school.

We thought it would be more fun for the kids to see the film with someone else, so we shot them in pairs. We set up a hidden camera to record their reactions and then watched in agony as one set after another viewed the film with multiple versions of total boredom.

By the end of the day, we knew we in deep trouble. We hadn't seen a giggle or anything even approaching a smile. One of the kids was so bored by the video that she got up and left. Every single child that the casting people brought had seen the film, and every single one of them was beyond uninterested. We were out of kids but had one unanticipated possibility. The assistant cameraman had brought his 3-year-old daughter with him because he was unable to find a babysitter. She was unquestionably adorable. Giving her a shot on camera couldn't hurt. So, with nothing to lose, we gave her a try.

In filming, just as in life, the unexpected occurs with regularity. But most of the time those occurrences are unhappy surprises. This time it wasn't. The girl was fabulous – expressive, excited, fully engaged, and so extravagantly animated that the little boy watching with her was unable to contain his own pleasure.

We wrapped for the day knowing we had killer footage. All that was needed was an equally killer Voice Over.

From the moment we conceived the commercial, we had only one person in mind: Burgess Meredith. He was old, but his voice had aged well. Even better, he was deeply embedded as a fixture in Disney's extended family.

We knew he was well past his prime but were unprepared for the bent and weakened man who showed up to the recording session. He was able to get through two takes and, with prodding, attempted a third. We begged for a few pick-up lines, but it was clear that even though he was willing, his voice was not.

He hadn't given us much, but what we had was wonderful. His voice is totally unique – warm, fatherly, even a bit mystical. With deft editing it was possible to assemble something very close to magical. Combined with the adorable, emotionally charged kids, the TV spot turned out to be all we hoped it would be.

What happened next was of little surprise. The <u>Beauty and the Beast</u> videocassette broke all previous sales records – and by a significant margin. I modestly take credit for that success although, grudgingly, will admit that Walt's participation might have been a contributing factor.

Part 2

Advertising Maven

An Interesting Story

Just as constructive criticism is often less than joyfully welcomed, information that follows the phrase "let me give you some good advice" is also seldom appreciated.

But, in the spirit of the exception that proves the rule, I once received some advice that was so good, I continue to employ it with consistent success.

At no cost or obligation, I cheerfully re-offer it.

On occasion, we find ourselves in the company of someone we have just met and, after the usual topics of weather and sports have been pummeled into submission, we are in a quandary about how to continue the conversation. The awkward silence that follows, quickly gives way to discomfort and, possibly, even a mild sense of panic.

Here comes the advice: Ask the new acquaintance these two questions.

Question #1: What do you do for a living?

The next question is even easier. It's so easy, in fact, you don't even have to pay attention to the first answer.

Question #2: How did you get into that line of work?

That's it. That's all there is to it.

The answer to the second question is always some version of "Well... actually that's an interesting story."

The fact that, almost without fail, the story will not be remotely interesting, is of little consequence. What's important is, from that moment on, you're off the hook. All you need to do is listen and feign interest. The "interesting story" is about to be told in excruciating detail.

Assuming that your eyes do not glaze over, and you are able to suppress disparaging yawns, even if you don't utter a single additional word, your new acquaintance will remember you with fondness for your extraordinary conversational skills.

With that in mind, this is the answer to your unasked question about how I came to be an advertising maven.

It was all a mistake.

In the spring of 1964, I was about to graduate from college. In addition to realizing that my carefree days of panty raids and student pranks were nearing an end, I also came to the unhappy conclusion that unless I took some relatively decisive immediate action, my next pair of footwear was likely to be combat boots, and my next destination was likely to be Viet Nam.

Although I disagreed with the reason the United States was outfitting so many men my age with uniforms, supplying them with rifles and sending them to a country that few of us knew anything about, I had more personal concerns. I had an inordinate fear of death and/or dismemberment.

Admittedly, my options were limited, but I knew there were several ways to avoid being drafted.

Either physical or mental impairment was sufficient to generate 4-F status. But my health was good and, although there were many who would surely question my mental stability, my college degree was likely to be more than enough to invalidate that excuse.

At the time, gay men were unacceptable to the military, so indicating a less than macho sexual preference could be a deal breaker. But even though I had limited experience with women, I wasn't about to switch teams.

Marriage was also a get-out-of-the army free pass. But that required commitment of another kind and a willing partner. Not a viable option.

The only other available route to avoidance was a student deferment. Even though my fascination with college courses had long since been extinguished and I was anxious to get on with the rest of my life, pursuit of a post-graduate degree seemed infinitely superior to the military alternative. Professors vs. sergeants. Books vs. rifles. Dorm rooms vs. trenches. Classroom discussions vs. incoming artillery. The choice was difficult, but I was up to the task.

I applied to graduate schools.

My undergraduate degree indicated that I had a double major in philosophy and English. But my enthusiasm for philosophy and its seemingly unending search for truth (although with no apparent desire to ever reach that elusive goal) had dissipated long ago.

My interest in English had little to do with literature or anything produced in the previous century. My focus was on contemporary writing – preferably my own. So, I made a list of universities that were highly rated for journalism or creative writing and fired off applications to the six that I thought were best.

My first choice was Stanford. It was the only school where I had any connections but, even though one of my father's friends held a senior position there, for reasons that are still puzzling, I decided I wanted to be judged on my own merits. Apparently, the judgment was more severe and more negative than I hoped. Stanford turned me down.

But four universities accepted me and a fifth, Northwestern, offered an assistantship. The money I'd be earning, combined with the waiving of tuition, made the choice easy.

In September, I arrived in Evanston, Illinois. The weather was beautiful, the professor I was assigned to assist was cordial, and I was thousands of miles away from Viet Nam. Life was good.

Things changed quickly.

By October, temperatures dropped. Significantly. Frost comes early to Chicago and consistently outstays its welcome. After 4 years in North Carolina, I was poorly prepared for a never-ending winter. By my birthday in April, I was still chipping snow off the car's windshield and holding a lighter to my car key to make it hot enough to melt the ice that had frozen over the door lock.

As a bonus, I was miserable at Northwestern. I knew I'd be attending classes in the Medill School of Journalism, but I was unprepared that those classes were designed to help me achieve my Master's Degree with a major in advertising.

I had no interest in advertising and had no idea why I had been placed in that program. But as much as I wanted to quit, I envisioned forced marches in uncomfortable footwear and the very real potential of significant bodily harm in a country not noted for medical facilities. I decided to stay the course.

In addition to my quite reasonable fear of death, after 4 years of accepting money from my parents to cover the costs of college, I thought it was time for me to be responsible for at least some of my expenses. And, because the Medill School of Journalism had an impeccable national reputation, there was always the possibility that, while there, I might even learn to be a better writer.

One of the things I learned almost immediately was that there is a significant distinction between journalism and creative writing. I loved writing. Journalism... not so much.

Apparently, there are rules for journalism. The idea that there are rules for writing had never occurred to me. How could there be rules for creativity? It turns out, that although there is a lot about journalism that certainly entails ingenuity, perseverance and imagination, the actual writing part is not high on that list.

The first assignment in my journalism course required us to write a news story based on a meeting our lab class had with a local politician. I wrote what I modestly admit to being a pretty clever story about the frustrations of political life. Unfortunately, my cleverness was unappreciated. The professor wrote the "correct" story and read it to the class. He was very clear: this is what the headline should be, this is what the sub-head should be, and this is the way the story should unfold - paragraph by paragraph. Anything else was unacceptable. Anything else was, simply, wrong.

Once I understood the concept, following the rules was easy. But, as far as I was concerned, the sentences I was putting together had nothing whatsoever to do with writing.

My journalism class was problematic for another reason. My assistantship required that I maintain good grades. But, when the mid-term marks came out, I received a "C" in journalism. It was accompanied by a note from the administration informing me that I was now on probation caused by inadequate academic performance.

The "C" made no sense to me, so I made an appointment to meet with the professor. I wanted him to explain the reasons for such a poor grade. Before saying anything else, he apologized for not recognizing me. Although my lack of visibility was hardly a compliment, it was at least understandable. He taught a lecture class with more than 200 students, so I was just another anonymous face to him. Still, he was very obliging and, along with me, reviewed my work, my class participation and test scores. We had, by then taken two tests. My grades on both were good. On the first test, I had the second highest score in the entire class, and on the mid-term,

I had the highest grade. So, he checked my laboratory performance. I'd done well there, too. Not only had I done all the work and turned it in on time, but I had received an "A" on every assignment. He was perplexed, but he persisted and eventually located the problem. I had been tardy. I had arrived a few minutes late to two of his lectures and, for each unpunctual arrival, he dropped my grade one letter. His explanation was simple: reporters can't be late for an assignment. No excuses are acceptable. If you're not there when it happens, you miss the story.

There was obviously no point telling him that I lived miles from campus and that snow, ice and closed roads sometime made travel difficult. It wouldn't have made any difference. From then on, I made it a point to arrive well ahead of the appointed hour and, at the end of the semester, my final grade reflected my work and not my transportation skills.

But even getting an "A" in his course did nothing to improve my interest in a journalism career. Unfortunately, the advertising classes I took weren't much more interesting. Most of the course work involved studying cases of actual businesses that faced problems or responded to potential opportunities. Our task was to determine the best way to work through the situations and come up with a way to make the business more successful or, at the very least, allow it to remain solvent. Our analysis and suggestions were then compared with what the company had actually done and the results those actions had achieved.

The professor treated the case studies as if there was a single correct solution – and it always happened to be whatever the company chose to do. He was wrong of course – even if he was the one doing the grading. I hated his rigidity and lack of imagination, but I was surprisingly intrigued by the cases, and gradually began to get a feel for the potential power of both advertising and the opportunity for creative solutions to real world business problems.

Even that small glimmer of interest, however, was far from fulfilling. My experience as a student at Northwestern was never good, and, more often than not, very bad. I had little respect for my professors, little interest in the courses I was taking and was only there because of the student deferment that kept me out of Hanoi. The trade-off, while much less than ideal, was nevertheless superior to fearing for my life on a daily basis.

I have never been known for my reticence to state an opinion, so when asked about my experience at Northwestern I was painfully truthful. It took me a while to realize that my long list of complaints about the courses, the professors and the other students was not working in my favor. Most people in Chicago, I learned, had great respect for Northwestern and were surprised by my negativity. Eventually it dawned on me that the accuracy of my fault-finding might be misplaced. Even worse, my complaints did not serve me very well. It took me a while to change my responses. But eventually, by praising the university, I found that my positive review was both greatly appreciated and consistent with what everyone wanted to hear. As a bonus, I was more highly regarded because I showed such appreciation for the wonderful education the university was providing.

Already, I was grooming myself for a career in advertising.

Although I was well on track to receive a Master's Degree with a major in advertising, I had a few additional hurdles to clear. Because my undergraduate work had included absolutely no classes in economics or business, Northwestern required me to catch up. That wasn't a problem. The additional time in school meant an extension of my student deferment, so I was more than willing to do the supplementary work. The only slight issue was that, because of the extra courses, my schedule was out of sequence with the school's regularly scheduled post graduate offerings. That meant I had a few months break between courses. During that time there was little for me to do other than fulfill the obligations of my assistantship and work on my thesis.

As part of the research for my thesis I arranged to meet with some executives at the Chicago Tribune. I had a long list of questions and was well prepared for the meeting. But not the outcome.

Like most people, I had to interview for my first job. But unlike most people, I was the interviewer, not the interviewee. In fact, it wasn't until well into the conversation with the Tribune executives that I began to realize that the topic had changed dramatically. The discussion had turned from my thesis into one that I was eminently better qualified to talk about: me. It took a while for it to dawn on me that the people I was interviewing were, in fact, trying to assess my interest in working for them. Apparently, I was no more astute then, than I am now.

To make a short story even shorter, they offered me a job. It never occurred to me to question anything about the position. I never asked why it was available or why it was being offered to someone they barely knew and whose skill level at anything other than conversation about a college project was entirely unknown.

The salary, while absurdly low, was also much more than I had ever earned before. I had limited experience as an employee. I spent several summers as a camp counselor where the compensation essentially consisted of tips from grateful parents when their child was returned to them with all limbs intact at the end of the summer. The relatively easy access to the conveniently located girls' camp - and, as a consequence, the girls' camp counselors – was an obvious a benefit, albeit not a financial one.

Stories about counselor mistreatment of campers abound. Some are even true. The one about filling a sleeping camper's hand with shaving cream and then tickling his nose is pretty much a sure thing. The curious look on the child's face when he realizes he's breathing shaving cream is a laugh riot - or at least a response worthy of the effort. The theory that placing a sleeping camper's hand in a pail of warm water will encourage peeing in bed is more difficult to authenticate. A hand dipped in water is pretty much an immediate wake-up call, even for a very sleepy 8-year-old.

My limited work experience included spent a few months as a part-time stock boy at the less than fashion forward men's clothing store, Robert Hall where I was an important cog in the greasy wheel responsible for selling cheap suits to even cheaper customers.

When a new store opened near my home, I was hired for the munificent sum of 95¢ an hour and began working part time as soon as high school started in September. When the holiday season approached and business picked up, the manager realized he needed an additional cashier. He tested the mathematical skills of all the stock boys and, because my ability to both add and subtract was better than his, I got the promotion and an enormous 20¢ an hour raise. When business slowed after the Christmas rush, forking over my new extravagant salary presumably crushed the store's bottom line. I was unceremoniously furloughed, fired, and essentially, let go.

The chain of Robert Hall stores (and its companion, Kinney Shoes) is no longer in existence - a demise I attribute entirely to my forced departure from the company.

On occasion, I am reminded of my experience in the clothing business because, based on the knowledge acquired at Robert Hall, I am still capable of folding a suit or sports jacket and placing it into a suitcase without fear of creasing. Sadly, as Casual Friday becomes Casual Every Day, that skill has become less and less necessary, and my folding skills fail to evoke the gasps of wonder they once did.

Accepting the offer to become a junior copywriter in the Chicago Tribune's advertising department was a no-brainer. I had been itching to have a real job long before I graduated from college and the idea of being paid to write was, for me, the equivalent of being paid to watch sports. As an indication of their desperation to have someone fill what was so clearly a position of little import, they agreed to let me work on a schedule they knew would be interrupted when, a few months later, I would need to take time off to complete my Master's Degree.

If there is a pecking order at a metropolitan newspaper – a qualification that is definitely appropriate for the Chicago Tribune - it is safe to say that, for a writer, being in the advertising department ranks roughly on a par with the guy who excitedly joins the circus and then spends his days cleaning up after the elephants. The ranks of newspaper writers include editors, columnists, beat reporters, cub reporters and, at the very bottom, obituary writers. All of them - every single one - view the ad guys with justifiable distain.

Unlike the Mad Men who created multi-million-dollar advertising campaigns, enjoyed 3-hour martini lunches, and filmed commercials in exotic locations, my assignment at the Tribune was somewhat less enviable. My task was simply to convince mortuaries, used car dealers and just about anyone or any local business, that running ads in the Tribune was the best possible way to improve their bottom line. My attempts to accomplish that goal did not involve expensive television commercials, clever radio spots or even full-page ads in glossy magazines. That would have required the purchase of media - and why do that when the Tribune was a medium unto itself?

There is no way to sugarcoat it. Essentially, the ads I developed were nothing more than filler. When the editors laid out a page, quite often the stories they wanted to print didn't fill every single line. Sometimes the empty spaces were tiny; sometimes they were slightly larger. They were never anything even close to the size of a full-page because if the space left over was too big, the story was simply eliminated. But if the people who laid out the pages of the Tribune found emptiness anywhere, I was the one who was called on to fill it. Not brilliantly. Not necessarily effectively. But, at the very least, right to the edge.

I started immediately, working full time during my two-month break from Northwestern, and then part-time while finishing my degree. Once the diploma was in my back pocket, I was back at the Tribune full time, working my way up the corporate ladder from a position where, if I jumped high enough, I could almost reach the rung at the very, very bottom.

It would be a bit of an exaggeration to claim that the work I did was on the cutting edge of advertising. It would even be an exaggeration to claim that the work I did approached mediocrity. But just because I was a total beginner was no reason to think I wasn't up to the task. From the very first I was able to churn out acceptable drivel with alarming regularity. Although it was hard to take pride in my daily accomplishments, there was an upside: I now had reason to rightfully claim membership in the advertising community.

After about a year, my 6'x 6' cubicle began to feel even smaller, the challenge of doing mundane work began to seem less interesting, and it became clear that it was time to move on. Because very little of the work I produced at the Tribune offered the slightest hint that I might have any creative ability at all, I put together some speculative ads, created a "book" and started interviewing at actual, honest-to-goodness advertising agencies.

At the time, my knowledge about advertising agencies was minimal. I knew they made ads and commercials, but not much more than that. I had no way of evaluating the quality of their creative work or their marketing acumen. But I did understand – completely – that when one of them offered to double my salary, determining whether to accept was not going to require deeper analysis.

The advertising agency I joined, Post Keyes Gardner was, at best, functional. Their client list was unimpressive, their marketing expertise was less than incisive, and their creative output left pretty much everything to be desired. With such low standards firmly in place, expectations for a standout performance by new employees were not high. My limited experience and almost non-existent proof of talent was more than sufficient.

At the time, Mr. Post, Mr. Keyes, and Mr. Gardner were either ensconced in executive suites that were off limits to mere employees or, more likely, had long since departed from the agency and, quite possibly, life itself. A few years after I joined the company, it was absorbed by another Chicago agency and the name disappeared forever. For Messrs. Post, Keyes and Gardner, an era had ended, but the tragic loss was mourned by few.

My welcome to the advertising agency world was hardly a joyous one. A few days before I started, a much loved, mid-level creative director died. He had been seriously ill for several months, but because there was hope he would return; his office had been re-decorated as a welcome back gift. Death has an inconvenient way of changing plans, and because no other offices were readily available for me, I was temporarily placed in his.

Other than the executive creative director's posh suite with multiple sofas and its own bathroom, the office I was assigned to inhabit was, by far, the nicest in the entire creative department. It was also completely inappropriate for the newest, greenest, most junior person there.

That point was made abundantly clear several times every day when friends and former co-workers of the recently deceased executive stopped, peered in the doorway, and felt compelled to let me know how unworthy I was to be occupying his office.

Mercifully I was eventually moved to a suitable cubicle devoid of windows, new furniture or good taste. But the damage had already been done. I was labeled as the guy who schemed to get Frank's beautifully decorated office and was, quite possibly, responsible for his death as well.

As unsuited as I was for an executive office, I was equally ill-prepared to write copy for almost any of the agency's clients. Their two biggest accounts were Maybelline and Brown & Williamson Tobacco.

Maybelline was – and, for all I know, may still be – the company that made eye make-up products for the budget-minded. Because I had the wrong genital components combined with a total lack of experience with make-up, I was kept far away from that account. The closest I got was stepping on a tube of mascara when exiting a meeting with my copy chief during which I had been chastised for writing an incomplete sentence.

There was no danger that I'd be asked to work on the Brown & Williamson account because it was too important to the agency. It was still the 60's and smoking was very much in vogue. Tobacco was big business and cigarette advertising was certainly no place for a junior wordsmith. I was frustrated about never being asked to participate because I had a well-rehearsed speech at the ready - one which included my moral objection to the dangers of inhaling anything other than cannabis and therefore my righteous refusal to work on a cigarette account.

Even though Brown & Williamson was the agency's largest account, the two cigarettes they produced were hardly best sellers. Filter tipped brands were definitely on the ascent, so Raleigh (the regular one) and Bel Air (the menthol one) were at least in the right category. But they were heavily outspent by competitors with much better brand images due to much bigger ad budgets. Marlboro, the category leader, was smoked by rugged men (which made it surprisingly appealing to women as well), Winston offered the possibility of delivering good taste in spite of having a filter ("Winston tastes good like a cigarette should"), Parliament with its recessed filer offered sophisticated appeal, Kent actually had the balls to make health claims due to its "micronite" filter, Tarreyton was theoretically so good, people would rather fight than switch, and others like Viceroy, L&M and Benson & Hedges offered imagery as well as celebrity endorsements to enhance their appeal.

With limited sales and, consequently, a limited budget, Raleigh and Bel Air had no choice but to try a less traditional approach. They carved out a marketing position based on value and practicality. Each pack came with a coupon that could be used, much like Green Stamps, to redeem valuable prizes. The premise was pretty basic: you're smoking a lot anyway, now there's a way to make it worthwhile. So, in addition to lung cancer, you might be able to get a handsome lighter or perhaps a genuine imitation leather key case. I never checked the catalog to see how many coupons were required for chemotherapy sessions, but I suspect the quantity was significant.

With their meager ad budget and peculiar marketing concept, it was hardly surprising that Raleigh and Bel Air were among the earliest casualties in the filtered cigarette category.

Just because I was never asked didn't seem to be sufficient reason to keep me from offering suggestions for TV commercials. I showed one to the creative director in charge of the account and he said he was going to keep it in hopes that I'd get rich and famous someday so then he could use it to blackmail me.

This is the commercial I wrote:

The camera pans down a line of male and female physicians   We know they are doctors because some have stethoscopes hanging around their necks, some are in surgical greens and others are in lab coats. All of them are smoking, visibly enjoying their cigarettes.

Music plays while the camera moves along the line. There is no conversation and no announcer until well into the commercial.

Anncr. (Voice Over): 9 out of 10 doctors who smoke, recommend Raleigh cigarettes for their patients who smoke...

As the camera reaches the 10th doctor, it is revealed that he is not wearing pants. His back to the camera and a lit cigarette is protruding from his ass.

Anncr. (Voice Over): ... there's always an asshole in every group.

Dissolve to beauty shot of a package of Raleigh cigarettes

Logo and Line: Raleigh cigarettes. Definitely not for assholes.

Even though I was kept at a safe distance from the agency's premier accounts, there was plenty of work for me to do for the simple reason that no one else wanted to do it. If television commercials are at the top tier of the advertising totem pole, at the base are brochures, trade ads and promotional materials. That's pretty much where I hung out. My work for a company that made juke boxes somehow failed to achieve national recognition and the same ambivalence greeted my efforts on behalf of the paper company that was introducing an admirable addition to their lineup of available colors. Even my best efforts on behalf of the Santa Fe Railroad could do little to encourage people to pay a premium for a long train ride instead of a short plane trip.

One of my assignments required me to write clever phrases for the covers of matchbooks that a client was going to hand out at a trade show. Nothing I wrote was as memorable or as valuable as "close cover before striking" but just being asked to write matchbook copy was a low point that made me re-think my career path.

Although I was clearly ensconced in the world of advertising, the glamor of the business continued to escape me. And, as nearly as I could tell, that glamor was also evading pretty much everyone else at the agency where I worked.

I suppose it's not uncommon for the honeymoon period of a new job to begin to wear off at some point. But it took longer than necessary to dawn on me that Post Keyes Gardner was not a particularly good advertising agency. Their creative work and marketing advice was, at best, nondescript, unimaginative and not particularly helpful. They were one of many advertising agencies that could boast no point of difference and no real success stories, yet somehow managed to stay in business for reasons that are not easily explained. Some of their clients were equally inept, some had been with the agency for years and remained due to apathy, neglect or perhaps relationships between senior officers based on friendship, favors or the realization that changing agencies required too much energy and would likely yield little in the way of improved results.

As brilliant as my work continued to be - and clearly, my match book covers will long be remembered - it did little to vault me into the top tier of creatives - even at an agency as undistinguished as Post Keyes. But there were other reasons why my personal star never got around to shooting while I was there.

My student deferment had run out and, although I had not yet received my draft notice, there was no question it would be arriving very soon.

My options were severely limited. Like many others, I could move to Canada – a concept that was more desirable than risking my life in Viet Nam for a cause I did not believe in. As a last resort, I probably would have made that move but, if possible, I preferred to stay in America. So, the only other possibility was finding an opening in a National Guard or Army Reserve unit.

Through a friend, I learned about a National Guard battalion located in the south side of Chicago. This one had been formed during the Korean War and provided a few hundred poorly trained soldiers to the conflict. Some of them survived but many did not. The ones who returned didn't make up the full complement of a fighting force and eventually there was a need for a few hundred part time soldiers to fill the vacancies. I was one of the first to slip into an empty slot. Others who followed later had to force their way in.

Because the fear of soldiering in Viet Nam was so great, there were many who were more than willing to do anything they could to join a National Guard unit. One of those hopefuls, whose father owned an appliance store, offered a refrigerator to the captain in charge of enlistment. Another offered a TV. Others were more straightforward and simply offered cash.

When it became clear that there were significant benefits for adding soldiers to the unit, the paucity of remaining openings was beyond frustrating for the officers in charge of enlistment. Clearly money was being left on the table and they were determined to find a way to pick it up.

Their solution was simple, albeit not very well thought-out. The commanding officer invented a phantom unit. Once enlisted, the men who paid (often handsomely) to join the ghost battalion didn't have to do very much. They didn't have to go through basic training, they didn't have to wear uniforms and they didn't have to spend a weekend every month in a dusty armory marching in formation for no apparent reason. Most of all, they didn't have to worry about being sent to fight in Viet Nam. What they had was lifesaving: paperwork proving that they were officially members of the National Guard.

It was a beautiful scheme until – predictably - it fell apart.

One of the phantom Guardsman had a brother who was in the regular army while stationed in Viet Nam. After his brother died in action, the guilt was overwhelming. When he told his story to the newspapers the walls came tumbling down. The officers who created the non-existent company ended up serving time in jail. I have no idea what happened to the men who paid the bribes, but my assumption is that many were eventually drafted.

My time in uniform, though relatively brief, was not the happiest. I think "miserable" would be a more appropriate description.

Although being in the Guard meant I would not be sent to Viet Nam, it did not mean I would be exempt from basic training. So, along with about 50 other Chicago recruits, I boarded a train bound for Fort Dix, New Jersey where I was issued a new wardrobe, given a very short haircut and, for the next 4 ½ months, learned how to become a combat ready infantryman.

My drill sergeant did his best to train me in the art of warfare but realized relatively quickly that I was not destined to be a worthy soldier. Not even close.

Even though the ad agency did not provide wardrobe, meals or sleeping quarters, working there was still preferable to being employed by Uncle Sam. It turns out that, to the surprise of no one including myself, I was poor military material. I didn't shoot accurately, didn't march well with others, and consistently proved inept at following orders. Often, my poor soldiering was explained to me in colorful language, and on one occasion, there was a more official indication of my failings as a G.I.

The Article 15 that I received for referring to the salmon croquettes as "camel shit" enhanced my reputation among my fellow recruits but did little to earn the admiration of my commanding officer. The punishment for my offensive language seemed surprisingly severe because I had never encountered a sergeant capable of completing a profanity-free sentence. But the condemnation was written up, signed, and enforced. In addition to 14 days of extra duty, my penalty included the loss of an entire month's pay … the munificent sum of $15. For obvious reasons, my Article 15 is framed and, to this day, displayed with proper pride on the wall above my desk. I have always been frustrated, however, that I was misquoted. I did not, as stated on my Article 15, ask the sergeant, "what kind of shit are you serving today?" The fact that I referred to the salmon croquettes as "camel shit" was not only a more accurate description of the food being dished out but infinitely more clever. It was also the reason I became known as "Camel Shit Krakow" for the duration of my time in basic training.

After 4 1/2 months of being told what to do and where and how to do it by non- commissioned officers who, truth be told, did not always have my best interests in mind, I returned to Chicago, much the worse for wear and convinced that a career as a full-time soldier was an unlikely possibility.

Re-adjusting to civilian life was understandably difficult, but in the minute or two that it took to make the transition, I also realized that greener pastures existed beyond Post, Keyes Gardner. Even though I was unproven and inexperienced, my aspirations transcended mediocrity. So, almost immediately upon my return, I began looking for a job at another advertising agency.

My career at Post Keyes Gardner was never destined to be long-term. Even more than an increase in salary, I wanted a chance to prove and improve my creative chops.

During my relatively short stay at Post Keyes, I produced very little, learned very little and earned very little. But, once my foot was firmly jammed in the door of the advertising business, I was able to pry it further open.

For most people, the ladder to success is more like a gentle slope. Little by little, knowledge is gained, mentors are found, accomplishments are recognized, opportunities are presented, and, over time, the direction becomes clear, and a planned route towards the top begins to form.

For me, that's not what happened. Although I have had several businesses of my own with partners who continue to be friends for life, my next job in advertising was more than I could have hoped for.

At Hurvis, Binzer and Churchill, I did my best work, was part of an extraordinarily talented group of people, and had the most fun I've ever had working for someone else.

From the outhouse to the penthouse

At the age of 25 I was a junior copywriter with a portfolio consisting of some relatively obscure promotional in-house ads for the Chicago Tribune and, from my four-month stint at a local advertising agency, a few undistinguished trade ads for a paper company and a juke box manufacturer.   In short, nothing impressive. Nothing even close.

My meager compensation was, understandably, commensurate with my output.

Two years later, based on industry awards and job offers, I was the hottest advertising writer in Chicago. At the city's annual awards show, I left carrying armloads of trophies and, on an almost monthly basis, turned down opportunities to double - and later, triple - my salary.

This is how that remarkable transition occurred.

Based on little other than persistence and a heartfelt appreciation for the work they were doling, I was hired by Hurvis, Binzer and Churchill, a fledgling year-old advertising agency that was turning out the most remarkable work I had ever seen.

Because one of their employees had been drafted, there was an opening in the writing department, and because their shallow pockets did not provide the luxury of hiring a top-flight, established talent, they settled for me and my understandably affordable salary requirement.   After joining the agency, on my first day, in a meeting with Mac Churchill, the writing partner, before being taken on a tour of the agency, I asked when I would get the opportunity to meet the other writers. His response was typically Mac. "The writing department is assembled."

I should have been intimidated. After all, I was not just the new member of the writing staff, I was the entire writing staff. But I was too young, too enthusiastic, and too naïve to be concerned. As it turned out, there was good reason for my confidence. Even though I didn't realize it at the time, I had been training for this job my whole life.

Growing up, I always thought I'd be a writer. So, I wrote a lot, and I got a lot of guidance from my father. One of the main things he taught me was the value of editing. He encouraged me to try to find ways to make the writing better – clearer, more interesting, more amusing, or more convincing. I took pride in marking up a first draft, crossing out words, adding new ones, and re-writing entire paragraphs. When I looked at an edited page, the more marks I saw, the better I felt. Each of those marks, and each of those changes, indicated improvement. I never thought of the editing process as drudgery. It was the part of writing I enjoyed most. So, at a time when most high school students were pleased to have any written assignment completed, I looked forward to figuring out how make it better.

While the willingness to edit was surely helpful when writing essays for my high school English classes, it proved invaluable at the agency. Writing ads and commercials has specialized requirements for brevity and clarity. And because I had been training myself to write that way for as long as I could remember, every day was a treat.

Clever headlines came naturally to me. Humor, irony, understatement and over statement were embedded in the way I thought and spoke. Body copy required diligence. Every extra word was not only a word too many, but also endangered the possibility of anything being read at all. But, although on rare occasions, long copy seemed to make sense, for the most part, the goal was to write as short and persuasively as possible. I also determined relatively quickly that it was a good idea to have a last line that thanked the reader for taking the time to read all the way through. At the very least, I felt there was a benefit to ending the ad with a smile.

There were just the two of us doing all the writing. Based on experience alone, it would have been reasonable to split the duties somewhat evenly - with the majority of the important work being done by Mac. As it turned out, the workload began to shift relatively quickly. Within a year I was probably doing 90% of the writing while Mac took over other responsibilities at the agency.

At the time, there were stirrings of change in the advertising industry. The age of Mad Men was slowly beginning to fade and, along with it, the 3-piece suits and the 3-martini lunches. Taking its place was the brilliant work from the New York agency, Doyle, Dane, Bernbach. Their advertising was clever, memorable, and right on point. People not only noticed their ads for Volkswagen and Avis, but astonishingly, even looked forward to reading them.

Like many others, I was awed by the consistent quality of the Doyle Dane work. (Curiously, the creative member of that partnership and the one rightfully credited for their outstanding creativity and fame was Bill Bernbach – the one name that always seemed to be omitted when talking about the company). But, as exceptional as their advertising was, I felt that at Hurvis, Binzer and Churchill, our work was even better. The difference was art direction.

Doyle Dane ads definitely had a look. Their work was clean, simple, and both easy and enjoyable to read. There was no flashiness. The ads were not intended to call attention to themselves – the only goal was straight forward communication, often laced with humor. Our ads – or at least many of them – differed significantly because they were designed to stop readers in their tracks. The ads almost jumped off the page. They were visually arresting. Often stunning. Always powerful. The reasoning for the strong visual statements was based in the belief that an unnoticed ad was essentially useless. Once we had the reader's attention, we followed the Doyle Dane formula for headline and copy – make the point, make it memorable, and make the reader feel good about taking the time to read it.

For me, being the writer for almost all of the agency's work was anything but a burden. I didn't think of the assignments as something I had to do but, instead, something that I was lucky to do. That attitude had everything to do with the art directors I worked with every day.

There were three – each with unique skills and personalities. All of them had a consummate desire to do nothing but brilliant work. They were incapable of ordinary.

Rollin Binzer was the creative force of the agency. In a few years, he became the creative force of the entire Chicago advertising community. Rollin was an indomitable presence who exuded boundless enthusiasm, style, persuasiveness, and positive energy. He had many abilities, but the one that stands out is that, without exception, everyone who worked with him felt what they did together was the best work of their lives. That was true for photographers, illustrators, directors, designers and, of course, me.

Each of the other two art directors, while much less of a presence than Rollin, had extraordinary skills. Frank Biancalana, a recent college graduate, was someone for whom the word "impeccable" was woefully insufficient. Everything he did was designed, re-designed, and re-examined until any conceivable flaw has been beaten into submission.

Peter Coutroulis, also newly escaped from a university, was a bottomless source of ideas. He began every day with a mountain of thoughts, happily accepted rejection of any of them for any reason, and then filled the void with yet another barrage. His thought process didn't follow any linear path. Often his concepts were the kind of ideas that generated a response combining equal parts of admiration and "how in the world did you ever come up with that?".

The ratio of one writer to 3 art directors made more sense than might immediately be apparent. Although conceiving an ad was almost always the work of two people, once the idea was in place, the responsibilities differed greatly. Writing the copy and perhaps tweaking the headline was my only responsibility. Even with multiple edits and often complete re-writes, a finished ad seldom required more than a single day's effort. But, for the art directors, the task was on-going. Choosing the ideal photographer or illustrator involved research. They constantly reviewed portfolios and made mental lists of talented people with unique skills. Choosing the right photographer was only the first step. There were endless meetings and detailed discussions about casting, wardrobe, and props. The decision process took days; often many of them. The photography session invariably required a full day of shooting and was immediately followed by lengthy evaluations to determine which shot worked best. Then each photo was retouched. Designing the layout of the ad, selecting the typeface for the headline and copy often required constant adjustment. So, although my work was usually completed comparatively quickly, for the art director, finalizing the ad usually required at least an additional week, and often much more.

As a very new agency with few business relationships to help launch it, none of our clients would have made any Chicago's "Who's Who" lists. They were more likely to be on a "Who's that?" list. When I started, the companies we represented included a funeral home, a grocery store (not a chain of supermarkets – just a single store that sold groceries), a company that made engraving plates for printing, and a radio station focused entirely on a Black audience. It was an unlikely group for brilliant advertising. But the work we did for every one of them won awards. Consistently.

Although we recoiled at being referred to as a "creative boutique" the description was certainly apt. The quality of our creative work was not just our strong suit – it was, essentially, the only card we had to play. In most advertising agencies, the important people were the account executives – the ones who were the main point of contact with clients. Researchers, media planners, media buyers and a full complement of secretaries and assistants all provided support – but the account guys (and at the time, they were pretty much all men) essentially called the shots. They also held sway over the work developed by the creative department – a small group usually located in areas where clients were unlikely to see them. Members of the group could be identified by their peculiar wardrobes but sadly, seldom by the actual quality of their work. The creative department – including production people and any support staff – probably represented no more than 20% of a typical advertising agency. For us, the percentage was closer to half.

Some of the other players

Although not a single client hired us because of our business acumen, there was a partner who was, at least in theory, a successful marketer. Tom Hurvis, we proudly told prospective clients, was at one time the youngest vice president in the history of Colgate Palmolive. It wasn't as if that was ancient history, either. Tom, though already beginning to bald, was, like Rollin and Mac, in his early thirties.

Because the agency was so small, even though all of us in the creative department saw Tom every day, we knew very little about him. Discussions about research, strategy, positioning, and market variables were all beyond our interest. We were totally focused on making ads that made our agency and our clients, famous.

Tom didn't fit the mold of a 1960's version of Mad Men. No one would ever claim that he looked good in a suit. He did wear them but, as a general rule, they were ill-fitting and, like the man himself, totally lacking in style.

As a bonus, he stuttered. Not badly and not all the time, but there was unquestionably a hitch to his presentation. Eventually, he got all the necessary words out - usually in relatively appropriate sequence - but his tone was not mellifluous, and his explanation was often less than convincing. His traditional claim in new business meetings was "we can double your business" – a statement seldom met with either appreciation or belief.

In an agency of equal partners, Tom was clearly the least equal.

So, when the agency eventually dissolved (Rollin wanted to move to New York and Mac wanted to live in Florida and concentrate on real estate), expectations for Tom's future were not particularly high. Had they been higher, they still would have been woefully insufficient.

Tom's first venture after leaving the ad agency had something to do with chemicals that he bought and sold in limited quantities. He quickly realized that the process was complex and inefficient. Availability was often limited, prices seldom related to supply, and accurate information was almost non-existent.

He remedied every one of those problems simultaneously by forming the Chemical Exchange. Almost immediately, it became the place to list chemicals for sale or post a request for a chemical that was desired.

In addition to taking a healthy cut of the action for every completed transaction (and there were a lot of them), Tom soon realized that the Chemical Exchange provided him with valuable information that was unavailable to anyone else.

One of the things he learned was that a chemical critical to the manufacture of antifreeze was in short supply. Knowing that, he essentially cornered the market and then scraped up enough money to buy Peak, a small, struggling antifreeze company. Then he raised prices considerably. On the chemical. And on Peak.

While others in Chicago braced for winter, Tom waited patiently. And then cashed in. The money he made by selling the chemical to other antifreeze manufacturers provided a staggering profit. Sales of Peak antifreeze put those profits into orbit.

From there, Tom bought and sold other companies. On occasion, he made mistakes. But there were a lot more hits than misses.

By the time he retired, Stuttering Tom, the least known and least important partner in the agency, was worth a billion dollars. Probably more.

The agency's staff was tiny. Even though there was an unusually high percentage of creatives who fully embraced their responsibility to dress and behave outside the norm, the others provided plenty of character as well.

Our bookkeeper suffered from commuter anxiety. To avoid the frustrations of being stuck in traffic during rush hours, she negotiated a unique working arrangement. She arrived two hours early and left an hour before everyone else. For someone whose entire responsibility was based on numbers, the math seemed a bit out of kilter. But she outweighed me by about 100 pounds, so I kept that astute observation to myself.

Al Foreman was in charge of print production. His job was to negotiate with type setters, printers, and engravers. He made sure prices were fair, quality was good, and deliveries were timely. His was an important function, requiring limited creativity but enormous attention to detail. Because his office was near the creative department, he was affected by the general spirit of the agency. On his desk he kept a 3-dimensional sign that read, "NONE OF US IS AS SMART AS ALL OF US" - admittedly, not particularly clever, or even helpful. But Al improved the sign immeasurably by placing tape over the last few letters. To his credit, the tape was intentionally poorly applied, resulting in a message that was much more appreciated: "NONE OF US IS AS SMART AS AL".

In the early days, there was only one account executive. John was Brooks Brothers from top to bottom and handsome in a predicably clean cut, collegiate way. He possessed all the attributes of a client-pleaser – a firm handshake, a ready supply of off-color jokes, and a consistent willingness to say "I got this" whenever a restaurant or bar bill was presented. He lacked intensity, insight and was hardly a brilliant marketing mind. But he fit the account guy stereotype because, although married, he certainly had an eye for the ladies. One in particular. She was the agency's Eye Candy - tall, slim, and attractive in a sultry, sexy sort of way. Her job title was "traffic". Essentially her responsibility was bringing each ad to everyone who had anything to do with it, and then making sure they approved and initialed it before it went out for publication. It wasn't that difficult a job but, on many occasions, the task exceeded her capabilities. It took about a week from the time she started at the agency until she and the account guy began their covert affair. It took less time for their secret to be known. And, based much more on incompetence than impropriety, not much longer before both were no longer employed.

In the advertising industry, even minor award competitions carry weight. And, as would be expected, the bigger the show, the greater the significance. At the time, Manhattan was the hub for most national advertising. It's where many of the corporate businesses were headquartered, and, as a result, the biggest agencies were nearby. But in New York, advertising was considered far down the line for artistic and creative talent. Manhattan was the hub for theatre, magazines, art, books, and newspapers. Those endeavors, quite reasonably, gobbled up the cream of the creative set. America's other huge city, Los Angeles, was a hub for music, film and TV production. As such it was well known for actors, writers and musicians – all of whom looked down on the advertising industry.

But in Chicago, a city that always seemed to be fighting to justify its place among the Big Three, advertising had an outsized presence. Winning an award in the Chicago Advertising Show was a major achievement. Winning a gold medal was even better.

For the agency or the creators, winning "best of show" was monumental.

At the time, there were a few hundred advertising agencies in Chicago. A few were small, but many had a staff of hundreds. There were several with more bookkeepers and accountants than the total number of employees in our entire agency. But, at the Awards Show, we were, in a word, dominant. So dominant, that one year the rules of the show were changed, and no gold medals were awarded. Instead, only certificates of acceptance were distributed. That was done because, after the initial judging was completed, our tiny agency had received gold awards in pretty much every category. The show organizers feared – probably correctly - that the big agencies might react to their humiliating losses by choosing to reduce their participation in the following year's show. With fewer entries, the future of the show would be in question. So, an appropriate business decision was made. And even though we didn't take home our usual sack of trophies, we felt a different kind of satisfaction, knowing that the quality of our work was so intimidating, it almost permanently shut down the Chicago Advertising Show.

The attention we received from awards, and the glowing reports our clients continually offered, put us on a trajectory for more business. In short order, we picked up a local cookie company, the maker of a chocolate flavored breakfast cereal and Ft. Howard – the company that made the paper towels and dispensers found in many public restrooms. It was a long way from being an impressive client list, but we were definitely growing and continually hopeful that a breakthrough account would make us famous, wealthy or, preferably, both.

As is often the case, when the opportunity arrived, we hardly noticed. The new client was yet another small Chicago company with hopes of becoming just a little bit more successful.

But, although none of us realized it at the time, the Tipping Point had arrived.

The Rise and Fall of Screaming Yellow Zonkers

The Screaming Yellow Zonkers saga is, at its core, a tale of two companies. One invented the product, manufactured it, sold it to retailers, warehoused it, distributed it, and paid all the bills. The other company came up with the name, the package design, and the radio and television commercials that were responsible for the product's almost instant success.

I worked at the second one.

There are few people under the age of 60 who have even heard of Screaming Yellow Zonkers. The name rings no bells and the only box of Zonkers they might have seen would be empty, offered on E-bay, and priced at 50 times what it originally cost when completely filled.

In the beginning, there was little about the product that hinted of future success. It was just another popcorn snack with an acceptably pleasant taste. The lack of uniqueness offered no indication of what was about to happen. 1. The product would become a nationwide phenomenon, and 2. It would only have a brief moment in the sun before falling swiftly and completely from grace.

The product was conceived by Lincoln Snacks, a relatively small Chicago company that had achieved a moderate level of success with two previous popcorn-based products.

Fiddle Faddle, was an inexpensive popcorn coated treat covered with caramel and sold in a colorful cardboard package. Because of its low price and sweet flavor, it became relatively popular.

Poppycock was a more expensive version of Fiddle Faddle. Almonds, pecans, and a honey glaze were added and, instead of being packed in an ordinary cardboard box, it came in a fancy tin. Because of its comparatively high price point, Poppycock was often offered as an unusual, yet appropriate, hostess gift when invited to someone's home for dinner.

With two comparatively successful products already in place, Lincoln set out to expand the business they knew best – popcorn: specifically, popcorn with a twist.

After some trials and errors, they came up with a potential winner. Research groups seemed to agree that the popcorn with a sweet butter flavored coating was indeed quite tasty. Even better, the test results indicated that the product was potentially quite marketable if priced about the same as Fiddle Faddle. Happily, that very affordable price, not coincidentally, was part of Lincoln's plan from the very beginning.

There were plenty of reasons to add the new popcorn treat to Lincoln's product mix. It was in their wheelhouse, so it could be produced affordably on their existing equipment. Although a new package would have to be designed, the same box that was used for Fiddle Faddle would surely suffice. Sales and distribution teams were already in place. Even though new products always come with justifiable concerns about acceptance and profitability, this one seemed like a natural extension to their line of popcorn snacks.

All that was missing was a name and package design – two critically important elements.

After brainstorming sessions within the company proved unproductive, Lincoln decided to get help. They called all the usual package design suspects and came up with the usual results. Nothing excited them. Nothing felt quite right.

So, they decided to extend their search and look beyond traditional sources.

Hanging by a thread somewhere on the extreme outside of those potential sources was our advertising agency, Hurvis, Binzer and Churchill. We had, by then, built an impressive reputation as a highly creative group – big on humor, bold visuals, and style.

But we were anything but a perfect fit. There was nothing in our resume to indicate that we had even the slightest experience designing packages or naming products.

Our client list was also less than impressive. We had no national accounts and only a few local and regional ones. But we did have a national reputation because we had won a ton of awards for creativity. Although our art direction and writing staff was tiny, we often dominated agencies many times our size in advertising competitions. It was not uncommon for us to leave the award shows with more trophies than we could easily carry.

Given that combination of talent and inexperience, Lincoln felt we might be at least worthy of an initial meeting. After letting us taste their new popcorn concoction, they handed us a white box and asked us one question: what should we put on it? Then they added another request: please don't make it ordinary.

About a week later, we returned with the obvious answer: we told them that they should name the product Screaming Yellow Zonkers.

They agreed that our suggestion wasn't ordinary and was certainly memorable. But they had a few concerns. So, not unexpectedly, they wanted to do some testing. Our idea, along with others they thought worthy of examining further, was shown to a focus group. Actually, several.

Focus groups, it should be noted, are often where good ideas go to die. The participants are often focus group pros who come for the free donuts and a little financial compensation. They are happy to offer their expert opinion on things about which they know absolutely nothing. In their daily lives at home or at work, no one cares about their opinions, but here, their thoughts seem to carry great weight. So, in exchange for the soft drinks and snacks, they are more than pleased to tell the marketing experts huddled behind a two-way mirror, precisely what they ought to do.

As is often the case, results of the focus group research were less than encouraging. Although some submissions from other companies were found to be acceptable, everyone in every single focus group absolutely hated the name Screaming Yellow Zonkers. Hated, hated, hated it.

Among the landslide of negative comments, these thoughts came up consistently:

"Screaming" is a disturbing and unpleasant act. It reminded people of children wailing and throwing temper tantrums.

"Yellow" is the color of cowardice. Few people enjoy being fearful – and being afraid of a treat made no sense at all.

"Zonkers" made people think of hitting and causing pain.

So, by actual count, the name was 0 for 3. Individually the words were problematic. Collectively, they were simply awful.

What happened next will surely go down in the annals of package goods history. In response to the overwhelming and consistently negative comments, Lincoln Foods said something that, to the best of my knowledge, no client has said before or since. "Sure, the test results are terrible. But let's do it anyway."

Once the name was settled, there was no possibility of designing a conventional package. Essentially, we asked ourselves, "what are the rules for traditional package goods?" Then we made sure we broke as many as possible.

Package goods rule #1. Don't put food in a black box. Never. Never. Never.

So naturally, that's where we started. Surely a black box would stand out on the shelf.

Package goods rule #2: Always use photography. It's the only way to convey the most important element for food products - taste appeal.

So, we made sure that all the visuals on the box were cartoon-styled drawings.

Package goods rule #3: use clear, simple language to explain the product's benefits.

We wrote the funniest things we could think of and most of them had little to do with quality or taste.

Not surprisingly, Lincoln's salespeople were concerned. They explained why it would be an uphill battle to encourage retailers to carry a product with such an unusual name and especially one that came in such an unusual package. Based on experience they anticipated a negative response from stores. Lincoln's sales team complained bitterly about their new assignment. But the "let's do it anyway" philosophy prevailed and, because they appreciated their regular paychecks, the sales team reluctantly loaded up boxes of Zonkers and started knocking on doors.

What happened next surprised just about everyone. Grocery Store Buyers - the ones who decide what products make it to the shelves – are notorious rule followers and unwilling risk takers. But they thought the product was amusing. And, they had to admit, Zonkers also tasted pretty good. So, in accordance with the theme of the times, they went with the flow. Their attitude was, "what the hell – it's not a vitamin supplement, it's only an inexpensive snack. Let's put it on the shelves and see what happens."

This is what happened: Zonkers was an instant hit.

Because the package looked so different, it was impossible to ignore. Amidst a sea of colorful boxes, the black one stood out. People picked it off the shelf and, out of curiosity, tried to figure out what such peculiarly named product was all about.

They started to read the box and started to laugh. Then they read some more and laughed some more. Other shoppers wanted to find out what was so funny, so they also picked up a box. The laughter increased and crowds grew. The price sealed the deal. People didn't know what was inside and really didn't care because Zonkers clearly delivered a lot of amusement for only 39¢. Soon, boxes of Zonkers began filling shopping carts. Lots of people bought one. Many bought more than one because they wanted to give it to someone who they were certain would get a big kick out of it.

Many stores sold out completely the very first day.

Everyone who bought a box felt the need to show it to someone else. And, quite often, that someone else went shopping almost immediately.

Word of mouth started the ball rolling. But it wasn't just customers and friends who were talking. New York Magazine put Zonkers in their "Best Bet" section. The next week, sales in Manhattan skyrocketed.

Stores did more than re-order – they doubled and tripled their orders. And still they were unable to keep up with the demand.

All this happened with zero advertising and pretty much the same amount of promotion. But Lincoln realized that they had a tiger by the tail, so it was clearly time to find out how successful Zonkers could be. Unquestionably, there was an upside. But how up was up?

Lincoln ordered radio and TV commercials and our ad agency was more than happy to oblige. The assignment and the challenge was essentially this: come up with the funniest commercials of all time.

We were more than up to the task.

Because the concept of cartoons was so firmly established with the box, the commercial we conceived was animated. It began with a decidedly unattractive man who had the misfortune of also having an oversized leg that he dragged behind him.

The Voice Over began this way: "Once there was – there existed – an ugly, ugly man…" Because most advertising includes a product benefit, we included some ridiculous claims. As the story unfolded, it turned out that eating Zonkers changed this ugly man's life in every possible and wonderful way. He became handsome, wealthy, and extremely attractive to beautiful women.

By the end of the commercial, Zonkers had made it possible for him to have an abundance of wealth, love, and happiness. But all was not perfect - he still dragged his leg behind.

After the commercial was presented and greeted with gales of laughter, the president of Lincoln Snacks revealed that his father suffered from a paralyzed leg. His father not only walked with a limp, he dragged his foot behind. It is hard to know whether we were more surprised by that information or by his next statement: "what the hell, the commercial is hysterical - let's do it anyway."

A primary force behind the commercial was the person who wrote it, Allan Katz. When he joined the agency, Allan had no experience in advertising, but a lifelong relationship with humor. It was no surprise to any of us that he was soon invited to join the writing staff of Laugh In and later became one of the most successful writers and producers in Hollywood.

When Allan first began working with us, he was quite familiar with Chicago but had not travelled very often or very far. So, when he went to New York to meet with the animation company to supervise production of the commercial, it was a very big deal for him.

After a brief get together to discuss the project, we all went out to dinner. As is often the case, the production company, feeling the need to impress, chose a well-known, expensive restaurant.

There were about a dozen of us seated around a large, oval table. A formally dressed waiter proudly placed enormous, leather- bound menus in front of each of us and then made the rounds to take our orders.

Allan was first. He was understandably uncomfortable. There were too many items on the menu and too many explanations. In addition, he had no idea what the protocol of the ordering process would be. Were people having appetizers? Were salads included – and would it be improper to ask? He was in New York for the first time and seated with a group of people he just met. So, he did the prudent thing. He asked the waiter to start with someone else.

As the rest of us placed our orders, Allan continued to study the menu. Even given the additional time, he was still unable to make a decision. But the waiter had completed his circle and now all eyes were on Allan.

I sensed his distress but also knew what was coming. For Allan, the greater the discomfort, the greater the opportunity for humor. With an impatient waiter and everyone at the table looking at him, Allan still took too long before announcing his decision. Then, with assurance, he closed the large leather menu and said decisively, "I think I'll just have the roast cock."

Once the TV commercials started running, Zonkers sales escalated even higher. Because money was rolling in and the energy and excitement was high, new ways to promote Zonkers were explored.

We already had a full stash of TV and radio commercials, print ads, and even a second package being written and designed. But surely there was more that could be done.

The idea of a Screaming Yellow Zonkers Circus poster made about as little sense as anything else that preceded it, so work began immediately.

Once again, Allan wrote the bulk of the copy, but the opportunity was too appealing to allow him to do it all. Many of us jumped in with ideas, and a few of them even passed muster.

Responsibility for the design and finished art for the poster was assigned to Push Pin Studios. Even getting them to accept the job was a major coup. At the time, Push Pin was unquestionably one of the best – and certainly most famous - design studios in America, if not the entire world. The two founders, Milton Glaser and Seymour Chwast, led a team of extraordinarily talented designers. But, for this project, they were going to do work themselves.

Because the poster would be offered as a special premium, it needed to be completed relatively quickly – soon enough to be included as a special offer on the next iteration of the Zonkers box.

Push Pin sent some early concepts, but it became clear that a hands-on effort was required to keep the process moving, so Pete and I went to New York to make sure the schedule was met.

The meeting at Push Pin will remain as one of the most uncomfortable I have ever attended and almost certainly one of the most difficult. We met with Milton Glaser to see how the finished art was progressing. Our expectations were understandably high but even if they were much lower, we would have been beyond disappointed. We were surprised to see that the actual work was being done by Seymour Chwast. His style of illustration is quite wonderful, but also totally inappropriate for a circus poster. The only saving grace about the meeting was that Seymour was out of town and didn't have hear the rejection in person. But Milton was there, and we were faced with the impossible assignment of telling one of the most famous designers in the world that the work of his studio was unacceptable.

Under normal circumstances, turning down an artist's work is difficult. But saying "no" in person to Milton Glaser was an unenviable task. By then, he was already astonishingly well-known and deservedly well respected. Years later he became even more famous for designing the I (heart) NY logo, becoming a co-founder of New York magazine, and being the first commercial designer/illustrator to have a solo show at the Louvre in Paris.

Because we held him in such high regard, Pete and I were thrilled just to be in the same room. But once we saw the work, there was no possible way for us to accept it. For understandable reasons, Milton wouldn't back down. He correctly told us that the preliminary layout and sketches had been approved. That didn't leave us much wiggle room. But eventually we agreed that Push Pin would be owed money for their work even though we would not be using their illustrations in the final poster. Pete and I were badly shaken when we left. There are better ways to spend an afternoon in Manhattan than saying "no" to a legend.

By then, a lot of money and a lot of time had been wasted, but the need to have a poster had not changed. Because we had never considered that Push Pin's work would be unacceptable, we were in a bind. With few options available to us, we called Charlie White, a good friend, and an even better artist. That evening he and his agent came to meet with us in our hotel to talk about the possibility of his taking over the project.

I'm not sure how we became regulars at the St. Regis Hotel but somehow that had become our home when we worked in New York. The St. Regis had – and continues to have - a well-deserved reputation as a beautiful, traditional, exceedingly expensive hotel. The production companies, photographers, and artists we worked with were all impressed that we stayed there. Pete and I, however, were clueless. Someone had made the reservations and we showed up. We knew very little about New York and assumed that we were just in a relatively convenient hotel that had available rooms.

My first inkling that the St. Regis was more than a step up from the ordinary occurred at a time when Rollin and I were shooting a commercial in Manhattan. After a full day on location, we returned to the hotel, exhausted, sweaty, and looking very much the worse for wear. Joining us on the elevator was an elderly couple – a blue-haired woman and her impeccably dressed husband. As the elevator doors closed, she looked us up and down with great disdain. For her, sharing the tight space with long haired, unkept, jeans-wearing hippies was beyond unacceptable. Our mere presence in the elevator was troubling. With a sense of sadness, she turned to her husband and told him what he had almost certainly realized himself, "The St. Regis isn't what it used to be." Rollin didn't miss a beat. He smiled as he told her, "I'll tell you what lady. If you shave off your moustache, I'll shave off mine." The rest of the elevator ride was spent in cold, stony silence.

Usually, we stayed in standard rooms, certainly not a hardship. But on this visit, we were given significant upgrades. Apparently, there were problems with the air conditioning on the lower floors, so Pete and I were both placed in enormous penthouse suites. It was in one of those distinctly over-the-top suites that Charlie White and his agent came to meet with us to discuss the possibility of him doing the Zonkers circus poster.

It's important to note that Charlie is a brilliant artist and, under normal circumstances, would have been a top consideration for the assignment. Charlie was a master of the airbrush technique and his work for us in the past had never been anything less than outstanding. But because the opportunity to work with Milton Glaser seemed too great to pass up, we originally gave the job to Push Pin. Charlie was hardly a second choice. There was no question he'd be able to do a brilliant job. The only question was if he had enough time to do it. Given our previous experiences with him and his less than stellar ability to deliver work on anything even close to a timely basis, there was plenty of reason for concern.

That concern was echoed repeatedly by his agent. Charlie loved the idea of the poster and was enthusiastic about taking on the assignment. He was ready and eager to go. His agent spent the entire meeting shaking her head and explaining to him about the commitments he had already made and why, no matter how appealing the job might be, it was simply something he could not and should not accept.

Spoiler alert: Charlie did the poster. Although he came nowhere near delivering the art on schedule, his work was, as anticipated, nothing short of spectacular. The poster was a major hit at the time and now, is an even a bigger deal. Recently, one was listed on Ebay for $2,500 – a bit more than the $1 original price. (Plus, of course, the box top proof of purchase that added a whopping 39¢).

After our discussion about the poster project, and after his agent left, shaking her head in disbelief that he still wanted to do it, Charlie told us there was something he wanted us to see – the amazing Maxwell Parish painting downstairs in the King Cole bar of the hotel. Even though we had stayed at the St. Regis many times, we had never gone into the bar. Entry required coats and ties. It wasn't that we had neglected to bring coats and ties; neither of us owned them. For us, dressing up meant a T-shirt with no illustration or writing on it.

Because Charlie was insistent, we went downstairs and tried to follow him into the bar. We didn't get far. The maître d' stepped in front of us, barring our entrance, and chastised us for inappropriate attire. Frankly, from a visual standpoint, our lack of coats and ties was just a warm-up. At the time, Charlie's hair was very long, he had puffy mutton chops and, instead of the required suit and tie, he was wearing overalls. That was pretty much the same way he looked a month before when he took his children to Disneyworld and was denied entrance due to his unacceptable appearance.

Charlie barely missed a beat. He was incredulous that we were even being slightly delayed. He pointed to the two of us and told the maître d' that we were not only important guests of the hotel, but we were staying in penthouse suites. Then he charged into the room with us trailing behind. Because of the commotion we were causing, there were more than a few displaced looks from the correctly wardrobed people already seated. But they had no idea how uncomfortable they were about to become. Charlie stopped in front of the painting, completely awe struck by the brilliance of the work. He fell to his knees, spread his arms in appreciation and, because he simply couldn't help himself, was compelled to express his admiration. I'm pretty sure that this is the actual phrase he delivered at full volume: "Can you fucking believe this?"

There is no question that his assessment was absolutely correct. The painting is exceptional. And there was no one in the room who could possibly appreciate it more than Charlie. As a phenomenal artist in his own right, Charlie didn't just see a painting that was overwhelming in both scope and detail, he also understood the talent, effort and energy required to create it. For him, being in front of that painting was nothing short of a religious experience. Nevertheless, I think that everyone else was pleased when, after a few moments of admiration, the three of us were escorted out of the room. No one – including us - was disappointed that we were gone.

Although he was enthusiastic about accepting the challenge of creating the artwork for the circus poster, Charlie's delivery of the finished art was, not unexpectedly, more than a little behind schedule. At one point – already well past the drop-dead delivery date - when the art had still not arrived, we called to tell him that we absolutely, positively needed to have it in two days.

To our amazement, a package from his studio arrived two days later. There was, however, a small problem: the painting was only about 2/3 completed.

Charlie had a totally defensible excuse. Because we told him we needed the art in two days, he made sure he got it to us right on schedule. In his mind, he had fulfilled his assignment. If we had specified that we needed the finished art, he would have told us that was impossible.

Eventually, the poster was completed, printed, and offered to the public. Although it was late, it more than lived up to expectations. Just as the commercials and package were a big hit, so too, was the poster. Because of the quality of the art, design, and hysterical copy, it became an instant classic. The promotion worked brilliantly and sales of the second box were even better than anticipated. Screaming Yellow Zonkers was now well established as a certified hit.

But the tidal wave of success was short lived.

The unanticipated drop off in sales began slowly at first. Then the flood of sales eased into a trickle. It took a while to figure out why.

For the uninitiated – and that certainly included all of us who worked on Zonkers – there is something known as a "Snack Scale." It's not a judgement of quality or price but, nevertheless, all snack products fit somewhere on that scale.

The numbers run from 1 to 9. On the lower end of the scale are salty snacks – potato chips, pretzels, peanuts, and the like. The saltier the taste, the lower the number. On the upper end of the scale are the sweet snacks – candy bars, cookies, donuts, and the like. The sweeter the snack, the higher the number.,

The scale has nothing to do with preference or quality. There are some number 1's that sell extremely well and some that don't. The reason for sales could be based on price, packaging, taste, availability, or any combination of factors. The same is true for the higher numbered snacks. Some sell well and others don't. Some are loved and some are completely ignored.

But all snacks, no matter where they fall on the scale, have a common attribute. They are seldom consumed alone. Almost always, they are accompanied by a drink. And the beverages consumed differ significantly.

When enjoying salty snacks, people tend to drink beer, water, soft drinks, or something that quenches their thirst. Sweet snacks are often accompanied by coffee, tea, milk, or a beverage that pairs appropriately.

Again, this is not a quality judgement. it's just matter of personal taste. But because snacks and beverages usually require some sort of pairing, finding the right combination is no subtlety. It is critically important.

Screaming Yellow Zonkers, like all other snacks, had their place on the scale. Zonkers were a #5 – right smack in the middle. They were tasty, but neither salty nor particularly sweet. The position on the salty/sweet scale had absolutely nothing at all to with enjoyment. Most people liked the taste of Zonkers. But Zonker's unfortunate placement in the very middle of the scale caused a peculiar and unanticipated problem. Eating Zonkers made people thirsty, but they had no idea what to drink to quench that thirst.

Maybe it doesn't sound like much of a problem. But it turned out to be the deal breaker. There simply was no way to sugarcoat the issue: no drink seemed appropriate. After snacking on Zonkers, people felt two things: thirsty and unsatisfied.

There is no question that the Screaming Yellow Zonkers package was a huge hit. People snapped up the boxes and gave them to friends. Many amused their friends by reading the copy out loud. The box was hysterical, but the Zonkers inside left an unfulfilled taste in the mouth.

If Lincoln Snacks had been in the business of selling packages, the story would have ended differently. But since their business was selling popcorn treats, there was a relatively abrupt, unhappy conclusion.

For a very brief moment Screaming Yellow Zonkers was a sensation. But the demise came quickly.

It was an exhilarating ride while it lasted. But it didn't last.

Shades of Success

The old saw goes something like this: "success has many parents, but failure is an orphan."

While that may account for over-populated orphanages, the larger truth is that there are many ways to determine success. Some are more elusive than others.

For youngsters who have been encouraged to participate in organized sports, trophies are often awarded simply for showing up. Elementary school students may be rewarded for trying hard by receiving an "A for effort."

While there are those who recoil at the thought of rewarding participation because it sends the wrong signal for real world encounters, it is worth noting that even in the hard scrabble world of business, success is not always easily discerned.

For example:

If a company doubles sales, is that a success? What if the sales came by extreme price cutting or a marketing effort so expensive that the increased sales actually resulted in decreased profits?

If a company reduced the price of a product and lost money on every sale for a full year, is that a failure? What if the price cut forced their main competitor to lower prices to the point where they went out of business? Then, the following year, with less competition, the company was able to raise prices and be profitable from then on.

If a company's sales are down 50% for a full year, is that a failure? What if those sales came at a significant price increase and an equally significant decrease in production costs, resulting in an improved bottom line?

As another old saying goes, "it all depends ..."

During my many years in advertising, I have worked with clients big and small, confident and befuddled, aggressive and fearful, challenged and challenging. Not surprisingly, I have experienced both success and failure. But occasionally, and often to my surprise, both occurred simultaneously.

A Child Shall Lead Them

There was a time – actually, a considerable time – when there was such a thing as The Telephone Company. Not several phone companies. Just one. Ma Bell was it.

Bell Telephone – like all monopolies – was granted astonishing latitude on just about everything – prices, equipment, quality, and service. If it was possible to conceive of anything that would raise profits or make customers more miserable, it would surely be implemented.

For decades, if anyone objected to anything the Bell company offered, the options were essentially limited to these two: 1. suck it up and accept the unacceptable, or 2. do without phone service entirely.

What a difference a few decades make. Today, telephone behemoths beg customers to sign contracts and offer freebees up the wazoo for the privilege of providing them with service. Reliable phone service is taken for granted by everyone, everywhere, and every child over the age of 2 is not only skilled in the use of a smart phone but likely uses it for hours every day.

That was not always so. As recently as the 1970's, there were some areas in the U.S. that had no phone service at all, and many others where access was severely limited.

In 1973, when I first started doing advertising for Mountain Bell, (the division of the Bell Telephone Company that was responsible for serving Colorado, Arizona, New Mexico, and a few other nearby states) phone service for all was little more than wishful thinking.

At that time, a nationwide network of telephone poles and telephone lines was still very much a work in progress. The gaps – and there were many - meant that some customers in the Mountain Bell area were forced to share party lines. Two, three and sometimes four homes shared the same telephone line. So if the line was already in use, nobody else could make a call. Or because privacy was not a viable option, discrete busybodies had total access to listen in on any conversation that took place on the shared line. For those who preferred to call on their own time schedule, sharing a party line was problematic. For eavesdroppers, it was a dream come true.

Although a shared phone line seems beyond the limits of imagination in these days of ubiquitous cell phones, for some residents in the rural mountain states, even party lines were a luxury. In more than a few less populated areas, telephone poles had yet to be constructed and, as a result, residents there had no phone service at all.

While that was obviously a problem for people who wished to communicate with each other, it was also a problem for Ma Bell. After all, even a monopoly has difficulty charging for a service that does not exist. So, motivated as always by the desire to generate additional profit, creative minds at the company were tasked with inventing new ways to charge existing customers even more.

Raising prices was always an option. But occasionally, even avarice driven companies display some restraint. The urge for greater profit, however, is strong and difficult to resist. The only thing that truly prevents even higher prices for what is often less than adequate service is the nasty issue of governmental oversight and the very loosely imposed regulations that constantly interfered with the monopoly's natural desire to overcharge.

So, at Ma Bell, the search was always on for more subtle ways of gouging the public. Because the best minds in the company were assigned to that task, there was never a question that a solution would be found.

Even though there were surely geniuses at the phone company, it didn't require a Mensa IQ to realize that there were only 2 requirements for connecting people by phone. They had to know each other's phone number and, of course, in those pre-pushbutton days, they needed sufficient manual dexterity to dial it.

Friends and relatives happily shared those numbers. But for everyone else, the phone company provided the necessary assistance. That was accomplished in two ways:

1. Free of charge, books jam packed with names, addresses and phone numbers written in the tiniest possible print were distributed to everyone who leased a phone. Although phone books were often enormous and the miniscule type was difficult to read, at least the desired information was somewhat accessible.
2. Directory assistance operators were available 24 hours a day. Anyone could dial 411, provide the operator with a name and address, and the requested phone number would be offered – sometimes even cheerfully.

Printing and distributing the phone books and paying the salaries of directory assistance operators was obviously a significant expense. But, because both seemed necessary, the phone company provided them at no additional charge. A key word here is "additional." That's because, both ways of obtaining a phone number were included as part of the monthly fees for renting a phone and having access to phone service. Those fees were never inexpensive, and continually increased. But, even Ma Bell, realized there were limits to the amount that could be charged. So, the challenge went out to the company's most devious minds: surely there was a way to eke out additional profit from customers who were already overpaying.

Option #1, charging for phone books was rejected almost immediately. It was simply a step too far, too soon.

Option #2, exploring he opportunity to monetize the directory assistance operators seemed more feasible.

Eliminating those operators entirely would, of course, save the company a lot of money. But removing a service that so many people counted on would almost certainly be viewed as an unacceptable solution. Even though upsetting customers was a regular occurrence for the phone company, removing directory assistance operators seemed more than a bit extreme.

But what if there was another way to skin the directory assistance cat? Why not charge for the service? The earned money could, at the very least, pay the operator salaries. And if the price was sufficiently high (and why wouldn't it be?), maybe there was even a potential to throw off some profit.

Even the greedy monopoly monsters realized that springing new charges on an unsuspecting public would not be appreciated. But with determination and cunning, they came up with a solution. They engineered a sneak attack.

Their devious plan involved running some TV advertising to make the public feel that the Directory Assistance service was being over-used; perhaps even overwhelmed. (It wasn't, but honesty was not a significant component of the plan.) Because of this supposed over-use, and to keep up with ever-increasing demand, the phone company regretfully explained they might – I repeat "might" have no choice other than to start charging for the service. But, because their kindness and concern for their customers was limitless, they offered a remedy: charging for the service could be avoided if people relied on their phone books a little more. If the public responded by decreasing their calls for directory assistance, there would be no need to initiate a charge.

Of course, the phone company knew that was a ridiculous idea. Why use a clumsy, difficult to read phone book when the needed information could be provided so much more easily simply by dialing 411 and speaking to a real live person?

It is worth noting that phone books did offer some useful benefits. They were so heavy that anything needing flattening could be pressed beneath them. They were so thick that strong men found the concept of ripping them apart both challenging and worth betting on. And they were seemingly free - usually arriving on doorsteps, unannounced when least expected. But realistically, they were so enormous that keeping them in anything resembling a convenient location was simply absurd. And, for anyone over the age of 40, the size of the type was far too small to be of any functional value whatsoever.

The scheme was both simple and devious: use PR and news stories to warn about a possible charge if directory assistance usage continued unabated. Additionally run some ineffective advertising to encourage the use of phone books. But when customers failed to comply – as they surely would - the phone company could use that failure as justification for inflicting new charges for directory assistance.

There are scientists who will explain that, given the weight of its body and the size of its wings, it is impossible for a hummingbird to flap those wings fast enough to fly. However, the hummingbird, being unaware of that impossibility, flies anyway.

We, at the ad agency, were in a similar predicament. We were blithely unaware that we had been given an impossible task. So, in our naivety, we set about creating a commercial designed to reduce the number of calls to Directory Assistance. We were told that judging the effectiveness of the commercial would be very easy. They'd just count the number of calls. The fewer the calls, the more successful the ad campaign. What we weren't told was that the real goal of the campaign was abject failure. The less effective our TV campaign, the happier the phone company would be.

The commercial we produced wasn't cute or even particularly clever. It was based entirely on reason. We cast a four-year old boy and had him explain the situation as he understood it: There was a problem with directory assistance. Sometimes when people really need help from a directory assistance operator, they couldn't get through because all the lines were busy. So, he suggested that if people looked up the numbers themselves, the problem could be solved. Not everyone had to comply, of course, and he offered a reasonable example. It was OK for him to use directory assistance because, after all, he was so young, he didn't know how to read.

The kid did a brilliant job. Frankly, that was not surprising. He was already famous for a commercial he had done the year before with his two older brothers. For years, Life cereal had been positioned as an adult product, but the company saw opportunity to increase sales by appealing to children. In what became one of the best-known commercials of all time, his two older brothers refused to even try the cereal. Instead, they shoved it in front of their little brother because they knew that he hated everything. But he tried it and enjoyed it. The phrase "Mikey likes it" almost immediately became part of the national lexicon. Mikey was the boy we cast for the role.

The commercial we shot for Mountain Bell was clear, easily understood and made total sense. As soon as it started running, it began to make a difference. And every week that it was on the air, it worked even better. In short order and against all odds, calls for directory assistance plummeted.

The execs at Mountain Bell were not pleased. In their minds, and according to their plan, the commercial was decidedly not a success. We had done our job too well. We solved a problem the phone company really had no desire to solve.

They had every right to believe that the commercial would be ineffective. After all, for notoriously lazy Americans, getting an operator to offer a phone number would always be preferable to the arduous task of finding a phone book and looking up the number all by themselves.

Ma Bell's plan to charge for directory assistance had already been set in stone and was scheduled to be put in action. Financial projections had been circulated. And as is typical with big companies, failure to meet those expectations would not be happily accepted. Unfortunately, the unanticipated results of the advertising campaign threw a monkey wrench into those plans.

The script the phone company had carefully prepared for customers was now undeliverable. It was now impossible for them to say "well, we tried to warn you, but you wouldn't listen. Even though it pains us immeasurably, we are now forced to charge for calls to our directory assistance operators."

Despite succeeding at what we had been asked to do, in the great scheme of things, because we had done so well, as far as the phone company was concerned, the result of our advertising campaign was a disastrous failure.

What happened next was entirely predictable. The "successful" commercial was pulled off the air. Once that happened, calls for directory assistance gradually began to increase, and, after an appropriate waiting period, the phone company reluctantly, and with great remorse, announced to their customers that, painful though it was, they had no choice but to charge for what had formerly been a free service.

For our ad agency, the applause for a job well done was significantly less than deafening. We had triumphed when incompetence was required. We had flown like hummingbirds when we should have flown like penguins.

The phrase "winning the battle but losing the war" seemed appropriate.

The elephant in the room

My career in advertising began in Chicago, evolved in Los Angeles, and eventually completed in New York where I was a partner at an advertising agency whose biggest client was MCI. Those letters mean almost nothing today because that company has long since disappeared, but there was a time when the airways were inundated by MCI commercials.

The greatly abridged story of the company's demise is that, after a decade of success, MCI was sold for several billion dollars. The sale turned out to be a complicated, bogus deal that put the mastermind who conceived the illegal transaction behind bars for years. But the money that the MCI senior management pocketed from the buyout was very real indeed.

Throughout the '90's, it was almost impossible to turn on a TV without seeing a commercial for both AT&T and MCI as they locked in a ferocious battle for long distance customers. An astute friend of mine observed that although he didn't know much about the phone business, he knew one thing for certain: both MCI and AT&T were making too much money.

For reasons that should be relatively obvious, as the advertising agency for MCI, there was little objection to the "making too much money" issue because a significant portion was winding up in our pockets as well. I use the term "our" rather loosely because, although I was officially a partner in the agency and a well-paid one at that, the truly filthy amounts of lucre somehow eluded my personal checkbook.

Even though MCI was socking away millions of dollars by offering all manner of money saving enticements on long distance calls, the company was also quite creative about finding other ways to increase their bottom line. One of the very first places they checked was AT&T's annual report. There, in black and white, was clear indication about a potential opportunity.

No tears needed to be shed for AT&T. While it is undeniably true that long distance competition from MCI and Sprint took chunks of their revenue, an unconscionable amount of money still streamed in – much of it from their strangle hold on collect calls. Every single collect call made in America went through an AT&T operator and was eventually carried on an AT&T long distance line. Not only were there thousands and thousands of collect calls made every day, but those calls were, by far, the most expensive and the most profitable.

MCI executives noted the lucrative tightly shut door and determined to pry it open. Admittedly it would be a daunting task, but they had the manpower and brain power to make the attempt.

Their first move was unexpected. They purchased the rights to a seemingly innocuous phone number (1 800 265-5328). With that in hand, they completely upended the collect calling business.

MCI's computer geeks created a technology that streamlined and eventually disrupted collect calling. Instead of dialing "0" to get connected to an AT&T operator and then paying exorbitant fees for the service and the call, MCI made the process a lot simpler and much less expensive.

All customers had to do was dial 1 800 COLLECT. (1 800 265-5328).

The number was easy to remember. The service was easy to use. The savings were impressive. And the concept was immediately embraced.

The success of the new service had executives at MCI doing cartwheels. Not only did each of the thousands and thousands of daily calls to 1 800 COLLECT generate substantial income for MCI, but each call also represented money that was no longer going to AT&T. Depleting AT &T's war chest was the source of unbridled joy - appreciated almost as much as filling MCI's coffers with gold. 1 800 COLLECT was a double whammy winner and an off-the-charts hit.

And the money-making ideas kept coming.

The success that Mountain Bell enjoyed by charging for directory assistance did not remain a secret within the Bell system. It was only a matter of time before every division of AT&T jumped on the bandwagon. Once the dam had been broken and directory assistance evolved from a free benefit to a money-making service, MCI followed AT&T's lead and happily cashed in on the opportunity. Both companies were more than pleased to provide "information" operators for a price – and that price was as steep as they thought possible, acceptable, or tolerable. At least until it could be increased.

As telephones proliferated throughout the country and long- distance calls became more and more commonplace, there was an obvious need to help people find phone numbers in other states and other cities.

But local operators only had information about local numbers so finding an out of state phone number was difficult, annoying, and time consuming. The process was piecemeal, inefficient, and, of course, expensive.

For starters, it required knowing the area code for the city you wanted to call. So your first call was to an AT&T operator who gave you that number and happily charged for that service. Next you used the area code to get to a directory assistance operator in the city you wanted to call and paid for that as well. After writing down the number, you dialed it and paid handsomely once again.

The system was clearly broken. But not for long. The geniuses at MCI figured out a way to make the process as simple as it could possibly be. All you'd have to do was dial one number for directory assistance anywhere. Anywhere at all.

But that wasn't the whole story. MCI, understanding the unbridled laziness of most Americans, wanted to make the process even simpler. All someone had to do was say "connect me" and the call would automatically be placed. MCI would then make money on the collect call and, for the first time ever, AT&T would not. For MCI it was a win/win. For AT&T it was a lose/lose.

Once conceived, there were only two things to do.

1. The easy part: Create the technology to make the whole process work. That merely required conceiving the enterprise, buying the hardware, developing the software, building the system,

and making sure that it worked flawlessly every time.
2. The hard part: Create an advertising campaign to let America know about the new number and new service.

Although we obviously could have accomplished both tasks, Pete, my art director partner, and I took on the much more difficult communication challenge.

Our assignment was clear: let everyone know that to find any phone number anywhere in America, there was only one number to remember: 1-800-777-777.

It didn't take us long to come up with the commercial. We began by asking ourselves a very basic question: Is there anyone or anything known for a great memory? And the answer came back: elephants. Surely, we weren't the only ones familiar with the phrase "an elephant never forgets."

The commercial we envisioned was simple and straightforward. On a plain, white set, a spokesman (James Garner was at the very top of our wish list) explained the new, universal number. As he spoke, an elephant walked on stage and stopped next to him. The commercial ended with the logo that Pete designed – an elephant's head, the universal directory assistance number (1 800 777-777) and the words "never forget".

Usually, when we present a commercial, we show a storyboard to indicate the way the action develops. But, because this was such a simple idea, we only showed a single frame. On a 2 by 3-foot white board were two images: James Garner and an elephant.

When we finished explaining the commercial, the client was ecstatic. She thought it was clear, simple, and undeniably memorable.

We were a bit taken aback by her enthusiasm because she had always been a tough sell. But this time she couldn't have been happier. She only had one issue – a very minor one. She loved the white space, but she didn't like the elephant.

Of course, the elephant was the whole idea – and without it, there was nothing other than James Garner in an empty white room.

I was completely flummoxed by her response and was about to offer some resistance, but Pete was undaunted. Almost immediately he said, "We agree. That's why we brought the storyboard for that commercial as a back-up." Then he flipped the cardboard over and showed her the back – a pure, clean expanse of totally white nothingness.

Once again, she was thrilled. "That's it. That's perfect."

And that's the commercial we ended up shooting. We didn't have an elephant, but we did eventually have James Garner.

When we met him, Garner was in his 70's and no longer a TV star. It had been more than a decade since "Maverick" concluded its years of success, and even syndicated episodes of "The Rockford Files" were no longer being aired.

Many of the notables who appeared in MCI commercials were faded also-rans who had been, at best, sidekicks on sit-coms. But Garner was still very much a recognized star. Even at his advanced age, he continued to be cast in feature films.

So, although we treated every actor who appeared in an MCI commercial with at least a modicum of respect, that respect was amped up for him.

It is not unusual for the bigger stars to request that the initial meeting with ad agencies be held in their homes. Not only is it convenient, but it affords them the opportunity to impress. As we all know from "Lifestyles of the Rich and Famous", many of them live rather well.

But Garner was not interested in entertaining visitors. So, we had to come up with a suitable location – someplace befitting his status as a Hollywood luminary.

There is no shortage of premiere hotels in Los Angeles. The Beverly Hills is surely the most famous, but for those in the know, the Bel-Air ranks even higher. Its location, tucked away in the most exclusive part of the city, is a plus. The limited number of rooms and the excessive rates add to the allure.

The decision to meet at the Bel-Air seemed a good fit for someone of Garner's status. To give the appearance that it was our normal haunt, instead of just booking a conference room, it was decided that key representatives from the agency would stay at the hotel. But because it was hard to justify the expense for the full duration of the production, we'd only stay for the nights before and after our meeting with

Garner. After that we'd move to our regular, more affordable digs.

While the rest of our group was quite pleased with that decision, for reasons that have to do with obstinacy and foolishness, I was not. I didn't like the pretense of the Bel-Air being our regular hotel. Pete and I usually stayed at The Niko, a wonderful, welcoming place that was tasteful in a very Japanese way – simple, uncluttered, and immaculate.

Everyone else was more than happy to be spending 2 nights at the Bel-Air, but I was determined to leave as soon as possible. Our first night had already been pre-paid, but I knew I could check out in the morning.

So, when registering, I informed the desk clerk that I was cancelling my reservation for a second night. And, given the brevity of my stay, I had a further request. I wanted the worst room they had.

As it turned out, my attitude – as is often the case – was not particularly helpful. I was indeed provided the worst room in the hotel. But it was fabulous. There were fresh flowers, ridiculously high-quality linens, and an enormous selection of lotions, soaps, coffee, and tea. The next morning, breakfast on the terrace was exceptional. Everyone else stayed and enjoyed another opulent, pampered experience. But, with my tail firmly ensconced between my legs, I moved out.

The meeting with Garner went even better than expected. Our timing could not have been more perfect. He was an avid golfer, and the day before, had achieved a lifetime goal – he'd shot his age. None of us were foolish enough to ask the number.

Although far from bald, his hair had definitely thinned. When we suggested making a piece to cover some of the gaps, Garner was uninterested. He'd seen his share of bad wigs before. But we told him that we'd have one made and, if he liked it, he could wear it. If, as expected, he felt it made him look foolish, it would never see the light of day.

The hair stylist we hired was, if not the best, certainly the most expensive. The piece she made was hardly a full wig – just enough to fill some thin spots. Garner surprised himself by liking it. He not only wore it in the commercial; he kept it. And, although I'm just guessing here, it is conceivable that there were other occasions when he put it to use.

The wardrobe discussion was important, but not difficult. Although Garner was still in great shape and would have looked good in pretty much anything, he liked the idea of not wearing a suit and tie. He didn't even want to wear a starched shirt.

The stylist brought several shirts to the fitting – all were fine, but none were perfect. She agreed to continue shopping, and because Pete and I had time on our hands, we went shopping, too.

Our first stop was Barney's – an exclusive men's store well known for high quality and even higher prices. We found a few shirts that seemed worthy of showing Garner, and because we were enjoying ourselves, continued looking. Pete was astonished to find a plain white undershirt that was priced a little over $100. That discovery set us off on a hunt for one that cost even more. Eventually, we found the winner – a V-neck version for $325. We didn't buy it, but that ludicrous price tag for an undershirt remains lodged in our memory bank.

Garner was – as anticipated - terrific. I did the best I could to write words he felt comfortable delivering. But there were some hard-sell phrases that the lawyers insisted on including, word for legalistic word. Garner was unphased. Even the clumsy, uncomfortable-to-deliver lines flowed effortlessly and believably.

For reasons that I don't recall, or maybe never knew, the universal directory assistance number was not the giant success that MCI anticipated. Perhaps the system itself was too complex to build and maintain. Perhaps the need for the service was smaller than originally projected. Perhaps the system never operated as flawlessly as envisioned.

There are, undoubtedly, reasons for the failure.

But I blame the elephant.

Even if the first time isn't the best, it's always memorable

Logo lines have been an advertising fixture almost from the get-go. Most are easily forgotten, but some live on - often long after they have ceased being used.

"Just Do It" hasn't been part of Nike's communication for decades but those 3 words are still inexorably linked to the company. Apparently, lacing up a pair of Nike shoes or donning a baseball cap with the swish logo is all that is required to have done it – even though precisely what has been done remains somewhat elusive.

Coca Cola has offered many logo lines. "Things go better with Coke", "Have a Coke and a Smile" and "It's the real thing" were all used until they were used up. The theory is that, although drinking Coca Cola has always been refreshing, eventually the advertising could use some re-invigorating.

There are many goals for logo lines. Although memorability is always hoped for, even when that is not achieved, if the clever phrase sums up a company's attitude or a product benefit, the line is deemed to be at least somewhat successful.

Morton Salt proudly claimed that "When it rains, it pours" to underscore their product's unique benefit in an era when most salts (well, at least the un-iodized losers) clumped and clustered when the humidity was high. As technologic improvements in salt preservation made Morton's uniqueness easy to duplicate, the line was summarily dropped. Ever since then, the salt business changed dramatically, and the price of salt escalated. Now there seems to be little problem forking over big bucks for pink Himalayan Sea Salt, Italian Black Truffle Salt, Saffron Fler de Sea Salt and, the most expensive salt of all, Amethyst Bamboo 9x, the salt highly praised by South Koreans. Not a single one, however, offers anything close to a memorable logo line.

Hallmark's "When you care enough to send the very best" is an attempt to justify the absurdly high prices for a few words and a cute illustration on a piece of folded paper. To be fair, on occasion some of the words do rhyme, and the sticker price always includes an appropriately sized matching envelope. To be even fairer, it's obvious that Hallmark is on to something. There are probably few women over 30 without a stash of cards tucked away, awaiting the appropriate time to send a heartfelt birthday, anniversary or sympathy message written and illustrated by someone else. The card selected somehow always manages to strike the precise note of profound sadness or rollicking sense of humor that could only come from her – or, as it turns out, a giant greeting card factory.

As an advertising copywriter, I was often assigned the task of writing a logo line. It was something that I enjoyed and, although I never wrote anything quite as memorable as "just do it", I did enjoy some minor successes along the way.

My first one was for a regional paper company. Like most of their competitors they offered a large selection of papers in a variety of colors, sizes, and textures. And, like most paper companies, they sold everything at relatively similar prices.

Since an advertising message along the line of "we sell paper, too" wasn't likely to do much for their business, they looked to the ad agency to come up with a clever phrase or, even better, a point of difference. Because we were asked to create a distinction where none existed, we felt no need to be tethered to facts. Whether true or not, we suggested a campaign designed to lead customers to believe that the company was capable of creative solutions for even the most difficult paper dilemmas. In other words, even though they were in the business of selling paper, we recommended that they position themselves as a company very much oriented toward service.

With all due respect, this was hardly a breakthrough concept. Every corporate leader happily embraces the "problem solver" description. It's about as original as an executive who thinks of himself or herself as a "people person". Or anyone who proudly boasts of having a good sense of humor. Or being a hard worker. Blah, blah, blah. Nothing new here.

For me, writing a line for the paper company turned out to be typical of the challenge I'd be given for the remainder of my career. Essentially, my assignment was to say pretty much the same thing that every other company was saying but to do it in a way that at least sounded somewhat unique. Happily, there was general agreement about the company's marketing proposition. They wanted to be known as the paper company that solves problems - a decidedly superior position to the alternative: the company that causes them.

This is the line I wrote: "The answer is yes. What's the question?"

I'll pause for a moment to allow you to catch your breath over the brilliance of those combined sentences. But you have to admit, they are a significant improvement over my runner-up idea: What's your problem, asshole?"

Even though I was a new employee only recently escaped from grad school and, as such, firmly entrenched at the subterranean level of the creative staff, because I had written the line, I was allowed to attend the client presentation. My bottom-feeding status didn't require me to participate but, just being there, was a big deal for me. The fact that the client liked the line – actually, liked it a lot - made the agency happy. But their approval did much more for me.

As the meeting progressed, it eventually dawned on me that I was the in real world, and a real client was praising my work. Unlike receiving a good grade for a school project, having client approval had nothing whatsoever to do with effort. They weren't pleased just because I tried really, really, hard. All they cared about was the result.

That was the moment I felt, for the first time, that I had achieved status as a professional writer. So, for the me there is no question that the logo line I wrote was a success.

Of course, from a business standpoint, boosting the égo of a junior copywriter is not the critical measure of accomplishment. It's possible, although improbable, that the logo line and ads I wrote for the paper company had a positive impact on their business. But I have absolutely no idea what happened.

That's because, months before the campaign began to run, I reported for basic training in the National Guard.

And that part of my life, I can say with absolute certainty, was definitely not a success.

All the news that's fit to abuse

When I lived in Los Angeles, I wrote some screenplays that didn't get produced (shocking, I know), some TV pilots that were made but never picked up (true brilliance is seldom recognized at the network level) and a lot of television commercials that did little to save the planet but nevertheless generated sufficient income to provide food and shelter for my family.

One of the ad agencies I worked for at the time had the local ABC-TV affiliate account. Local stations, even in a huge market like Los Angeles, don't do much original programming. Almost everything aired on their channel is either produced by the network or is a re-run of a movie, sit-com or some previously recorded show. With minor exceptions, the only content the network affiliates generate are the local news programs. Since the viewership for those news shows is essentially the only place where incremental revenue is generated, the task for the station is abundantly clear - do whatever it takes to improve and maintain ratings of the local news.

Because TV viewers enjoy looking at attractive faces, news anchors and many on-air reporters are often valued more for their visual appearance than their insightful analysis of the day's occurrences. That doesn't explain why the men who deliver weather reports tend to be extremely quirky, but it does account for the female meteorologists who are appropriately well proportioned and often squeezed into tight fitting dresses.

Our job at the agency was clear: increase viewership by making whatever news team has been assembled seem more appealing, more informed, or more reliable than they actually were.

It's not an easy assignment because the news doesn't vary very much. If there is a fire, a robbery or the city council is considering raising taxes, it's hardly secret information. Sports results are straight forward and prognostications about tomorrow's weather are essentially equally inaccurate, regardless of the source.

The decision about which news show to watch is based almost entirely on the appeal of the on-camera team. Not surprisingly, people like to watch people they like. So, even though commercials may attempt to make one news team seem more friendly, intelligent, honest, or reliable than the others, it tends to be a message without meaning. It's hard – frankly, nearly impossible – to change someone's mind about who they trust or where they prefer to get their information.

Nevertheless, advertising agencies are handed the assignment of promoting whatever real or imagined positive qualities the news team may have to offer. And if the commercials that are created don't increase viewership, at least there is a handy place to lay the blame.

Just as ad agencies have no voice in determining the formula of soft drinks, the percentage of cashews in a tin of mixed nuts, or the price of a detergent, their job is to promote the news team that exists; not the news that could be improved by, for example, replacing the ex-jock dufus who gets so excited about an upcoming game that he forgets which camera to look into.

As anyone who has ever watched local news knows all too well, the difference between news teams is often difficult to discern. Most look like this: The anchor is an older man who is quite capable of reading out loud, although almost completely incapable of delivering a coherent ad lib line; an attractive, younger female co-anchor who may also check another minority box by being either Asian or Black; a sports guy, (always a guy) preferably someone who played professionally; and a quirky meteorologist who is beyond fascinated by wind currents and fluctuating barometric pressure.

Plus, or minus very little, that's the group. Finding something unique about this essentially vanilla team is often difficult. But occasionally a bone is hurled in the agency's direction.

For us, the bone was the new hire at the ABC affiliate. Because ratings were in the toilet, the general manager was willing to try almost anything to shake things up. In an act of bravery or desperation, he hired the brother of the current anchorman and placed them side by side, at the news desk.

A brotherly tandem of anchormen was certainly a first although not necessarily an improvement. Still, it was a point of difference and one that became the focal point of the ad campaign.

The line I wrote, "It's not like watching news, it's like watching family" felt just about right. Unlike other lines I have written in the past, it wasn't an exaggeration because, at least this one was unquestionably true.

But, just as many families have their squabbles, this pairing was not without friction. As it turned out –

and much sooner than the network executive hoped – it became apparent that viewers didn't like the new brother at all. Frankly, they hadn't much cared that much for the original one either. Ratings continued to tank, both brothers were sacked, and my quasi-acceptable line met its demise as collateral damage.

The search to replace the brothers began immediately and in earnest. Fortunately, the station already had a ready group of possibilities. Wherever there is a desk and a TV camera, there are anchors-in-waiting. The general manager of every station in the country has an ever-growing pile of demo tapes of hopefuls who are willing – and beyond anxious - to relocate to a better situation in a more prominent market. Los Angeles, because of its huge population and location in the heart of the TV entertainment industry, is at the very top of almost every anchorman's wish list. An unlimited number of candidates, pushed forward by their less than subtle agents, lawyers or representatives, eagerly made their availability known. But, after taking a chance – and failing, miserably - the need to get the right person the next time was a major priority. One more mistake and, in addition to a third deposed anchorman, the general manager would also likely be seeking employment.

While the search was going on in earnest, the contract for the number one newscaster in LA was about to be re-negotiated by his employer, the CBS affiliate. Whether completely or only partially true, he was reputed to be the prototype for the empty-headed, pompous anchorman on the Mary Tyler Moore Show. The remarkable similarities were undeniable – a thick shock of white hair, an ingenuous smile, and a voice quality that almost made him blush with self-appreciation. Even though he was a card-carrying, blathering fool, his ratings were impressive. He'd been sitting in the CBS anchor chair for over a decade, and for almost the entire time, he was the top-rated local news guy.

Realizing the ABC was in a tricky situation and more than just casually interested in a making an important move to bolster ratings, the general manager of the CBS affiliate made sure he had his bases covered. He called the head of KABC-TV and asked – friend to friend, leader to leader – if there might be even a remote interest in stealing their white-haired news reader. Understandably, he was greatly relieved to learn that ABC's general manager planned to go in an entirely different direction and had no interest in anyone so old or so inept.

The next day, in a major shake-up of the local news scene, KABC-TV announced their decision. They had signed the former CBS anchor to a long-term contract.

Stunned, the CBS honcho called his "friend" at ABC. He needed an explanation. After all, he had been told – actually, he had been promised - that what just occurred was not even a remote possibility.

The explanation from ABC general manager couldn't have been clearer: "This is business. I lied."

Now, with a respectable looking, white-haired, familiar face reading the news from a teleprompter and, fortunately, not straying very often from the written text, ABC's ratings began to creep up. Actually, way up.

Once solidly back in the desired #1 position, moves were made to solidify the station's leadership.

In addition to the regular nightly news reporting, stations often include some "feel good" segments – stories about pet adoption, a remarkably gifted 5-year-old pianist or an amazingly accurate face of Jesus spotted on a rotting avocado. But the head of KABC decided to go even further. He organized a documentary team to create special local reports. These were not designed to be about news of the moment. Instead, they were 2-minute videos about dedicated people who were working hard to make Los Angeles a better place. Sometimes the stories were about employees of the station who volunteered for local charities. Sometimes the topics were about programs to feed the hungry or house the homeless – all conceived and funded by the station. The goal was to show that KABC-TV was not just a station that reported news but was very much a part of the Los Angeles community and actively involved in making life better for the people who lived there.

It is true that the short films were self-serving. But it was also undeniably true that real work was being done and real people were being helped.

My task was to sum up the good deeds and good feelings in a few words – preferably memorable ones. This is the line I wrote:

"KABC-TV. Because there's more to life than news, weather, and sports."

The line lived for decades. And I'd like to think that the words and the advertising that we did for the station helped the ratings climb and continue to remain at the top. But I know the truth: the new anchor (actually, he was pretty old) and the station's very real commitment to be actively involved in the city were what made the difference.

Both the agency and the station were very gracious and gave me more credit than I deserved.

I modestly accepted their praise; told them I was truly appreciative of their compliments and humbly explained that I felt a larger bonus would have been a much more meaningful gesture.

Cars or Planes, what's the dif?

The same Los Angeles advertising agency was invited to pitch the business of a regional airline – Western Air. Even though, at the time, the price of air travel was heavily regulated, and all carriers charged essentially similar prices for similar routes, there were certain instances (usually specific flights to specific destinations) when Western was able to offer lower prices. To make a profit on those lower prices, they lowered just about everything else - beginning with their standards. For starters, Western's fleet of planes was old and not always kept in tip top condition. They flew at less than advantageous times and from distant gates. As a general rule, they were less than compulsive about adhering strictly to departure and arrival times. Schedules were treated less as a formality and more as an approximation. To no one's surprise, their poorly paid flight attendants provided the kind of service that should be expected from an airline lacking in frills or anything close to amenities. Passengers chose to fly with them only after all other possibilities were eliminated. Because they are no longer in business, I can say without much fear of contradiction, that Western was, at best, a pretty crummy airline.

That didn't mean that our agency – and many others – wasn't interested in their account. While representing the best product or the best service is always preferable, pretty much any business willing to pay a substantial monthly fee is one that almost any agency would be pleased to represent. There is a reason why used car dealers, insurance salesmen and advertising executives are similarly regarded for integrity.

Meetings and discussions about potential marketing platforms for new business pitches are always lively affairs. This is the time for free thinking and a great opportunity to demonstrate business prowess and creativity. Everyone jumps at the chance to get in on the action and ideas usually flow freely. But in preparation for the Western Airline pitch, the room was somber. Because we all knew the airline's abundant shortcomings, gallows humor prevailed.

I suggested "the airline to fly when no other is available". Although the line certainly rang true, it wasn't the kind of uplifting message likely to have Western's ticket agents scrambling to fulfill reservations. Another suggestion: "Pay less and take your chances" was in the right direction but equally unacceptable.

After the fruitless discussions concluded, it became clear to all of us that the occasional low price was the single benefit that Western offered. Admittedly, passengers paid heavily in other ways for those savings, but because low prices and saving money are always good things to promote, that's where we landed. If the ad campaign was to have even a shred of honesty or believability, we really had no other choice.

The creative teams went back to their offices and got to work. For new business pitches, good ideas flow effortlessly. At other times – meaning when the assignment is to do the work the agency is being paid to do - even mediocre ideas are often difficult to come by.

For reasons that evade me now, I was feeling either productive or in a willing mood to stretch the truth. Whatever the motivation, it didn't take long to come up with some words that sort of rhymed and were even partially on message.

This is the line I wrote: "There's only one question when you fly Western...what will you do with all the money you save?"

Once others at the agency agreed that the line was the one to pursue, the next step was a to call my favorite composer. In short order he wrote a terrific melody, I wrote some lyrics, and within days, we had ourselves a jingle.

To be honest, there are many other much more reasonable responses when questioned about flying Western. Here are just a few:

Why on earth did I allow my travel agent to book me on this airline? How is it possible to be 3 hours late on a 1-hour flight? Are there any seats on this plane that aren't broken? Are both of those engines supposed to be on fire?

For rather obvious reasons, we didn't bring up those questions during our presentation. In fact, to hear us explain the virtues of the airline at the new business meeting, the uninitiated or more likely the highly gullible, might have been sufficiently swayed to reconsider their previous objections to flying on Western Airlines.

As is the case with almost every new business presentation, after leaving the meeting, we thought we had done well. Apparently, that opinion was not fully embraced.

Short story made shorter: we didn't get the business. But, to make the story a bit longer, there turned out to be an alternative - and much happier - ending.

Even after the failed presentation, the music and the line reverberated around the agency. Everyone liked it. No one could get the tune or the words out of their head. So, the owners of the agency decided to re-purpose it.

We removed the reference to Western Airlines, but kept "what will you do with all the money you save?" and played the jingle for one of our accounts, the Southern California Toyota Dealers. We saw little benefit in explaining that the world's worst airline had rejected it and, instead, without embarrassment or shame, told them it had been conceived just for them. I'm certain that was the very first time – and perhaps only time - when truth has ever been stretched in a discussion about advertising.

The Toyota dealers loved it.

Of course, they did. The melody was memorable, the words were all about saving money, and saving money was the only message that the dealers ever wanted to communicate.

It is worth noting that, for car dealers, helping customers save money was not really at the tippy top of their to-do list. They were much happier up-charging for unneeded extras like undercoating, extended warranties, or luxury accessory packages –

because, after all, what car couldn't be improved by some additional chrome trim?

For the Toyota dealers, just like all other car salesmen, the actual goal was to extract every possible penny from every single buyer. But a catchy tune sung to the lyrics "thanks for letting us take advantage of you, sucker" was not in keeping with the image they hoped to convey. So, even though the money-saving message wasn't a precise fit with the way they did business, at least it was in perfect sync with the way they wanted to be perceived.

Because the jingle didn't explicitly state what the savings really
were, or even if saving money was a possibility, the words easily passed muster with the TV networks.
And for many years, that jingle ended every Southern California Toyota commercial.

I probably should have carried at least a modicum of guilt about being the guy responsible for promulgating misinformation. But the way I looked at it, anyone who swallowed whole a message offered in a TV commercial or by a car salesman, fully deserved the fleecing they invariably received.

Wow! Only $250 for undercoat? Great. I'll take two.

Wanna buy a suit?
My second most successful failure.

I accepted an offer to join an advertising agency that had a great reputation for marketing strategy and media buying but produced creative work that left a lot to be desired. The goal wasn't for me to save a sinking ship because the agency was very much afloat. But there was some hope that I might at least slap on a fresh coat of paint.

One of my first assignments was to come up with a new campaign for a chain of men's clothing stores. The commercials that had been running quite successfully for over a year focused on the store's main benefit. They sold suits and sports jackets at somewhat less than standard retail prices. Although the commercials made a big deal about the savings there was more than a little sticker shock at the moment of purchase. Even at a discount, men's suits can be very expensive.

Because the commercials promised such impressive savings, store traffic was good. But, just as with any campaign, the wear out factor eventually raised its ugly head. After running the same commercials for some time, the effectiveness began to wane. It was time for some new thinking and because I was the new guy, the task was handed to me.

My analysis of the company's business indicated that, in addition to changing the commercials, a change of the marketing approach might also be in order. I reasoned that after driving home the point about discounts for so long, that message was already indelibly imprinted and no longer needed repeating. But if low price wasn't the key to success, there didn't seem to be a lot to say about the company's stores. They were hardly the only place in town to buy men's suits and sports jackets.

I tried to come up with a point of distinction, but there weren't a lot of options. All men's stores look pretty much alike. There are racks of suits, display tables of shirts and sweaters, and a bevy of nattily dressed salesmen who are happy to offer more advice than is usually desired. But I was determined to find at least one unique benefit and eventually succeeded.

Just like other men's stores, this one provided alterations. And, just like other men's stores, for an additional price, those alterations could be completed the very next day. To me, this seemed to be an unexploited opportunity.

It is probably worth noting that I didn't reach that conclusion based on personal experience. There isn't a lot I have gleaned from my own familiarity with the process of purchasing suits or, for that matter, any new clothes at all. If I pick up a Hawaiian shirt at a thrift store, I've pretty much completed my new wardrobe purchases for the year.

But even I know that men and women have completely different attitudes about shopping for clothes.

For women, shopping for clothes is a highly desirable activity – it's what they do for fun.

Women love everything about the process. Just thinking about a day of clothes shopping is enough to get them excited. Being in a store, trying on lots of clothes – especially if the time is shared with another woman who can comment, critique, and participate - is a day well spent. Every bit of the process is enjoyable. Rejections are just as important as items that are perfect in every way. The time it takes to make a purchase – even if it's just a casual top – is time well spent. And, in the highly unlikely event that nothing is purchased, a day of clothes shopping with a friend is still a totally satisfactory way to spend an afternoon.

For men, the opposite is true. Shopping for clothes is a dreaded experience. Resistance begins days – often weeks - before. Once the fateful moment arrives, the pain increases. Every minute is excruciating. The longer it takes to find something acceptable, the worse the experience. Simply trying on a pair of pants is a stressful activity. Trying on a second pair is physically painful. For women, the decision process can take all day. For men, buying clothes is simpler and quicker: Does it fit? Good, I'll take it.

For many men, shopping for anything to wear is a chore – even if it's only a shirt or sweater. But shopping for a new suit involves a level of agony that is almost indescribable. A root canal would be preferable.

No matter how many times a man is assured that he looks good in a suit, he'll still do everything possible to delay shopping for one. If there is an important event coming up that requires anything approaching formal attire, this is the phrase that is repeated endlessly: "I already have a suit."

Women with an overflowing closet can still complain about having nothing to wear. Men will look in their closet, see the lone suit that was purchased within the past few decades and feel confident that they're good to go.

Eventually however, after days and sometimes even weeks of prodding and pleading, a man may be convinced to get a new suit. But any plausible excuse to delay the painful experience will be embraced. Even though he knows that the battle is lost and eventually he will endure the shopping experience, he will still do everything possible to put off the actual store visit for as long as possible.

For men, there is definitely a best time to shop for a suit. It's later. Maybe next week. Possibly tomorrow. But today is simply impossible.

That's why shopping for a man's suit often becomes a last-minute activity. The problem is that buying a suit at the last minute creates an unanticipated problem. Buying a suit isn't like buying a pair of jeans. You don't put on a suit and walk out of the store. Alterations are necessary. Always. And they take time. Several days or even a week is not uncommon.

But if a store can do the alterations in single day, then delaying the suit shopping process until the very last minute becomes a viable possibility.

The benefit is obvious: for the woman who wants her guy to wear a new suit at the christening, bar mitzvah or her best friend's 3rd wedding - even if he waits until a day or two before the event - it's still not too late.

My idea was to promote next day alterations. For obvious reasons, it didn't seem necessary to explain that there was an additional cost for the extra speedy service. I'm not sure it would have mattered. For men, anything paid for a new suit is wasted money anyway. And for women, simply getting their guy to get a new suit and tie is worth almost any price.

I condensed the message into a phrase I knew would be memorable. The line I wrote – well, to be honest, I borrowed it from a great song – was "What a difference a day makes."

The commercials were very simple and, fortunately, beautifully shot, While the lyrics to the song "what a difference a day makes" were sung, there were vignettes of men in various "before and after" situations. In the "before" shots each guy was casually dressed. They wore work-out outfits, old clothes for gardening or even pajamas. In the "after" scenes, each man was immaculately dressed in an exquisitely tailored suit.

Although everyone at the agency and client was pleased with the commercials, none of us were prepared for the reception they received. It was the only time I've ever seen fan letters – and there were lots of them – for an advertising campaign.

People told us that when the music came on, they ran to the TV to watch the commercials. Women loved them, talked about them, and looked forward to watching them. And, because it was women who often engineered the suit buying process, sales soared. Business boomed. Profits escalated.

The owner of the agency puffed up with pride. The campaign was not just successful, in Los Angles it was famous. His friends and competitors in the advertising business begrudgingly acknowledged his accomplishment. This was his moment and he basked in the glory. Until...

He lost the business.

The success of the campaign and the accompanying increase in sales and profits made the business ripe for acquisition. A few months after the campaign began running, the company was bought out by a competitor.

The agency was left with a pile of awards, a fistful of fan letters and a lovely, handwritten thank you note from a grateful - and now very wealthy - former owner of a chain of men's clothing stores.

An actual, honest-to-goodness, successful line

Unquestionably, the best line I ever wrote was for the first Cheech and Chong film, <u>Up in Smoke</u>.

It was one of my very favorite assignments despite the film's poor quality, non-existent plot, and the mediocre vision of Lou Adler, a night club owner, music producer and talent manager who was a first-time director almost entirely devoid of filmmaking ability.

None of that mattered. Lou Adler was hardly an auteur, but the film was never intended for discriminating viewers of cinema. The target audience was stoners and absolutely nobody else.

Cheech and Chong were well known for their dope-oriented humor. They were a one joke marijuana team that could boast several hit records and sold-out performances across America. For those inclined to believe that smoking dope added to the humor of just about anything (which was limited to every single person who has ever smoked a joint) they were very, very funny.

While the film was unlikely to draw hordes of bible thumpers, right-to-lifers, or nursing home residents, it was must-see viewing for their many, many fans.

As far as I was concerned, the only thing the advertising needed to do was not get in the way. Just as importantly, I felt the film shouldn't be promoted as something for everyone. It was pure low brow, stoner humor – made by dopers, for dopers. There was no conceivable way that anyone else would find it the least bit amusing. But for Cheech and Chong fans, seeing the film was a no-brainer. All they needed was assurance that the movie would be the anti-establishment, cannabis-drenched comedy they anticipated.

From the very beginning, there was nothing about my involvement promoting the film that resembled anything I had experienced before. For starters, the only person I met with during the entire process was Lou Adler. And he was more than just a slight deviation from the corporate norm I was used to working with.

Usually – which is an only slightly under-stated way of saying "always" – any meeting about advertising occurs in a relatively formal setting. The discussions take place in an office building, usually on a high floor and quite likely in a conference room. There are often too many people in attendance. Most of them represent the client. Typically, that group is made up of a high-level decision maker whose main job is to appear thoughtful before saying "no" (albeit sincerely and with appropriate acknowledgement of effort) while a group of subordinates support that decision with knowing nods.

Not this time.

My first meeting with Lou – and all subsequent meetings – took place in his office – a large, stunning home, high in the Malibu Hills and directly overlooking the Pacific Ocean.

Lou was rich. Very rich. He made much of his fortune as a music producer. The Mommas & The Papas were an early discovery, and Carole King's Tapestry album was done under his supervision. He has a wall filled with gold records and, from all appearances, plenty of gold coin to go with it. He also owned two successful nightclubs on Sunset Boulevard. The "Roxy" was the downstairs venue where a mixture of unknown and big-name bands appeared, often in front of sold-out crowds. Upstairs, "On the Rocks" was an exclusive private club where entrance was strictly enforced. As nearly as I was able to discern, the only people allowed inside were the ones who showed up in person and expressed a willingness to pay the cover charge and purchase the over-priced drinks.

I have no idea how rich he is but the house/office where we met offered a pretty good indication. It was a large, lovey home on an acre of some of the most expensive land in Los Angeles. It was perched on the crest of a mountain directly overlooking the Pacific Ocean. Part of that acre had been turned into a go-cart course for his young son (because, as everyone knows, swing sets and jungle gyms are so last year). But the house, as impressive as it surely is, was little more than an afterthought.

Lou always wanted to live on the Pacific Coast Highway so he could claim the ocean as his back yard. Although most of the real estate in Los Angeles is expensive, land along the coast, and especially in Malibu, is at a ridiculous premium.

But just being on the coast was not nearly good enough for him. He was very particular. Only one specific site was acceptable. He found the plot of land in the precise location he coveted and then bought it. Unfortunately, there was a house already there, so it had to be torn down. Then, just to make sure that he didn't have annoying neighbors, he bought the houses on either side. After razing the original house, he designed the replacement himself. But, because he knew that building it would take time and require constant attention, he bought a house on the hill that overlooked it. That's where he lived and kept a watchful eye on the beach house until construction was completed. Once he moved in, he turned the temporary home into the office where we met.

Another indication of his wealth accumulation was his seat at Laker games. A front row seat costing many thousands of dollars was not good enough. He sat directly on the floor, around mid-court, and next to his good friend, Jack Nicholson. Whenever the camera panned over to Jack (something that happened at least once during every telecast), the shot invariably included a bearded guy in a white cab driver's cap. That guy was Lou Adler.

That's how rich he was.

The location of our meetings was not the only thing I found unusual. Lou, not surprisingly, because of his music and entertainment connections, had access to some excellent weed. He was the first person – and, even to this day, the only one I ever met - who did business while stoned.

Being high didn't mean he wasn't paying attention. One of my most distinct memories of several meetings was the time when, in the middle of our conversation, he picked up the phone, dialed and then spoke very quietly to the person on the other end of the call. Essentially, his portion of the conversation went something like this:

"This is Lou. I'm here in my house, looking across my pool at my beautiful view of the Pacific Ocean. (Pause) And there are no workmen here to spoil my view. (Pause again). That's right."

He then quietly hung up the phone and we resumed our conversation. Less than 5 minutes later, two pick-up trucks screeched to a halt behind the house and teams of workmen furiously set to work.

Apparently, corrections are made quickly when you speak softly and carry a big checkbook.

I don't remember much about our discussion. But I am quite certain that the customary buzzwords "tactics", "strategy" and "prime prospects" were never uttered. We both knew what needed to be done.

The line I wrote was intended to laser focus on the people who were going to see the film anyway – and to make sure that they knew it would be just what they expected to see – two stoners, baked out of their minds, wreaking havoc in every scene.

This is the line I wrote. "Don't go straight to see this movie."

It was at least semi-clever, a bit anti-establishment, and, clearly, a joke about getting high. But that's not why it was such a good line.

For the Cheech and Chong fans – really, the only ones who had any intention of seeing the film – it was nothing more than an unnecessary reminder that toking up before entering the theater would, as it always does, boost the enjoyment level. Just between us girls, this audience was more than likely to smoke up anyway, but true stoners always appreciate encouragement.

Although there was a slight – very sight – double entendre, no one had any difficulty understanding the intent of the line. Everyone who saw the ad got the joke. Up in Smoke was clearly a film by the wasted, for the wasted.

Lou liked the line and gave me points for not being a typical ad guy.

But the real reason the line was so good had little to do with cleverness and more to do with outrage. The ad generated a ton of publicity. In every newspaper where the ad ran, there were articles written about it and often several letters to the editor. The non-Cheech and Chong fans all objected – and objected strenuously – to advertising that clearly encouraged drug use. After all, at the time, smoking marijuana was illegal, considered to be immoral and, even worse, enjoyed by people with long hair who have been known to occasionally miss Sunday school and sometimes neglect to return borrowed tools. The outrage was visceral. The great unwashed appreciated the marijuana humor but the washed were deeply offended and wanted to make certain that their displeasure was known.

For every ad that ran, there were at least a half dozen complaint letters written to newspaper editors.

People who were against smoking weed were united in their desire to boycott the film. But since they weren't going to see it anyway, their reactions and their furious condemnation of the advertising worked against them. The negative attention actually increased interest and helped jack up ticket sales.

<u>Up in Smoke</u> was a big hit. It almost certainly would have been a hit without any help from me. But, for one of the few times in my career, I feel justified in taking at least some credit.

Usually, I think my ads are successful if people like them. But because the line I wrote was so strenuously objected to by so many - this one turned out to be the most successful of all.

Full Frontal Nudity

Another line – actually, an entire advertising campaign – that generated attention far beyond the norm was for a new clothing store that was about to open in Los Angeles.

Their business concept was solid. Based on their ability to purchase designer clothes at closeout prices they were able to offer savings of 40-60% - often on famous name brands. True, these lines were discounted for a reason – they were no longer selling well, or the manufacturers wanted to replace them with new, more current merchandise. The lifeblood of stylish brands is their ability to stay ahead of the curve by continually creating new and different looks. There are obviously some people for whom being caught in public wearing last season's colors or styles is beyond humiliating. But, for many, the idea of saving about 50% on prestigious brand name clothing is very appealing.

Because the most famous brands were understandably reluctant to be associated with steep discounts, we were not permitted to use their names in the advertising. But it was important to at least give the impression – hopefully the assurance - that the clothes were high quality. Even though the store's entire premise was based on deep discounts, they did not want to appear to be just another cheesy store filled with discount racks.

The line I wrote seemed straightforward. It was "We can't take it all off. Just 40-60%". The visuals, however, were beyond unexpected.

The ads and TV commercials featured exceptionally attractive men and women – all with equally exceptional bodies. For fashion advertising, that wasn't so unusual. But what was truly unique for a retail store that only sold clothes, was that the ads paid no attention to clothing at all. All the models were shown full figure and completely nude.

We wanted the ads to be arresting, but we didn't want to be arrested. So, in every ad, a combination of shadows and discrete positioning of hands and legs covered erogenous zones. Nevertheless, there was no question that the models were not wearing anything at all. To say the least, the ads were highly visible. Most of them ran full page in the Los Angeles Times. On the day of the grand opening, we ran a two-page spread.

In the TV commercial, a bare shouldered, beautiful woman looked directly into camera and, in slow motion began to remove her top. The scene faded to black before her nudity was completely revealed.

We knew that for the ad campaign to work, the taste level had to be impeccable. Anything less and the ads and commercials had no chance to see the light of day. So, we hired an academy award winning cinematograph to film the commercials and one of America's finest – and most famous – fashion photographers to take the shots for the ads.

Because of the erotic nature of the visuals, getting past the censors at the LA Times was an issue. Conceptually, the ads were doomed from the beginning. But, when the publisher of the Times saw the quality of the photographs, objections weakened. I'm sure there were some lively internal discussions but, in the end, even though they knew that controversy was certain, the Times agreed to run the campaign.

The TV commercials were, to no one's surprise, initially rejected by every TV station. Because I had a relationship with the local ABC affiliate (I had done their advertising for several years and knew many of the important players) I was able to call the general manager of the station and make an appeal. When he saw the commercial himself and realized that it was done in such good taste, he over-rode the censors in his advertising department. His explanation to me – and to his employees as well - was that the station made money by selling advertising, not by rejecting it. And, because of his approval, his station received 100% of the store's TV budget.

Although we had anticipated that the ads and commercials would get attention, it was the additional coverage that put the campaign over the top. Several nightly news shows did specials about the campaign. They not only ran the commercials (for free) during the newscast but also did on-the-street interviews to see how people felt about them.

There was plenty of controversy – which we felt was more than fine. We knew that the more attention the campaign received, the more awareness would be created for the store. We anticipated some negativity but were pleased to find that there was a lot of appreciation for the taste level and quality of the photography. The LA Times also ran articles about the campaign. They explained why they felt it was acceptable, and even important, to allow nudity in their advertising - provided it was done in good taste.

On the day of the store's grand opening, the combination of the surprising visuals, the significant media buy, the news stories, and the promise of tremendous savings, had customers lining up several hours in advance. Once the doors opened, shelves were quickly emptied as buyers gobbled up the bargains. Sales more than tripled the original projections.   The store's biggest – and, essentially, only - concern was how quickly they would be able to re-stock. They even considered shutting down for a day to refill the racks that had been stripped bare.

For a flat-footed line about discounts on clothing, the advertising campaign was clearly an unbridled success.

But, for the store, although the grand opening was a monumental triumph, problems arose almost immediately. Sustainability reared its ugly head. With such strong sales, keeping the shelves and racks fully stocked was an issue. But, as it turned out, that was not their biggest problem. Well known, fashionable and expensive brands are understandably uncomfortable about being associated with discount stores and especially discount prices. So, even though no brands weren't mentioned by name in the advertising, when their association with the store spread by word of mouth, it was only a matter of time before many of those companies stopped fulfilling the store's orders. And, without designer labels to sell, there were only two choices: become a traditional clothing discounter or go out of business.

They went out of business.

Interestingly, the brand name clothing manufacturers learned something important from the experience.

They realized there was an unanticipated opportunity to unload their unwanted, unsold, dated merchandise. Eventually, they took advantage of that new-found knowledge by opening their own discount stores in huge, outlet malls. There, they were joined by other major brand name manufacturers that also sold outdated merchandise at significantly less than full retail prices.

A truism for business is that nothing speeds the demise of a poor concept faster than great advertising. Although the original idea for the store seemed solid, the unforeseen and completely unanticipated reaction to their success was the reason for its demise.

In short order, the store closed, and the agency lost a valued client. Both were unfortunate victims of success.

Whitewash

The U.S. Borax company (which, peculiarly enough is not a U.S. company but is, in fact, part of a Swiss-owned conglomerate) had several products that were essentially taking up space on supermarket shelves. Due to almost non-existent sales, the next step for those products was removal – first from stores and next from the company's portfolio. In what was generally considered to be a futile attempt to elude total extinction, our advertising agency was tasked with the responsibility of saving one of those products.

Borateem, a powdered bleach, had almost no name awareness and, as a consequence, almost no sales. Although we realized that reversing such a severely negative situation was less than a remote possibility, we were able to take some solace in the knowledge that we'd be paid a handsome fee until the proverbial towel was thrown in.

Borateem sales were understandably poor for a few painfully obvious reasons. Unlike 99.9% of all bleach sold in America, Borateem doesn't come in the familiarly shaped large plastic bottle. Instead, it is packed in a box that is all too similar to a package of Corn Flakes. And it's expensive. Even very large bottles of bleach – including Clorox, the number one selling and best-known brand – are almost free. Liquid bleach is essentially as cheap as water. In truth, most bottled waters are considerably more expensive and certainly preferable for quenching thirst. But, despite the advice of the former President and renowned medical expert, Donald Trump, drinking liquid bleach is neither refreshing nor an effective antidote to Covid-19.

Our agency was under no delusion about the challenge. In addition to the first two strikes against Borateem, there was a third: practically no one knew its function. Locating someone who could connect the name Borateem with an ability to whiten clothing required ingenuity, perseverance or, more likely, a relative employed by the company.

As an added bonus there was a 4th strike: its placement on store shelves. Liquid bleach comes in 3 sizes - large, jumbo, and humungous. Because the bottles are so heavy, bleach is always located on bottom shelves. Anyone who shops for bleach knows it is futile to cast a gaze anywhere other than downward. Locating a box of Borateem, on the other hand, required a willingness to participate in a scavenger hunt. Although at least somewhat appropriately situated in the laundry section, Borateem was usually hidden in plain sight somewhere on an upper shelf in a package that looks nothing at all like it could possibly contain bleach. And, oh yeah, don't forget, it is also a lot more expensive.

As advertisers, we knew there was nothing we could do about the lack of liquidity, the high price, or the elusive position on upper shelves. But with a sufficient media spend and a provocative TV commercial, we held out some hope that we might be able to encourage a few shoppers to at least make the effort to seek it out.

Although almost all signs pointed to total disaster, there were some positives. On the plus side of the ledger was the brand manager who headed the project. In most situations, the battle lines between client and advertising agency are clearly and unhappily drawn. The decision about which agency to hire is often made at a relatively senior level, but the people who eventually do the work are not always involved in the selection process.

As a general rule (in my experience it's roughly 99 times out of 100), the person who actually runs the business on the client side is seldom satisfied with the efforts of the creative team that has been assigned to him (or her). And the creative team (the same 99 times out of 100) thinks the brand manager lacks vision, gumption and quite often, manners, acceptable personal hygiene or, most assuredly, anything approaching good judgement. Neither has much appreciation for the other. Or likes the other. Or can tolerate being in the same room without expressing some indication of overt or implied hostility.

But the Borateem situation was a rarity for all concerned. Pete, my art director partner, and I both felt an extraordinary bond with the brand manager. For starters, we thought he was smart and perceptive – qualities that were both unexpected and enormously appreciated. He, for reasons that had yet to be proven, felt we were absolutely the right creative team to handle the assignment.

In violation of all known norms, we even hung out together, had meals together, and went to ball games together. Politically we were on opposite sides of any conceivable conversation, so we were careful to stow those topics in a mutual "do not discuss" zone.

All three of us were football fans and, even though tickets to Raider games were expensive and essentially unavailable, somehow between his connections and ours, we often ended up with good seats. On a fairly regular basis we spent Sundays together, often meeting up at the same unusual parking place – the front lawn of a home near the Los Angeles Coliseum. We found the owner's sales pitch irresistible: "Easy in, easy out. That's what parking's all about". That phrase, along with the audacity of parking on a front lawn, was, for my teenage sons who happily came with us, at least as memorable as anything that occurred on the gridiorn.

Although Pete and I had a long history of doing award winning work when we were in Chicago, our creative output in Los Angeles was consistently unimpressive. In our defense, we could offer two legitimate excuses: our clients and our advertising agency.

Because that justification probably seems both flippant and insufficient, a more complete explanation might be helpful.

So what follows is for everyone who has been dismayed by television commercials that are annoying, offensive, or just plain bad. Here then is the unrequested, and probably too lengthy, explanation for that sorry state of affairs.

The advertising business works in precisely the same way as pretty much everything else in life. A basic rule holds: whoever writes the check makes the decisions. In a service business like advertising, the check-writer is the client. And the only way to keep those checks coming on a regular basis is to make sure the client is happy. Occasionally that happiness is a result of business success. When business is good, advertising agencies are quick to take credit. When business falters, agencies are even more adept at pointing to other factors – competition, weather, the economy, a fickle public, or possibly even phases of the moon. Fault is never assigned nor accepted either by the advertising agency or, heaven forbid, the client, for anything they did or didn't do.

In Los Angeles, many of the commercials that Pete and I conceived and produced were for the Southern California Toyota Dealers – a group of people making unconscionable amounts of money. Most had purchased their dealerships years earlier when Toyota was just beginning to sell cars in the U.S., so the cost of entry was relatively low. As Toyota sales grew (and grew and grew and grew) their decision to become car dealers turned out to be extremely propitious. All of them, including those who could barely utter a complete sentence without resorting to profanity, felt justified in crediting their success to personal brilliance, deft management skills, and the good sense to hire an accountant who knew a trick or two.

In theory, advertising agencies have only one responsibility: to help improve a client's business. But, for the Southern California Toyota Dealer Association, that task was essentially irrelevant. That's because business was already good. Actually, incredibly good. Without assistance from an advertising agency, that happy situation was unlikely to change.

The reasons for Toyota's success were not complicated. As is often the case, quality and price played leading roles and Toyota had both bases well covered. Toyotas were perceived as not only among the most affordable cars on the road but also the most reliable. Whenever I told a Toyota owner that I did advertising for the company, the response was consistent: "It's the best car I ever owned." That kind of positivity was both atypical and welcomed because at least a few of the companies I'd done commercials for (a mortuary, a discount furniture store, and a used car dealer) were held in somewhat lower esteem.

Because the commercials we did for the Toyota Dealers were hardly critical in terms of generating sales, the only judgment about the advertising was based on the way the Toyota dealers felt they were being taken care of. The owners of our ad agency made certain that was never a concern by factoring in important considerations.

There is a technical term for those considerations. That word is "perks." Hard to get tickets to Dodger, Laker or Raider games were often made available. Reservations at exclusive restaurants somehow materialized. Special, private events conceived for the dealers and their wives, occurred with regularity. The door prizes at those events were always a highlight. For reasons that made little sense, even though a dealer probably had a color TV in every room of his tastelessly furnished opulent home, for unaccountable reasons, winning a TV as a door prize was always a source of unbridled glee.

The owners of our agency correctly reasoned that anything that built loyalty was worth doing and even over-doing. Unlike agencies that professed astute business acumen or breakthrough creativity, they knew better than to tread in those treacherously judgmental waters. If the agency had a slogan, it would have been "would you like fries with that?" Whatever the client wanted, the owners of our agency wanted them to have. The more absurd the request, the more they delighted in saying "yes." What that strategy lacked in self-respect was more than compensated by the agency owner's bank balance.

It was also the reason that the agency never took a strong position on any of the commercials we presented. We always showed alternatives and let the dealers select their favorite. When asked for a recommendation, we consistently demurred. Our response, offered with great sincerity but little truthfulness, was that we never presented anything we didn't think was worthwhile. If pressed, we might suggest 2 or 3 concepts that were among our favorites. That way, no matter what commercial ran and no matter what response it received by the dealer's wives or fellow country club members, we were always in the clear. After all, we hadn't chosen it. They had.

For me and Pete, the acquiescing attitude was a disappointing revelation. We had cut our teeth at a boutique Chicago agency that essentially said: this is the advertising you should run – take it or leave it. Whether deserved or not, we claimed to be experts. The owners of that agency explained their position by offering a medical analogy. If a doctor suggested that you take two blue bills every morning, but you preferred taking one red pill at night, you had two choices: take the blue pills or go to a different doctor.

That reasoning was applied to the work we presented when we were in Chicago. Clients either bought it or hired another agency.

A perfect example of that attitude occurred after one of the partners from the Chicago agency moved to New York and was hired to create a new logo for a Boston bank. Two weeks later, he showed up with his concept. The bankers were more than a bit perplexed because he only brought one design. Their reaction should hardly have been unexpected. After all, his fee was significant - $25,000. For that amount, they anticipated seeing a roomful of alternatives. His response: "I thought for $25,000, the least you deserved was conviction."

In Los Angeles, Pete and I had proven to be quite adept at creating the nondescript, inoffensive, mediocre work that satisfied the Toyota Dealers. But we realized that the Borateem situation was entirely different. For the first time in years, we had a chance to do something exceptional. Even better than the opportunity to demonstrate our creative chops, was the prospect of doing advertising that would be judged, not by uncaring car dealers, but by actual sales results. We relished the assignment because we knew that, for the first time in a very long while, we had a client who actually believed in the power of advertising. Because of his confidence in us, we were determined to rise to the challenge.

There are times during the creative process when good ideas flow readily, and great concepts arrive in a matter of minutes. But there are other times when the magic is elusive, and the most valiant efforts only produce lackluster results. Even great athletes experience poor games, sometimes in succession. Unfortunately, for us, the slump seemed unending.

After several weeks of earnest, determined effort, we still didn't have anything that met our expectations. The agency owners, however, were anxious to present the work. They felt – not incorrectly - that the longer we waited, the more concerned the client would be. And because they were used to mediocrity, they thought many of our ideas were more than good enough. In truth, the commercials we had developed were both on target and fairly clever - they just weren't as good as we hoped they'd be. But, with time becoming an increasingly important factor, a client presentation already long past it's sell-by date was scheduled.

As is often the case, the client meeting provided mixed results. Our friend, the brand manager, nodded appreciatively as we showed the storyboards and explained the commercials. He readily agreed that we had some solid ideas. But his response was lukewarm at best. We all sat in awkward silence for a while and then he asked to be excused. When he returned, he told us that he was able to get us more time. He was positive we could do better. The owners of the agency were understandably upset because we hadn't made a sale. Under normal circumstances Pete and I would have been frustrated, too. But being granted more time made us ecstatic. We wanted very badly to hit a home run, but so far, had only managed a ground rule double.

As the saying goes, we went back to the drawing board. And continued to be frustrated. We knew from too many past experiences that sometimes an assignment can be worried to death and the sought-after solution never materializes. There simply is no telling when the creative spark will ignite. But we knew it was there somewhere – it just needed help finding its way to the surface.

We continued to slog through – and eliminate – a host of semi-acceptable ideas. Eventually, however, after too many late nights, we came up with something that, for the first time, felt exactly right. It not only had the potential of being memorable, but it also was laser focused on Borateem's sweet spot.

Although the many obstacles facing Borateem were certainly quite real and undeniably difficult to overcome, there was one significant product benefit. Unlike liquid bleach, Borateem, because of its powdered form and milder ingredients, is comparatively gentler on clothes. That was more than just a subtle difference. Regular liquid bleach - strong, effective, and inexpensive as it surely is - has a major negative. Even when used properly, liquid bleach is tough on clothes. The right amount can make clothes whiter, but when used excessively, an entire load of wash can be ruined.

Our idea was to do a parody of the film, <u>Jaws</u>. We envisioned a pair of pants and a shirt floating in the water, appearing at least a little like a human form but also, obviously, just clothes. A white shark-like shape moves menacingly through the water. A closer look reveals that it isn't a shark, but, instead, is a bottle of bleach – easily identified because all liquid bleach comes in similarly shaped bottles. Eventually the bottle reaches the clothes, attacks them, and after a brief struggle, the shirt and pants are destroyed.

An ominous sounding voice (we hired a guy who did an on-point imitation of Orson Welles) warns about the destructive power of liquid bleach and, in the end, offers up Borateem as a safe, effective alternative. The logo line summed up the message: "Borateem. The safe, great white."

From the moment we explained the idea, there was total acceptance – a very rare occurrence. The safe position when considering any major business decision is always to withhold approval. That's because there are seldom consequences for saying "no". Saying "yes", on the other hand requires boldness – something in short supply at most companies and in most board rooms. But the owners of the agency loved our idea and couldn't wait for us to make the presentation. When we explained the concept to the brand manager, he was beyond pleased and felt appropriately self-satisfied for granting us additional time.

The final step in the approval process was a formal presentation to the executive VP who flew in from Switzerland for the meeting. That also went well for essentially one reason: Pete. When presenting a concept – especially one that he genuinely likes – Pete can be mesmerizing. He doesn't just describe the story line – he lives it. Sometimes when he finishes, there is applause. This time we had to settle for enthusiastic approval.

The next challenge was a minor one – all we had to do was locate a bottle of bleach that could swim or else find a young one and teach it the backstroke.

We handed that assignment off to a brilliant director and, because of its clear blue waters, flew to Bimini for the shoot. As we soon learned, the benefits of producing a film in Bimini are pretty much limited to beautiful water.

In the U.S., tiny communities are often referred to as "one street towns". Bimini is a one street country. It is a wafer-thin island with only one road that runs almost the entire length. Not surprisingly, there are very few cars. By actual count there is one: a Mercedes Benz convertible, owned by Adam Clayton

Powell's grandson. With no apparent destination, he seems to be a constant fixture on that highway to nowhere, waving proudly as he passes people at breathtaking speeds of up to 15 miles an hour. Powell, the elder, was originally from Harlem and held the distinction of being the first Black man or woman elected to Congress. He made Bimini famous because he kept a home there – one he often visited on the government's dime and in the company of women who, on most occasions, were not his wife. When forced to resign for a bucketload of improprieties and financial irregularities, he retired to Bimini. Following form, his seat in the House was taken by Charles Rangel, who years later, was requested to vacate his position for tax dodges so unethical even politicians disapproved.

Although Bimini is a country, it functions more like a small fishing village. There are boats to rent, a few places to eat, and many places to drink. All schedules operate on Island Time - in a word: later. With little to do and fewer places to do it, there seems to be no reason to rush. Understandably, nobody does.

Our first dinner at a restaurant taught us all we needed to know about timely service. After being seated, we were ignored for at least ten minutes before our client decided to take matters into his own hands. He stood up, prevented the waiter from returning to the kitchen and delivered a lecture specifying our group's importance to the economy of Bimini and our entitlement to more attentive service. Had the waiter listened carefully, he would have learned that our group had booked the entirety of the best hotel in Bimini ("best" being a relative word), that we were going to be in the country for a week and that we intended to spend a lot of money. In other words (actually, these were his exact words) "while we're here, we own this island." The waiter listened attentively, nodded understandingly, and from that moment on, completely ignored us for the rest of the evening.

In Bimini, the availability of film production equipment is essentially limited to...well, there is none. Everything we needed had to be brought with us. And all of it was packed on the sea plane that flew us in from Miami.

Chalk Airlines was, at the time, the oldest sea plane service in the world. That statement is no longer operative because neither is Chalk Airlines. Due to an unfortunate incident involving a wing falling off and all 20 passengers dying, Chalk no longer offers a half hour flight between Miami and Bimini. Because Pete is uncomfortable flying first class in a 747 even after consuming two double Bloody Mary's as liquid fortification, squeezing into a tiny propeller plane that took off and landed on water was not an experience he was looking forward to. He was petrified during the entire flight – apparently with good reason - and didn't regain anything approaching normal coloring until long after we landed.

During a typical commercial production, Pete and I are obsessively involved. We pay close attention to camera angles, props, wardrobe, the way actors deliver lines, and pretty much everything that takes place in front of and behind the camera. But in this production, we had absolutely nothing to do. Because most of the filming was done under water and because we were on a boat, it was impossible for us to see what was being shot. Without actors, there was no dialog to check. So. while the filming took place, we gave ourselves an important assignment: we fished. To attract fish to our lines, we threw chum in the water. Even though the scattered chum performed as desired, for reasons we found personally annoying, we were requested to stop using it. Apparently, in addition to attracting smaller fish, the chum also attracted sharks. Showing absolutely no concern for our attempt to ward off boredom, the divers who were propelling the bleach bottle underwater made it known that having their lives endangered was not mentioned in the job description when they signed on for the production.

The film footage turned out to be all we hoped it would be and the ominous music soundtrack mimicking the foreboding theme from <u>Jaws</u>, provided the final, finishing touch.

From the moment the commercial was completed, expectations were high. And they were all realized. No one was surprised when, later in the year, the commercial won just about every major national award for advertising excellence.

Although trophies and gold medals are certainly appreciated, we all knew that the real judge of success for the commercial would not be measured by peer approval or awards. In the final analysis, we'd be cheered or booed by what happened in the marketplace. And here, too, the commercial was a huge hit. Sales spiked immediately. And continued to rise.

Amidst all the back-slapping positivity, there was a minor hiccup – a lawsuit. Universal Studios had a legitimate gripe. They argued that the parody of the well-known <u>Jaws</u> music might cause people to believe that Borateem was endorsed by their company. Their point was emphatically made by a team of impeccably dressed attorneys who seemed to have little appreciation for our cleverness.

My first reaction was to check with the composer who created our soundtrack. He admitted that he had been influenced by a previous composition. But he hadn't copied from the Universal soundtrack; his point of reference was precisely the same as theirs – the brilliant composer, Rimsky Korsakov.

The validity of that explanation notwithstanding, the lawyers from Universal remained unimpressed. In response, Borateem's attorneys reasoned that a legal battle, even if won, would be expensive. So, as is the case with most lawsuits, an out-of-court financial settlement was agreed upon and both sides left the negotiating table firmly convinced that the outcome was unfair.

With that issue settled, the commercial continued to run, and sales continued to remain strong. A plateau was reached but it was a high one – much higher than even the most optimistic expectations.

Based on the success of the commercial, the next logical step was to produce a sequel. Fortunately, for us, the idea for this one came much faster. Instead of visualizing the bleach bottle as a shark, we turned it into a torpedo that travelled at high speed under water until it crashed into the floating clothes and blew them to smithereens.

The presentation process was repeated. Once again, the executive vice president flew in from Switzerland for the meeting. Pete and I had done the first one on our own, but this time, the two owners of our agency wanted to attend. The first commercial had been such a hit and because the account was critically important to the agency, they both wanted to be there in person to share in the glory.

About an hour before we left, one of them realized I was wearing a bowling shirt with someone else's name carefully embroidered over the front pocket. Because of the importance of the meeting, he asked me to change and put on a coat and tie. I was a bit surprised by the request because there was nothing remotely usual about my attire. I wore bowling shirts every day, and for good reasons. For starters, as most professional athletes realize, bowling is a sport that, much like gymnastics, pole vaulting or wrestling, requires not only superb athleticism, but also freedom of movement. So, for purely practical reasons, bowling shirts are quite comfortable. As a bonus, they are also extremely silly, completely tasteless, and come in a variety of absurd colors.

Because all my bowling shirts were purchased second-hand, each was emblazoned with the name of someone else – a feature that proved to be particularly valuable for new business meetings. The introduction period of those meetings is often a bit awkward, but my shirts served as an immediate ice breaker. In a room where just about everyone was in a suit and tie, it was a no-brainer to make fun of the guy in the lime green bowling shirt whose name really wasn't "Rocky" but, was in fact, "Howie. Once the get-to-know you period ended and the meeting moved on to the business at hand, I usually remained relatively quiet   Eventually, however, after the meeting progressed or, what was more common, regressed, someone seeking a break from the serious

288

discussion would ask, "I wonder what Howie thinks about all this?" Because they were anticipating befuddlement or a frivolous comment from the guy in the ridiculous shirt, anything I offered that was even remotely coherent, was deemed to be nothing less than pure genius. At the end of the meeting, regardless of what else had transpired, everyone remembered Howie, the bowling shirt guy.

The second Borateem presentation, like the previous one, was held in the same upscale, wood paneled conference room with an enormous table surrounded by about a dozen oversized leather chairs. Rooms like this are intended to provide a sense of importance and formality – neither of which was a good fit for either Pete or me. But, because we had both been there before and enjoyed such a positive experience, the two of us were completely comfortable.

The agency owners did not share our sense of ease. The surroundings and the participants were unfamiliar, and the perceived importance of the meeting weighed heavily on them. They were intimidated by the room as well as the presence of the Executive Vice President who had flown in from Geneva and who sat directly across from us, looking every bit the part of an important international senior executive in his impeccably tailored, obviously expensive suit.

The agency's owners felt it was their responsibility to open the meeting, so they did. Both were both visibly nervous. After a few very brief and uninspired remarks, they quickly turned the presentation over to me and Pete.

Before I could start, the Executive VP asked why I wasn't wearing a bowling shirt. He said that when we met before, my attire had really amused him, and he was looking forward to seeing the name I'd be sporting this time. At that moment, I could have shot a quick "I told you so" glance to the owner of the agency, but to my credit, although I felt totally vindicated, I resisted the temptation.

When it was Pete's turn to present, he stood, leaned across the table, and flicked a piece of lint off the Executive Vice President's suit jacket. He said something like, "Ian, that piece of shit has been bothering me the whole meeting. It's got to go." Although the owners of our agency were horrified, as expected, the VP laughed and graciously thanked Pete for the wardrobe improvement.

Just as he had at the previous meeting, Pete captivated the room with his explanation of the new commercial. Everyone loved it – no one more than the VP. He told Pete that, even though the original commercial was wonderful, he thought Pete's presentation was even better.

We hit the repeat button and produced the second commercial the same way as the first. Same director, same production company, same trip to Bimini and same disinterested waiters.

There was a slight setback when the commercial was finished. The networks had a problem with the explosion at the end. They felt – and were absolutely correct – that we had vastly over-stated the damage liquid bleach can do to clothes. Quite reasonably they requested that we add a disclaimer. Pete wrote the line, and it was perfect: "Explosion blown totally out of proportion". With that minor adjustment, the commercial was approved, aired nationally, and continued to generate strong sales results.

The feeling of satisfaction over a job well done was pervasive. The owners of the agency were ecstatic. Not only did they have a national success story to brag about, but they also had award-winning commercials that greatly enhanced the agency's creative credentials.

The celebration was so enthusiastic and so inescapable, it was almost impossible to fathom the moment when everything imploded. Seemingly out of nowhere, a shoe dropped. And, immediately afterwards, a second one fell. Euphoria turned to anguish.

In one fell swoop, the agency and the brand manager were fired.

We were all stunned by the news. We didn't just feel that we had performed well – we knew that we had. And we knew that the most senior executives at U.S. Borax absolutely agreed. Everyone was thrilled with the commercial and the sales results.

But that wasn't the problem. The problem was that we weren't all playing the same game. In ours, we were heroes. But in theirs, we were only pawns.

We thought we were building a brand. But the senior management at U.S. Borax had no such expectations. They never believed that a quirky, expensive product like Borateem could sustain success and profitability. From the very beginning, their plan was to spend heavily for a very short period and pump up sales quickly. But immediately afterwards, they knew they would stop all advertising and allow the product to become a "cash cow" - a product that exists totally on its own, without any promotional support. I suppose the concept is possibly based on the idea that it doesn't have to cost very much to get milk from a cow. Provide the cow with access to a pasture, and that's about it.

The benefit for U.S. Borax was clear: when marketing expenses are reduced to absolutely nothing, a much greater portion of sales becomes pure profit.

Of course, the executives realized that by eliminating advertising, sales would diminish and continue to slide downward as time went on. But they also knew that without spending millions of dollars on ads and commercials, even with reduced sales, Borateem could still be profitable ... for at least a few years.

So, the dominos fell.

After achieving the hoped-for spike in sales, Borateem became a forgotten product. With no need for brand supervision, there was no need for a brand manager. And because there was no need for marketing advice or TV commercials, there was no need for an advertising agency, either.

For U.S. Borax, it was the best imaginable win. For everyone else, it was the best imaginable loss.

Lights Out

Some people know, even from a very early age, exactly what they want to do when they grow up. Most of us don't. And even if that's not true about others, it is most certainly true about me. Which, for purposes of this story, is all that counts.

Without any specific plan about the way I was going to earn a living, like many others, I knew that, after college, I'd probably stumble around a bit trying to find a place where I fit in, where my minimal skill set seemed appropriate, and where the compensation would be sufficient to stave off starvation, homelessness, and preferably, both.

But I got lucky. While working on the thesis for my Master's Degree (a degree I sought not because I felt a compelling desire to further my collegiate education but because a continued academic pursuit allowed me to obtain a deferment from the military at a time when too many men my age were dying in Viet Nam). I interviewed some executives at the Chicago Tribune. Although the quality of my thesis was barely sufficient to pass muster, for some reason, I impressed the people at the Tribune enough for them to offer me a job as a copywriter in the paper's advertising department. An offer was proffered, I suspect, less because of my journalistic brilliance and more because of my willingness to work for less than minimum wage.

While the road forward was not completely paved for me, the path soon became clear. Although writing was clearly my strong suit, becoming a reporter was definitely not in the cards. But, with a full year of actual produced ads in my hip pocket, becoming a copywriter at an advertising agency seemed to be a natural step in the right direction. I began interviewing and, much to my surprise, received several offers. Using my extensive mathematical abilities, I accepted the one that paid the most.

The salary – which essentially doubled what I had been earning – turned out to be only one of the benefits.

I soon learned, even at the entry level, that working in the creative department of an advertising agency offered some highly desirable benefits. The office environment is usually more than pleasant, dress codes are either unwritten or unenforced, there are often young, clever, attractive people pretending to be busy or, at the very least, actively flirting, and although the workload may sometimes become overwhelming, the rules for completing assignments seldom are.

As a bonus, people in the creative department (they're the ones who come up with the ideas for commercials and ads that are intended to encourage people to buy what they don't need with money they don't have) are held to different standards than the rest of the office crowd. They are forgiven for keeping peculiar hours, arriving at work wardrobed as if every day was dress-down Friday, and in general looking the part of artists or writers even if they have displayed limited talent in either of those pursuits.

Of course, there is the element of stress that is standard issue in the ad biz. There are difficult bosses, unrealistic deadlines, and necessary interactions with clients who are often over demanding and under appreciative. But all of that is nicely balanced by the opportunity for advancement, travel for production (sometimes to exotic locales) and the benefit of working with talented filmmakers, actors, photographers, artists, and composers – some of whom are sufficiently famous to be name-drop worthy.

So, most days – and most situations – are pretty good. But the days when the agency is pitching new business are always the best.

There is a good reason for that. Actually, there are several reasons.

High on the list of positives is the very real chance to not only obtain a new account, but perhaps even more importantly, the relatively unfettered opportunity to prove that the agency is good at what it's supposed to do despite all existing evidence to the contrary.

The situation for new business pitches is completely atypical. Just as a waiters note that they could accomplish their task much better if they didn't have to deal with customers, the same is true for those who toil in the mines of advertising. For ad agencies, clients are both the reason for and the bane of their existence.

Everyone understands that without clients, there would be no advertising agencies. But clients – even the best ones - make the job a lot more difficult. Unfortunately, many are not the greatest arbiters of good taste or brilliant thinking. Many, in fact, are ill informed, inflexible, unimaginative, and demanding.

More often than not, they are every bit as inept as the advertising agency people who work with them.

But at pitch time, there are no clients – only potential ones. Unlike actual, existing clients, prospective clients usually offer few rules and make few demands. That, combined with an unusual receptivity – even an enthusiastic attitude about hearing new ideas - makes the opportunity much more interesting. There is, of course, good reason for their essentially unconstrained attitude towards the ad agencies that are pitching their business: if they were satisfied with the current ideas and the current work, they wouldn't be so actively looking for a replacement.

When pitching new business, the agency is at its hyper best. Positive energy emanates from every office. Account people and creative people who are often at odds are now in total sync. They not only talk to each other; they even listen to each other and seem to forget, at least for the duration of the pitch, that the people they are working with are annoying, self-serving dolts.

Of course, the reason for all the positivity comes down to one thing - money. Putting aside the ridiculously inconceivable concept of running a more efficient operation, there are essentially only two ways for an ad agency to increase profit.

1. Be competent. This requires being so good at what they're supposed to do that their clients become more successful. As a result of that success, those clients spend more money on advertising and the agency's fees are increased.
2. Get new business.

The first way should be the obvious and best solution. But for any number of reasons, it isn't. The contributions of the advertising agency's efforts are difficult to verify. Although advertising may be an important aspect of any business, it is by no means the only one – and not even the most essential. If business improves, the reason may or may not have anything to do with the marketing strategy or the quality of the work that the agency produces. Nevertheless, as might be expected, when profits go up, the agency clamors for credit and when the business takes a downward dive – or even declines slightly – the agency is quick to place the blame on market conditions, competition, production issues, delivery times or any other real or imagined issue.

But new business – like new romance – offers only the promise of good things to come. At the very least, it is a break from everyday doldrums and provides the opportunity to show how smart and creative the agency can be. Add in the possibility of winning the business and, by so doing, proving that the agency is superior to the others that lost, and it becomes clear why, at pitch time, every agency invited to participate goes all in.

Flash forward a decade or two. I am no longer the new kid, the junior copywriter on the block. I have moved on from Chicago and become the Creative Maven at a mid-sized Los Angeles ad agency.

A mid-sized advertising agency is neither fish nor fowl. With about 50 employees we were almost certainly too small to be considered reasonable contenders for any prestigious national account. Yet we were too large to bother with local merchants. Still, we had reason to believe we could play with the big boys.

Our two most important and most profitable accounts were both Southern California Dealer Associations: McDonalds - the nation's number one fast food business and Toyota - America's best-selling Japanese car. Both were undeniably impressive. Because Southern California is an enormous marketplace, each of the associations had a significant number of franchisees, some of whom served on an advertising committee. That group usually consisted of at least a dozen members. All were wealthy. Some were savvy entrepreneurs. None had a shortage of opinions.

The choices made by the advertising committees were, as might be anticipated, completely in line with other decisions made by committee. In other words: not good. Group think in advertising, just as in geometry, does not equate to the whole being greater than the sum of its parts. The much more applicable adage is "only as strong as its weakest link." And some of the links were as weak as moistened tissue paper.

Our agency earned its money not by strategic marketing thinking or brilliant creative work. The ads and commercials we produced were, at best, adequate. Not earth shaking. Not life changing. But not embarrassing, either. It is possible that, on occasion, our efforts might have helped, but since that is hardly a model to retain enthusiastic clients, the owners of our agency sought other means to maintain the business and, even more importantly, their monthly fee.

The agency "took care of clients." The men who served on the advertising committees (in those days almost all franchises were owned by men) knew they could call on the agency for favors. The answer, as expected, was always "yes."

Not surprisingly, the formula worked. The franchises all continued to do well – just as they almost certainly would have without benefit of our lackluster advertising. For obvious reasons, there was never a shortage of volunteers willing to serve on the advertising committee. And the monthly fee was not only secure but often increased.

The agency's ability to have on its roster the most important, best known, and successful regional businesses in California was certainly impressive. But because most of the work consistently fell into the "relatively acceptable" range – both in terms of creative quality and business effectiveness - clients in search of fresh marketing or advertising assistance seldom formed a line in our lobby.

That's why any opportunity to pitch new business was always enthusiastically embraced – not so much because it allowed us to tout our credentials but because it offered a chance to display our creative and marketing chops without being confined by client or committee assistance. There was a belief – I think correctly held – that our creative abilities greatly exceeded the current quality of our output. So, when invited, to pitch the business of Air Cal, a major California-based airline, there was no question as to whether we'd accept. We were, admittedly, a long shot, but at least we had a shot.

From the moment the gauntlet was thrown down, the entire creative department was a-buzz. After about a week of intense activity we had an internal presentation with one of the owners of the agency.

Two concepts emerged at the top of the pile. One was mine and the other came from a young, very talented writer. The owner needed to make an important choice and, although he surely had his own opinion, he felt he was in a tough position. He knew he needed both of us to be on board and for both of us to be fully committed to the cause.

He called the two of to his office and explained what we already knew. To accomplish all that needed to be completed in time to flesh out the creative concept for the presentation, a decision had to made about whether to go left of right. Because I was the senior creative person, a lot hinged on the veracity with which I defended my own idea. But I think I surprised everyone – probably including myself – when I recommended that we go with the concept that was not mine.

At that moment, all tension left the room. The direction was set and there would be no second guessing. To prove that I embraced the other concept, I immediately went to work writing a jingle/anthem based on the logo line that I had just endorsed. Then I called my favorite composer to set up a meeting so the two of us could get together to create the finished piece. Less than a week later we held the recording session. The result was a stirring piece – "California, you should see it through our skies" was uplifting, on target, and indelibly linked to the airline. Instantly it became the full-throated soundtrack at every agency meeting when the new business presentation was being prepared.

Although the agency was pleased to have been invited, we knew that the odds were stacked against us. Originally, about a dozen agencies were asked to submit credentials. For the final presentations, that group had been whittled down to 5. Unfortunately for us, the other four contenders were all excellent.

There are numerous theories about the order of presentation. Most feel that being the final presenting group is preferable because it provides the opportunity to leave a lasting impression. Some feel that going first is best because, with no other basis for comparison, the group that goes first automatically becomes the one to beat.

Invariably requests are made and, just as invariably, ignored. Because the order of presentation is decided by the client and is determined by criteria that is seldom revealed, agencies arrive when they're told to arrive and make their presentations within the time constraints that have been allocated. In truth, sequence is of little consequence. If wowed by a presentation, a victor is easily determined. And if an egg is laid, nothing else matters.

Generally, the group of agency presenters is relatively small – only heavyweights participate. That is not always the case on the client side. Because the presentation is often held in their corporate offices, travel is not an issue. As a courtesy, client attendees often come from a variety of departments and include some who are peripheral to the decision-making process. Everyone's votes may not carry the same weight, but few are at a loss for opinions. For this presentation, the airline gathered at least a dozen department heads, a few sub-heads and, to demonstrate their full-throated lack of discrimination, even a woman. The boardroom was filled.

Agency presenters are usually senior executives representing the three main departments – marketing, media and creative. If the agency has a strong leader, much of the weight falls on his shoulders. He's the one who makes the introduction, lays out the sequence of the presentation, serves as the MC who hands the ball off to the appropriate specialists and, in the end, ties it all up with a strong summation.

The owner of our agency was one of our major strengths. He was handsome, charismatic, charming, and disarming. He relished the spotlight and the opportunity to perform. For this presentation he was definitely on his game. He ran the show confidently and effortlessly.

We had agreed that the music and the logo line we were presenting would be the highlight of the presentation, so everything to be discussed was designed to lead up to the unveiling. The owner set the stage, the media and marketing VP's were flawless in their explanation and analysis. Then it was my turn.

My responsibility was to briefly outline the rationale for our creative recommendation. Then, instead of showing a storyboard and explaining about a commercial or two, I requested that the lights be dimmed. We were about to do something relatively unique at the time. We were going to show a video that we hoped would be a showstopper. Played against stunning visuals of California and backed by a full orchestra, a chorus of men and women sang their hearts out in praise of the remarkable state of California and of Air-Cal, its unofficial airline.

Before we showed the video, the meeting had been polite, formal, and businesslike. The group paid attention, took notes, and asked a few questions. But, overall, the atmosphere was, if not solemn, certainly serious.

Once the video ended and the lights went back on, everything changed. It was clear that we had done well. Actually, very well. Everyone in the room was smiling; everyone was enthusiastic. And then they did something that rarely happens in a new business presentation: they asked to see the video again.

We left the meeting riding an incredibly high. There was no question that we had succeeded. Of course, that didn't mean we'd won the business, but we knew that we had accomplished our mission and proved that we were, at the very least, a strong contender.

Confirmation of our good performance came two days later. The committee unanimously recommended us. Although there was still an additional hurdle to clear, they assured us it was only a minor one.

The Chairman of the Board had not attended the initial presentations, and, for obvious reasons, it was important that he support whatever decision was reached. My personal feeling is that his absence was hardly a result of a fully packed schedule, but instead, his desire to not waste time sitting through a bunch of presentations. He just wanted to be on board with the final decision. That meant we'd have to put on our show one more time.

Even though the entire group that saw all the previous presentations was 100% in agreement about recommending us, they felt it was important for the Chairman to see at least one other presentation in addition to ours. But only for the sake of comparison.

We were reassured - over and over again - that this was no longer a competition. The decision had been made and the business was ours. The next meeting with the Chairman was just for show. He would surely rubber stamp their recommendation.

And, oh, there was one other thing. They had a suggestion: "at the next presentation, don't bring the bald Jew." (Me).

Because of the offensiveness of the request – and the fact that the portion of the presentation that sealed the deal was the work I had been almost entirely responsible for producing – there was genuine discomfort at the agency about how to proceed.

But for me, the decision was easy: there was no question about insisting that I continue to participate. If we got the business, I knew I'd get my share of the credit. And I certainly had no need to be part of a dog and pony show for people who clearly had no desire to see me perform.

There was very little discussion about what to do. I was happy to be out. Until I wasn't.

What happened, happened quickly. The owner of our agency had a heart attack. At the time, we didn't know anything about the severity of the illness. All we knew was that he was in the hospital, and he was still alive. And we knew something else: there was no way he was going to be able to take part in any agency activities for the foreseeable future. He certainly wasn't going to participate in the re-enactment of our presentation to Air-Cal.

His absence was problematic on every conceivable level. He was not only our leader; he had been responsible for the presentation's heavy lifting. His style, his knowledge of the airline business, and his ability to connect with everyone in the room was a critical component of what the agency offered. He wouldn't just be sorely missed – in many ways he was simply not replaceable.

Nevertheless, he had to be replaced. The question was: who would do it?

There were no good answers. The other participants in the first presentation were clearly not capable of taking on his role. They knew their parts quite well but were totally lost about explaining the big picture. And bringing in another senior executive who was unfamiliar with anything that had been done before was simply out of the question – mainly because no such senior executive existed.

So, by process of elimination, the choice came down to the one person that we already knew was unacceptable: me.

From the standpoint of knowing the presentation inside and out and being familiar with the rationale and the strategy, I was the natural choice. But having me take the lead in a presentation where I was already marked as persona non-gratta would, to say the least, be more than a bit awkward.

No one – including me – liked the idea. But because there seemed to be no other reasonable alternative, the decision was made. I'd be the guy.

We also made another decision. Because the video had been such a highlight of the first meeting, instead of leading up to it, we decided to lead with it. We felt confident that the video would once again elevate the mood of the room and, in so doing, move the spotlight away from me and at least give us a positive starting point.

So that's what we did.

When the meeting I began, I stood in front of the group and told them that it was good to see so many familiar faces and made it a point to acknowledge the Board Chairman who, not unexpectedly, seemed less than overjoyed to see me.

I then did a very brief introduction, explained that we were pleased to be back a second time and really looked forward to demonstrating once again our marketing and creative abilities as well as our enthusiasm for partnering with them to bring their business to an even higher level of success. In other words, blah, blah, blah.

Then I asked that the lights be turned down so we could show the video.

The room darkened, the music swelled, the singers belted out the lyrics. The images of California in all its glory swept across the screen. It should have been a great way to begin. But it wasn't.

When the video ended and the lights were turned back on, instead of the praise and appreciative buzz we'd experienced the first time, the only sound to be heard was snoring. Really...snoring. Against all odds, and in spite of a soundtrack played at full volume, the 80-year-old Chairman of the Board had fallen asleep.

I surveyed the group to see who was going to wake him. Apparently, that was not in the offing. No one seemed inclined to take responsibility for poking the bear. I reminded them that they all - every single one of them – had seen the entire presentation just a week before. Since the only person who hadn't been there was asleep and would, as a consequence, not hear anything I said, I admitted that I was at a total loss about how to proceed.

After an awkward silence, it became obvious that no one had any intention of waking the old guy.

I waited patiently for a suggestion about what we should do. Eventually, it came: "Go ahead and do your presentation. But do it quickly."

Our group then spent about 10 minutes going through what had taken well over an hour to explain the first time. Every word was spoken against a backdrop of gentle - but constantly present and constantly annoying - snoring. The chairman never woke. He continued to sleep soundly while we folded up our presentation and quietly filed out of the room.

The phone call that came the next day came as no surprise. We didn't get the business. Apparently, our ability to serve as sleep inducers was insufficient to impress the boss.

The blame could be placed on a poorly timed heart attack (is there such a thing as one that is well timed?), the presence of the bald Jew who had been told in no uncertain terms to stay away, or an octogenarian who missed his nap time but was nevertheless capable of over-riding the recommendation of every single senior executive in his employ.

Not that we were bitter, but I can't say that there was much sympathy expressed when, a few months later, we learned that that Air-Cal had declared bankruptcy and gone out of business.

Reality Rears its Ugly Head

There was a time in the mid to late '90's when there was a ferocious battle between AT&T and MCI for customers who made long distance phone calls.

Television commercials for both companies were ubiquitous. It was virtually impossible to turn on the TV at any hour of the day or night without seeing one or more commercials for either – and often both – of those companies.

As is usually the case, the reason for the battle was the unconscionable amount of money on the line. Long distance operators had been replaced by computers. Telephone poles had been in place – and paid for – years ago. Expenses were essentially limited to maintenance of the lines and upkeep or improvements on the computers and cell towers that handled all the calls.

Even though there was a fortune to be made, the field was tiny. There were only two significant players in the game and the second, MCI, was a recent entrant. Sprint eventually joined the fray but never managed to come closer than a distant third in the race for the money. For years, AT&T was not just the leader, but by mandate, America's only provider for both local and long distance calls. As such, it was the bluest of blue-chip stocks.

Two developments changed everything.

The head of a tiny company figured out a way to re-sell a portion of AT&T's off-hour long-distance availability. It was a little – OK, very – complicated, but the deal seemed to make sense to AT&T because it generated additional income and required them to do nothing to receive it.

AT&T appreciated the additional funds because a major change had just occurred: they lost their monopoly. The company was broken into a half dozen U.S. regions. Essentially, there was no longer a mother corporation. But since there were no other telephone competitors, the break-up didn't have much impact. Still, the handwriting was on the wall – another competitor would inevitably appear. That made building a war chest for the coming battle seem like a smart move.

The earliest competition came from the little company that was already re-selling AT&T's long-distance access. That company was known as MCI, although what those initials stood for was pretty much of a mystery at the time, and now that the company is no longer in existence, nobody really cares.

But even with letters that were meaningless and not particularly memorable, MCI was up for the challenge. With few resources, but plenty of gumption, they set out to topple the giant or, at least become a major irritant. One of their main resources was clever marketing combined with the promise – and the actuality – of saving customers money on long-distance calls. MCI created calling plans that guaranteed significant saving for customers ... provided they were willing to sign a contract.

One of the calling plans was called Friends & Family. For groups that signed up together, all calls to each other were heavily discounted. Because the savings were so impressive, groups started signing up by the thousands. And, eventually, by the tens of thousands.

AT&T had enjoyed enormous – and unopposed - success for nearly a century. As a monopoly, the company was unaccustomed to competition and equally unprepared with a timely response.

Eventually, however, the sleeping giant awoke and began marking its territory with promotions of its own.

The long-distance war was on, and a new term joined the lexicon: "churn".

Participating in the special savings plans offered by either company required a contract. That contract was for a minimum commitment of 3 months. But, with new offers constantly being touted via television commercials, the desire to switch and save even more became irresistible. So inevitably, because the money saving offers were only for new customers, people moved from one company to the other as soon as their contract period was over. The constant 3-month movement back and forth became known as "churn."

While AT&T struggled to find an appropriate way to promote their offers, MCI hit on a reliable, albeit flexible, formula. An almost unending bevy of well-known celebrities (TV actors, comedians, and athletes) were used to hawk MCI's money-saving messages in television commercials.

All the performers in MCI's commercials were of a similar ilk. They were relatively recognizable, but none rose to A-lister status.

There was good reason for the choices. Many of Hollywood's best-known stars, for fear of devaluing their image, refused to participate in advertising at all. But the adage that "everyone has a price" eventually proved correct. A few very big stars were willing to accept outlandish checks for their appearance in commercials that ran exclusively in other countries.

But by dropping down a level – or several levels – plenty of notable performers were willing to appear in commercials if they felt they were being properly compensated.

Once the price negotiations were completed, MCI signed those celebrities to a 3-commercial deal. The arrangement was straight forward. All that was required of the celebrity were 3 days of shooting (1 day per commercial) within a reasonable period of time – almost always less than a year.

Although none of the notables were paid anything close to a million dollars, by any reasonable stretch of the imagination, all were extremely well compensated for their 3 days of work. When signing the contract, every one of them felt quite self-satisfied about having negotiated an excellent deal. After all, the work schedule was minimal, the location of the shoot was always convenient, there were very few lines for them to memorize, and no rehearsal was necessary. It was a very sweet gig that paid remarkably well for 3 days of exceptionally easy work.

The first commercial shoot usually went relatively smoothly. Even though scripts had been sent to the performers and their representatives well in advance, little attention had been paid. That was understandable. After all there were – at most – 20 words for them to deliver. And because they were professionals, they could practically do that in their sleep.

But once filming was about to begin, they realized for the first time that the words they were going to say were a bit more hard-sell than they anticipated. Not surprisingly, they often requested on-the-spot rewrites.

That issue was easily solved. After all, they had already accepted the script and they'd been paid in advance for the very few hours they'd be working. So, with reluctance, accompanied by whining, they went through the motions, did their job professionally and, at the end of the day, were very pleased to say goodbye.

At that point, they reasoned their job was done and, already, they were 2/3 of the way completed with their extremely well- paying assignment.

While the commercial was being filmed, they only thought about their single day in front of the cameras. Once completed, they felt certain the entire unpleasurable experience could be put behind them. After all, no one – other than the client, the ad agency, and the crew - had seen them perform and heard the uncomfortable words they had managed to choke out.

They never anticipated what was about to happen. The commercial – the one in which they delivered lines they didn't particularly care for and the one in which they were made to look like less than the brilliant actors they considered themselves to be and, instead, very much like people who sold their souls for cash - was about to air. And the commercial wasn't going to air just once. It wasn't going to air twice. Their commercial aired incessantly.

They were totally unprepared for the unwanted exposure. Friends began calling immediately – all of them disdainfully mentioning the commercial they had recently seen. And the calls kept coming.

The unanticipated embarrassment factor took over their lives. Everywhere they went, they were recognized – not as sit-com stars or professional athletes - but as shills for MCI. Seemingly every day, someone had something uncomplimentary to say about their performance in the commercial

One thing they heard with consistency was "I hope MCI paid you a lot of money for that."

Sadly, they hadn't. Not nearly enough for the daily – sometimes hourly - humiliation.

And that wasn't the worst part. The worst part was that they were only 2/3 done. There were still two more commercials to be shot. Two more commercials that would almost certainly continue to turn their lives upside down.

It should come as no surprise, that on the day commercial #2 was filmed – all was less than copasetic on the set. But, other than continuing to whine, there was little that the performers could do. They had already signed the contract and more importantly, had long since cashed the check.

So, they dutifully read their lines (unenthusiastically) and prepared themselves for the eventual humiliation they knew they'd be receiving once the new commercial aired.

Although the marketing team at MCI might claim that the continuing use of different celebrities was well conceived to keep their campaigns fresh, the reality was that none of the "celebrities" who appeared in any of the commercials had even the remotest desire to repeat their performance – regardless of how much they might be offered.

Apparently, even B-level actors have some semblance of pride.

How's this for pressure?
I had to write a script for
George Carlin

Many – actually, most – of the notables that had been contracted to do MCI commercials were well past their "Best Buy" date. Often, they had been second tier players on successful sitcoms. For the entirety of the show's long run, they'd achieved a certain level of recognition and enjoyed the lofty status of being among the 10% of SAG members who earned their living by acting and not by waiting tables.

But, when the shows eventually aired a final episode, because their skills were, to be kind, limited, job offers pretty much dried up. Even though they had once considered themselves to be stars, they now salivated over the opportunity to appear in TV commercials. In addition to the allure of once again performing for the camera, the fact that they'd receive considerably more than minimum wage was undoubtedly a consideration.

That was hardly the case with George Carlin.

When he agreed to do MCI commercials, he was arguably the most successful comedian in America. His one-man shows consistently sold out in colleges and major venues throughout the country. Year after year, his hour-long HBO special generated record setting numbers.

Equally impressive was the respect he earned. In the community of stand-up comedians, Carlin was royalty - universally admired by all who plied that trade.

I don't know why he agreed to become a shill for a long-distance telephone company and was sufficiently savvy to never raise that question to him. I knew that in his routines, he often targeted advertisers, pillaring them for their self-serving messages and wanton attempts at manipulation. So I found his willingness to appear in TV commercials for MCI more than a little surprising. The specific terms of his contract were never revealed to me, but I have no doubt that his remuneration was well into the "too good to pass up" category.

I had, by then, done many commercials with people who had rightful claims to the term "celebrity." I knew they had achieved a level of importance and expected a certain amount of respect that I seldom provided. I was fully on board with Alfred Hitchcock's assessment of actors. When told that he was reputed to treat them as cattle, he was quick to offer a correction. "I don't treat actors like cattle. They <u>are</u> cattle," he said. Like Hitchcock, I was happy to work with them, but I was hardly awed by their presence.

Meeting George Carlin was an entirely different experience.

Personally, I had great respect for his work and found it consistently intelligent and provocative. Even more importantly, I knew he wrote – and carefully considered – every word. So, the prospect of writing a script for him was beyond intimating.

Our initial meeting was scheduled to be held in his office. It's where he worked and where he was most comfortable. I had no idea what to expect. But I was certainly wary. Carlin's humor is hardly soft and gentle. His material may be a bit X-rated, but it's always incisive, smart, and often cuts to the core.

I didn't anticipate a cordial, welcoming, back-slapping meeting. I was prepared for a brusque encounter with someone who had very specific ideas, most of which probably had very little to do with the task at hand.

There were 4 of us in attendance. In addition to the two of us, Carlin's agent was there, as was the account supervisor from our agency.

Although I was concerned about the meeting, the account guy with me had worked himself into a state of absolute panic. Nervous and worried about just about everything almost all the time, he was hyperventilating long before we knocked on Carlin's door. His attendance was important if the discussion veered into specifics about claims or contractual obligations, but I knew that he would be no help at all in establishing a rapport or doing anything else to make it a productive meeting.

The best I had hoped for from Carlin was a curt, non-committal reception. Although there is always a twinkle to his performance, his on-stage persona doesn't leave an image of warmth, conviviality, and gentility. At best, I hoped he'd take a wait and see attitude before biting my head off.

Because of the trepidation about meeting him, I was totally caught off balance – and immediately put at ease – by his welcome. There was not a second of discomfort. He was relaxed, comfortable, happy to meet us, and interested in what we had to say.

I deliberately hadn't brought any scripts to show him. The purpose of the meeting was to give him a general understanding about the information he'd be asked to communicate in the commercials. Obviously, there were some specifics. But I also wanted to know what he'd be comfortable saying and what bridges he'd find difficult to cross.

As it turned out, he was – at least at this stage – willing to consider almost anything. He probably anticipated being handed a script with the expectation that he'd be required to perform it word for word. So the looseness of demands from our end was well received. And the plan for moving forward seemed to make the most sense. Because I was familiar with the assignment and the 30 second TV format - I'd take the lead by writing several preliminary scripts. He'd look them over and then offer revisions to make the words more his own.

Although that plan seemed reasonable, the concept that I would be writing for George Carlin – even if only for a commercial – probably should have been daunting. Surprisingly, it wasn't. As a longtime fan, I was familiar with his style and pacing, and because I had written MCI commercials for years, I knew the information that needed to be communicated. But what made the task less formidable, was the realization that he'd have plenty of opportunity to make revisions and improvements. So, I had no hesitation about offering ideas. Instead of being intimidated, I found the concept of collaborating with George Carlin to be exhilarating.

At our second meeting – again in his office – he was surprisingly accepting, even appreciative, of the work I had done. But, for me, the best part was about to begin. We huddled together at the computer, and he offered ideas about ways to make the scripts funnier. Not all the ideas worked, and many took too long to squeeze into a 30 second commercial. But for me, the process was an adrenaline rush. I think, once or twice, he even thought my suggestions were improvements. Even better, some of them made it into the actual spots.

Because we had worked together to finalize the shooting scripts, by the time we got to production, it was hardly surprising that he and I had formed a relationship. But I was far from the only one to receive positive attention from him.

Carlin was kind, generous, friendly, and appreciative of everyone he met. Because he was famous and undeniably funny, everyone on the crew reveled in his presence. During lunch break on most productions, actors - especially if they are celebrities - are often granted privacy and favored treatment. Many choose to eat specially prepared meals in their dressing room. Others prefer to be joined only by senior representatives from the agency or client.

Carin would have none of that. He flatly rejected anything even hinting at privacy or special treatment. He insisted on being in the middle of everything and everyone. He patiently waited in line for his meal and then ate what the rest of the crew ate. He happily posed for photos, signed autographs, and chimed in on even the most banal conversations. The only way an observer could tell he was anything out of the ordinary was because he was always in the center of things. And wherever he was, there was uproarious laughter.

The evening after the shoot, several of us went to see his show at the Newark Performing Arts Center. The audience loved it, and because we now felt a connection with him, we enjoyed it even more. After the applause died down, we went backstage to congratulate him – and thank him – for a truly memorable day.'

The MCI vice president who had been with us all day was a huge fan. She relished the opportunity to spend time with him and happily purchased one of his books. When she asked him to sign it for her, he took the pen she offered, wrote a few words, and handed it back.

She roared with delight when she saw what he had written and proudly showed it to the rest of us.

"Patty – Fuck you. George Carlin".

You can't handle the truth

Truth in advertising is a long-debated topic. But truth *about* advertising is much more straightforward. There are recorded facts and those, like it or not, are often well known and well documented.

It may be reasonably argued that advertising has always existed in one form or another, but the advertising that now influences our lives on a daily basis is a relatively recent phenomenon.

Although town criers announced events with regularity, it seems a bit of a stretch to consider those proclamations to be advertising. But, in all likelihood, it was probably not long after Johann Gutenberg brought us movable type that the first "Wench Wanted" personals showed up in the classifieds.

Putting aside posters and placards for the moment, it seems fair to say that, at least in the current era, signage alone doesn't qualify as advertising. To be considered the real thing, the information needs to be a part of some other communication – an unwanted intruder embedded into something viewed for other reasons.

Assuming acceptance of that explanation, it follows that the earliest advertising appeared in newspapers. The ads may have been an annoyance for readers, but the bargain was actually fair. Because ads helped cover the cost of publication, everyone benefited: the publisher of the paper made money, the subscribers received the news at an affordable price, and the merchants who bought the ads often saw a boost in sales.

Most would consider that to be a win/win/win. And it was. Until it wasn't.

To mix several metaphors, once the levee cracked and the horse escaped the barn, it was only a matter of time before advertising became the dog that wagged journalism's tail. There are surely those who wish to defend the integrity of honest, straight-forward reporting, free of outside influence. But the facts indicate otherwise. Profit has always been the goal of newspaper publishers and that profit arrived courtesy of advertisers who preferred praise rather than being reprimanded in the press for their occasional less than honorable activities.

With that uncomfortable understanding in mind, newspapers flourished and, along with - or perhaps because of them - so did their advertisers. Important information - what happened, what should have happened, what might happen, and where to get a really good deal on bonnets, petticoats, or buckle shoes - was affordably provided on a daily basis.

Newspapers became ubiquitous. They were hawked on street corners, delivered to front doors, and spilled on by coffee while eating breakfast or during crowded subway commutes.

Sometime after daily newspapers set the standard, a new form of printed publication – magazines - began to emerge. Although not published as frequently, what magazines lacked in immediacy was compensated for by in-depth articles of long-lasting interest. Newspapers were read and discarded the next day along with last night's garbage, but magazines often remained in homes for weeks or months.   And in the case of some peculiar hoarders, forever.

Along with magazines came a new kind of advertising. Instead of promoting daily specials warning that the best seats for viewing public humiliation of people pilloried at the stocks were almost all sold out, magazine advertising made it possible to provide messages about value and quality. It was now possible, for example, to extoll the virtues of installing a highly functional set of wooden dentures – perhaps even the same ones endorsed by G. Washington.

For advertisers, newspapers offered immediacy. Their message, simply stated, was "buy this now". Magazines offered the opportunity to build brand image. Stated simply: "why settle for less?"

With both sides of the coin neatly and completely covered, it was universally agreed that, from an advertising standpoint, things couldn't possibly get any better. But they did.

No one saw radio coming. Technically, because it isn't a visual medium, no one saw radio at all. But when it came on the scene, it arrived to almost instantaneous approval.

Radio offered something entirely new. For the first
       time, without
leaving the house and with no discernible ability other
       than
possessing sufficient dexterity to flip a switch or turn a
       knob,
whole worlds opened wide.

The unimaginable was now possible. People heard White Men
pretending to be Black, ventriloquists performing while moving their lips, and people of dubious talent appearing on a Talent Show. A primary reason for the enthrallment with this newly available bevy of entertainment was the price: absolutely free. Of course, in exchange for providing the free diversions, some of the programs had the name of the sponsor subtly embedded in the title. And somewhere in the middle of each program there were important messages extolling the virtues of tea, cod liver oil or cereal shot from guns. But, based on listenership, there was universal agreement that the mild annoyance of occasional commercials was a small price to pay for so much free entertainment.

Even the advertising was often painless. To compete with Coke, Pepsi conceived a new advertising concept: jingles. Ergo: this lyric:

Pepsi Cola hits the spot.
12 full ounces, that's a lot.
Twice as much for a nickel, too
Pepsi Cola is the drink for you.

By combining memorability with salesmanship, jingles boosted sales and provided a new avenue of employment for mediocre composers, singers, and poets.

With the affordability of newspapers, the accessibility of magazines and a full array of free radio programs, life was great. Only one thing was missing in this seemingly perfect world. And it soon arrived.

Television filled every conceivable void. Words, pictures, music, action, stories, comedy, celebrities, news, weather, sports – even a puppet show for the kids. All that was available in glorious black and white and accessible in the comfort of your own home. Even better, thanks to the concept of advertising that had been pioneered by radio, there was a cherry on top of the freshly baked TV cake: all the viewing was free.

Information and entertainment became omnipresent. All media flourished. The daily paper was a fixture in most homes. Radio became a welcomed companion for drivers who commuted hours every day. And magazines satisfied every conceivable interest, fetish, or perverted desire in depth, in full color, and on quality stock.

But television ruled.

After dinner – or, more likely, during a dinner that was served on TV trays – the television set was on and remained on until bedtime. Life without television was unthinkable. Television was more than entertainment. It was what America obsessed about, talked about, and relied on.

As television became all-consuming, it was more than coincidental that by 1960, the most successful advertising agencies in America were predominately focused on creating TV commercials. Unquestionably, that's where the money was.

It would be decades before social media unleashed its addictive force and upended what had become a well-fed golden goose. But, until then, television commercials were essentially the coin of the realm.

Any advertising agency worth its salt – or more specifically, any agency that was making a significant profit – did so based almost entirely on the budgets that their clients allocated for television commercials.

As a senior member of the creative department at one of those successful agencies, conceiving and producing TV commercials was essentially my only responsibility.

To justify my salary, my peculiar wardrobe choices (I only wore bowling shirts emblazon with someone else's name), and my perverse attitude about not arriving promptly at 9:00 a.m., I was expected to be skilled in all three stages associated with the development and production of TV commercials.

The first stage is conceptual. This is when a team - usually a writer and an art director - comes up with an idea or, preferably, several ideas. Some are rejected by the creative team (usually because they think their other ideas are better). Some are rejected by others in the agency for any number of reasons. Those reasons might be based on practicality (filming those concepts may be too expensive or too time consuming). They may be based on experience (the client had rejected similar ideas in the past). But the most likely reason for rejecting any idea is that it provides an opportunity for a person in position of authority to say "no" just because ... well ... just because. The concepts that pass the internal tests are then readied for client approval.

Stage two is the client presentation. This is when the creative team explains the commercial ideas and, more often than not, offers several alternatives.

This requires a combination of storytelling, performance, and salesmanship. The decision about which commercial to produce is often arbitrary - based on personal taste, opinion, and attitude. More importantly, the selection is often by committee and, as such, accounts for the many terrible commercials on TV.

The final step is producing the commercial. Because a TV commercial is like a movie – only much, much shorter - a lot is involved in the process. A production company and director need to be selected. Decisions need to be made about casting, set construction, location, wardrobe and much more. The shoot itself always takes at least a full day and is followed by post-production – the final stage when the commercial is edited and completed. From beginning to end, the process can last a few weeks, and possibly longer if the shoot takes place in an exotic location. The reasons for production in balmy climes often have less to do with a particular characteristic of the product and more to do with a desire to escape freezing weather during the winter, or perhaps an opportunity to visit Paris on the company's dime.

Although the first and third stages are critical, they pale in comparison with the second. That's because the advertising business is just like any other business and the adage holds true: nothing happens until someone sells something to someone.

In advertising, the commodities sold are ideas, strategy, marketing and, ultimately, ads and commercials. Most of that involves discussion, but only one involves more than a mutual nodding of heads.

At some point, after all the discussion and presentations, the client needs to pull the trigger. Someone has to say, "this is the strategy that we want to execute, and this is the commercial we'll use to do it."

What it all comes down to is very simple: the client has to "buy" an advertising campaign. Which is another way of saying the agency has to make a sale.

In a typical client meeting, an executive from the ad agency lays out the strategy and the rationale. That discussion can cover broad issues like competitive advantages and opportunities as well as tactical recommendations for spending the client's budget that could include specific media buys on programs that provide the most cost-effective time slots. Then it's up to the creative team to explain the commercials so the client can decide what they want to produce.

Explaining the commercials – often with visual aids like storyboards or even music – has been my job. In most situations, I'd present several options. Occasionally, for any number of reasons, the agency may have a preference. In that case, it would be my job to "sell" a specific commercial or campaign.

Unless the commercial happened to be one that I fully endorsed I always found the selling process to be a little tricky. I'm happy to answer questions or do my best to allay concerns. But, for purely personal reasons, I'm uncomfortable about even attempting to aggressively influence a specific decision – especially one that I don't fully support. I'm pretty good at explaining but selling is not my strong suit.

That's not to say I don't have respect for salespeople. Quite the opposite is true. Because selling is a skill I seem to lack, I marvel at those who can do it - often with what appears to be no effort at all.

I know some brilliant salespeople – some, I believe, could sell just about anything.

Here's a for-instance:

A friend's company was in dire straits because what had once been a solid business model had fallen out of favor, seemingly almost overnight.

His factory-made metal racks were specially designed to hold video cassettes at Blockbuster, a company with hundreds of stores.

Blockbuster's situation was, in a way, similar to Kodak's. Just as Kodak seemed to have been blindsided by the onslaught of videotape, Blockbuster was unprepared for the many new ways people were able to view films at home. Both companies ignored warning signs because their entire operation – factories, equipment, people, and systems - was geared to doing business in one way. Although they should have seen the handwriting on the wall, they didn't. And the result was catastrophic.

As Blockbuster began to falter, my friend's income stream slowed to a trickle. It became painfully obvious that he had to change directions. So, he came up with a plan that made sense on paper but required funding – a difficult challenge when his business was failing. As is typical, banks are most willing to loan money to people or businesses that can prove they don't need it. His conversations with friends and potential investors continued to be similarly unsuccessful.

But a true salesman does not allow "no" – or even a seemingly unending series of "no's" – to be an acceptable answer. In his search for funding, he read about a small bank that took pride in its support of small businesses. Their advertising featured a VP who boasted about maintaining a strong relationship with companies he helped with start-up funding and continued to support as they climbed the ladder of success.

My friend called, got the VP's secretary on the phone, and asked to speak with him. A trick he often attempted was to ask for the person by first name only – a guise that occasionally prompts an unsuspecting secretary to put the call through.

Although that ploy didn't work, it did present an opportunity to have a conversation with the secretary. Not surprisingly, because my friend can be quite charming, she eventually relented and got her boss on the line.

The VP wasted no time after picking up the phone. Essentially his question was: "Who are you and what do you want?"

My friend had a ready reply. He gave his name and then said he wanted to make two appointments. The first - to discuss a loan for his company as soon as possible. The second - to set a date 10 years in the future so the two of them could pose together for the cover of Time magazine.

That's a salesman.

Another for instance:

A major company, unhappy with their current advertising, decided to put their account up for review and invited a few agencies to participate. A good friend had recently joined one of those agencies as creative director and would therefore have an important role to play in their presentation.

Four advertising agencies participated in a very structured process. All the meetings took place on the same day in a hotel conference room. Executives from the company flew in from across the U.S to attend. Each agency was given 1 ½ hours – strictly timed – to make their presentation.

My friend's agency went through the standard procedure – an explanation of their credentials, a reel showing the agency's creative work for current clients, and an analysis of their thinking about how they could positively impact the company's future success. After that, it was my friend's turn. His task was to explain the commercials the agency had conceived and, hopefully, convince the executives in attendance that the work was distinctive, exciting, and precisely what was needed.

When it was his turn to speak, my friend stood, surveyed the room, and then, in a concerned tone, quietly explained that he was unaccustomed to appearing before such a formidable group and, because of that, was understandably uncomfortable and more than a bit nervous. He further told them that he had been working with someone who was helping him deal with his anxiety and he now knew what to do when faced with a stressful situation. He requested their indulgence and asked to be excused for a few moments.

He then opened the conference room door, stepped into the hall, and shut the door firmly behind him. Once outside, he took a deep breath and then let out a full throated, blood curdling scream that continued for a long, long time.

After that, he gently opened the door, re-entered the room and, with great sincerity, thanked everyone for allowing him that personal moment.

By then, the room had dissolved into hysterics. Unquestionably, what had just occurred was the highlight of their day. From that point on my friend had their rapt attention as he described the commercials. When he was done, instead of hearing the usual polite "thank you's", he received a lusty round of applause. And to the surprise of no one, his agency won the business.

That, too, is salesmanship. Unfortunately, that's also not me.

But there was an occasion when I came at least relatively close. Here's what happened:

I was the creative director of an advertising agency that had been very successfully doing work for the McDonald's dealer association of Southern California. Because of that success, the agency has recently been awarded the advertising account for the Northern California McDonald's group as well.

It's important to note that this event occurred in the mid-80's when everything was quite different – especially in Northern California.

Now, of course, the Bay Area has become the focal point for seemingly everything new and successful in America. Silicon Valley is where the money is. Apparently, *all* the money. But in the 80's, that was hardly the case.

At that time, San Francisco was a city with an inferiority complex. It wanted very badly to be considered a sophisticated urban center like New York. And, most assuredly, it didn't want to be compared to Los Angeles in any way.

The negative feeling about Southern California was so strong that they even came up with a shorthanded way of expressing distain. They referred to the city as "LA" - the most negative designation they could think of. That's because people in San Francisco recoiled at the idea of their city being known as SF. The problem was that in Los Angeles, the residents happily referred to their locale as LA. They actually *liked* the name.

The differences between the two California cities could not be more distinct. In Los Angeles, the major universities, UCLA and SC, while excellent schools, were likely to be better known for the quality of their athletic teams and their focus on film and entertainment. The major universities in the north, Stanford and Cal, also excellent schools, were better known for their progressive, counter-culture activities.

A case in point: When Stanford University felt, correctly, the political incorrectness of their nickname, "the Stanford Indian", the students were asked to vote on a replacement. The one the students chose "Robber Barons", while certainly both humorous and especially relevant due to a well-known but less than kind reference to the school's founder Leland Stanford, was hardly well received by the administration. The students were overruled, and the university became known as "The Stanford Cardinal." School officials went to great lengths to assert that the new name referenced the bird or the color and had absolutely nothing whatsoever to do with clergy members who seemed overly interested in sex with under aged boys.

Los Angeles was all about glitz, new money, and expensive cars. The city's most successful writers were not authors - they wrote screenplays for films and TV sitcoms. LA's most famous residents – and there were loads of them - were respected more for their physical attractiveness than their brains.

San Francisco was all about personal freedom, anti-establishment activities, intellectualism, and trees that needed hugging. Their celebrities were beat poets, long haired singers, gays, and politicians.

Both cities had eyes on New York.

Los Angles treated New York as a worthy rival – different in every way, but appreciated, nevertheless. The two cities shared a symbiotic relationship because, quite often, it was East Coast money that funded West Coast film and TV productions. And they shared residents as well. Many Hollywood actors, directors and studio executives were transplanted New Yorkers. Many were happy to consider themselves bi-coastal.

San Francisco viewed New York through a completely different lens. New York was seen as the cultured urban center on a hill - a place where international business, old money and sophistication blended seamlessly. People in Manhattan even read books, for goodness sakes.

Although Los Angeles couldn't care less about being compared to anyplace else, San Francisco wanted very badly to be considered the West Coast version of New York. Because there were not many New Yorkers who considered that desire to be anything close to reality, San Franciscans felt even more inadequate.

Back to the story.

I flew up to San Francisco for a presentation to the Northern California McDonald's dealers. This was a relatively important meeting because it was the third time that work was being shown to them. I hadn't participated in either of the first two meetings but was well aware that neither of them had gone well. None of the commercials previously presented had been approved. That meant no new commercials were produced and no new commercials had aired.

It also meant that no one was pleased. The McDonald's dealers wanted something new. They were tired of the commercials that were currently running and felt those ads had long since passed their sell-by date. Because the agency's very existence depended on satisfied clients, continuing to run commercials that were no longer appreciated was a sure path to a soured relationship.

Perhaps it's a bit of an overstatement but, in many ways, this was a make-or-break meeting. The dealers wanted to buy, and the agency was desperate to make a sale. Both were counting on me.

To help my presentation, I brought a portfolio with storyboards of the proposed commercials. But in many ways, I knew that the portfolio was little more than an empty case. The work inside was relatively ordinary and, unfortunately, not sufficiently dissimilar to the concepts that had already been turned down twice before.

There were many reasons why I hadn't been involved in the creating the work I brought with me. None of them mattered. Like it or not, the portfolio contained the commercials I had to present – and hopefully sell.

For obvious reasons, I dreaded the prospect.

The meeting room was packed. The advertising committee consisted of at least a dozen members. Because this was an especially important meeting, all were present. Representing the agency, were two of us – one of the owners and me.

He started the meeting by going over the situation and beginning to explain the rationale for future steps. He didn't get far. People who own McDonald's franchises are not known for their sophistication, reticence, or geniality. The interruption came almost immediately. Essentially the message was, "Cut the crap. Let's see the commercials."

From that moment on, it was my show. Like it or not, all eyes were on me.

I had been thinking about my presentation before we left, while on the plane and during the cab ride to their offices. But I continued to draw blanks. It wasn't until we were sitting in the meeting that I got an idea and decided to take a chance.

I stood, slowly looked around the room and then began with an apology - hardly a good way to begin any presentation. I told them that I was very sorry, but I couldn't show them the commercials that were in the case beside me.

There was immediate outrage. They couldn't believe what I was saying. They had come from miles away, set aside hours to be here and now it was all for nothing. They were furious and demanded an explanation.

I told them that it was all my fault and that I deserved every bit of their anger. I explained that I had recently come back from a visit to New York where I spent some time with friends who were also in the advertising business. They had shown me the new work they were doing for major national clients. That work was beyond impressive - it was simply amazing - fresh, unconventional, and just plain wonderful.

It was impossible for me to see the advertising they had created and not be energized. So, when I got back to Los Angles and met with the agency's creative teams, I revved them up by showing them what my New York friends were doing. Then I challenged them to equal it.

I told the advertising committee that our creative teams responded to the challenge with what I believed to be the best work they had ever done. That's what I brought. That's what I had in the portfolio beside me.

I was really excited about showing them the work because I was so proud of it.

But, sitting here in the meeting, I explained that it dawned on me where I was. I told them that it hit me like a brick. I realized that I wasn't in New York. And although the work I brought was good – actually, I thought it was brilliant – it really wasn't appropriate for their group. What I brought were edgy New York commercials. For Manhattan, they'd be perfect. But they were wrong for San Francisco. Unfortunately, the Bay Area just wasn't ready for this kind of breakthrough advertising.

I told them once again how sorry I was. And then I sat down.

What happened next was predictable. They demanded to see the commercials. And, of course, loved them all.

Just between us girls, I hadn't been to New York and the work was, at best, mediocre. But I did make a sale. So, at least on that one day, I guess I really was a salesman.

Down turns out to be a Major Up

I lived in Hollywood for almost 20 years and Manhattan for about 10.

During that time, I worked with A-listers, B-listers and dozens of men and women for whom the word "celebrity" is beyond well deserved. I've worked with Academy Award winning actors, writers, directors, and cinematographers. I've worked with golfers who won the LA Open and the Masters, Hall of Fame athletes and coaches, a Heisman Trophy winner, world famous comedians, the stars (and in some cases the entire cast) of many of the most popular TV shows of all time, and even candidates for President of the United States.

I've traveled with them in limousines and private jets, eaten with them at 5-star restaurants and roadside diners, and spent hundreds of hours kibitzing, complaining, and laughing with them during production.

I don't claim to be on a par with any of them. But I was definitely adjacent.

Not surprisingly, I have stories.

But what may be surprising is that my most memorable production story doesn't involve any of those people.

We were in Miami shooting a television commercial for the NBC network affiliate. It was a big production involving two weeks of shooting throughout South Florida. Our goal was to capture the blend of cultures that existed there – often uncomfortably. The mixture of elderly Jews, Cuban immigrants and African Americans was not always a harmonious stew. Tensions, tempers, and animosity, spurred on by high temperatures and even higher humidity, did not make for a blend of human kindness.

While it was obviously more than an over-reach to think that a television commercial could smooth the deeply held resentments and create an air of loving kindness, there was certainly something to be said for at least attempting to bring an air of positivity to the fore.

The soundtrack for the commercial had already been recorded. It was a song with upbeat lyrics about the wonderful mix of people in the Miami area who were actively doing things to make their own lives as well as the lives of their fellow Floridians more interesting, more meaningful, and more fulfilling.

Although the greater Miami area was home to many of the state's most famous and powerful citizens, those were not the people we set out to feature in the commercials.

None of the places we visited were national – or even local – landmarks. None of the people we interviewed were political leaders or icons of high society. No one was wealthy. No one was a well-known athlete or celebrity. All of them were relatively ordinary people engaged in activities that not only made their lives more interesting but also brought energy and happiness to others.

We met refugees who escaped Castro's Cuba and left their homes with nothing but the clothes on their backs. Less than a decade later they were prosperous business owners and community leaders. We met Mexican immigrants who made tortillas by hand and sold them by the thousands. We met a woman who convinced the city that the small hotels on South Beach were art deco treasures and encouraged the city's leadership to declare the area an historical landmark. She was personally responsible for starting the resurgence of the area and has been given full and well deserved credit for creating the Tipping Point that eventually turned South Beach into one of the most popular and most photographed sites in the entire country.

Those were the hits. But there were plenty of misses, too. We went down many roads that led us nowhere and met people who had little to say combined with the ability to say it poorly.

We had the most difficulty finding retirees who were actively engaged in pursuits other than mahjong, canasta or sitting poolside and discussing grandkids, humidity, medications, or bowel movements.

Somehow, we heard about a Jewish Community Center that encouraged a group of seniors to stay healthy – not by exercising, but by dancing on the beach at sunrise. Having attended many weddings and bar mitzvahs and observed firsthand the less than Astaire-like skills of enthusiastic Hora participants, we nevertheless thought that the potential beauty of filming at sunrise combined with earnest efforts of the elderly might hold some hope for a worthwhile visual sequence.

Because we were near the end of our production schedule and seemed to be coming up empty on other alternatives, we crossed our fingers, held our breath, and booked the group of seniors for an early morning shoot.

Amazingly, about a dozen people showed up. We were off to a good start. But, not unexpectedly, things began to deteriorate swiftly.

There was, unsurprisingly, some confusion about expectations. We thought we were going to film retirees who regularly danced on the beach at dawn. That was hardly the group that came. The ones who arrived sleepily had come for a different reason. They thought we were interested in filming retirees who would be willing to get up early for $50 apiece. They didn't dance regularly at sunup. In fact, they didn't dance at all.

Our crew was already there, and their equipment had been unloaded off the grip truck by the time the "dancers" arrived. So, even though the possibility of gathering useful footage was already beginning to seem remote, we had two choices: we could either leave or let the cameras roll. The cost would have been the same either way.

With nothing to lose other than a little time, we positioned the cameras and readied ourselves for the experience. As it turned out, we weren't even close to being ready for what we were about to see.

Elderly white people who have absolutely no sense of rhythm can, on occasion – even if it's only by sheer accident - move their legs and bodies in a manner that is indicative of something that could be deemed akin to dancing.

But even the most generous viewer of the disorganized movement that this group was engaged in would be hard pressed to explain what they were witnessing.

The seniors did hold hands and remain upright, but what they did with their feet defies description. Some leaned to the left, others to the right. Some kicked. Some swayed. Many came precariously close to falling.

And there was something else.

One of the couples had brought someone with them – a girl with Down Syndrome. Her age was impossible to determine - she could have been anywhere between 15 and 35. But her dancing skill was unquestionably determinable. Even in a sea of people with two left feet, she stood out as the one most wrong-footed.

Because the entire situation was such a fiasco, I thought that the addition of a girl with Down Syndrome was actually an improvement. Her presence added a touch of humanity that showed a lovely sense of kindness.

The client, however, was not impressed. Clearly the girl was not a senior, might not even have been Jewish and, what was undeniably certain, couldn't dance a lick. For the client, if there was anything even remotely salvageable from the shoot, the girl would have to be removed.

I was asked to make the request to have her taken away, but declined. I had all sorts of reasons: I thought everything we were shooting was totally unusable. I thought that the participation of a Down Syndrome girl at least added some humanity to the scene. But mainly, I didn't want to be the one responsible for making the girl feel that she was not good enough to perform with the group.

Because I refused, the task was handed off to someone else. I don't remember who went over to the couple that brought her, took them aside and explained what was desired. But I do remember that they spoke to the girl and walked her to a nearby bench. She remained there, by herself, while the group resumed its collective swaying and stumbling.

Eventually, we mercifully called a halt. The morning sun was beginning to shine fiercely, and the uncoordinated gyrations of the assembled masses had already captured on film. Prolonging the agony – for them and for the rest of us – would serve no reasonable purpose.

The producer thanked the participants, handed out the $50 envelopes, and we all said our goodbyes.

Because I was still uncomfortable about asking the Down Syndrome girl to be a nonparticipant, I felt the need to talk to the couple that brought her.

At first, I spoke with just the two of them. I explained that although I thought the girl added to the experience, I had been outvoted. But I was curious what they said that made her so willing to step away from the action.

I was totally unprepared for their answer. First, they looked at each other and smiled knowingly. Then the man explained, "It wasn't a problem. We used psychology on her."

I had no response. When an answer is that complete, there is nothing to add and nothing to question. But I did make a mental note to use that solution myself at some appropriate time in the future. Clearly, psychology is the answer.

By then the girl had joined us and we stood together in our little group of 4. I took a second to gather my thoughts and then spoke to the girl.

"I just wanted you to know how much I enjoyed watching you dance. It really was a pleasure."

There was silence for a while. Actually, too long. Then the woman (her mother, guardian?) asked her the same thing all parents request of their children, "what do you say to the nice man?"

Until then, the girl had not spoken. So, I had no idea what to expect. I wasn't sure if she could even speak, and, even if she could, if what she said would be comprehensible. But the one thing I was totally unprepared for was that she was about to give me the best – and certainly the most memorable - compliment of my life.

She continued to pause, look down, and compose herself. Then eventually, she raised her head, looked me straight in the eye and smiled. With total clarity and sincerity, she offered the only two words she spoke all day.

"Thanks, handsome."

Made in the USA
Middletown, DE
13 December 2023

44475765R00205